THE WILD VINE

THE
WILD VINE

A Forgotten Grape
and the Untold Story
of American Wine

TODD KLIMAN

CLARKSON POTTER/PUBLISHERS

New York

Copyright © 2010 by Todd Kliman

All rights reserved.
Published in the United States by Clarkson Potter/Publishers,
an imprint of the Crown Publishing Group,
a division of Random House, Inc., New York.
www.crownpublishing.com
www.clarksonpotter.com

CLARKSON POTTER is a trademark and POTTER with colophon
is a registered trademark of Random House, Inc.

Library of Congress Cataloging-in-Publication Data
Kliman, Todd.
The wild vine / Todd Kliman.—1st ed.
p. cm.
1. Wine and wine making—United States—History.
2. Norton, Daniel Norborne, 1794-1842. I. Title.
TP557.K55 2010
641.2'20973—dc22   2009033963

ISBN 978-0-307-40936-2

Printed in the United States of America

Design by Marysarah Quinn

1   3   5   7   9   10   8   6   4   2

FIRST EDITION

FOR MY FATHER, TED KLIMAN,
WHO TAUGHT ME TO TRUST IN MY OWN EYES
AND SHOWED ME THE COURAGE IT
TAKES TO CREATE

Whether bravely or cheerfully, you jettisoned anything about yourself that was a vestige and echo of a past form of life and vigorously settled into a new life-style—everybody's new life-style—and you became an American. In the great collective of the United States of our Western World, your halved self was transubstantiated into a new, bursting fullness. Your Americanness simply booms in one's face.

—GREGOR VON REZZORI,
The Death of My Brother Abel

The answer is never the answer. What's really interesting is the mystery . . . to seek mystery, evoke mystery, plant a garden in which strange plants grow and mysteries bloom.

—KEN KESEY

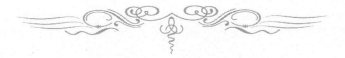

PART ONE

1

~~~~~~~~~~

C LOUDS OF DUST drift through the open windows of my rickety Toyota as it shudders along the bumpy gravel path of Champe Ford Road like a washing machine on spin cycle, stirring up sticks and pebbles.

The vineyard sits up ahead, just beyond a grove of ash and walnut trees so densely crosshatched that the road through it resembles a tunnel. It's a sunny, sweltering late spring day in Virginia's hunt country, but having entered the tunnel, it's as if I've entered a different realm altogether. Light and sound disappear. The heat, meanwhile, has not been dispelled by the intersecting bands of shade but becomes more concentrated, and the air has the odd, uncirculating stillness of a locked vault, of something trapped, a gathering of ghosts.

I emerge onto a steep and narrow road to find a woman standing outside the tasting room with her hand over her brow, squinting into the slanting afternoon sun like a land surveyor. I'm late. Even before I cut the engine, she bounds out to meet me in her pale yellow blouse and white skirt.

"Hiya," she says, giving me her hand. "Jenni McCloud." She doesn't squeeze but instead, at the moment her fingers come into contact with my palm, allows them to go limp—a delicate gesture meant, I suppose, to reduce the effect of their size.

I apologize for keeping her waiting. She waves me off. "No worries," she says, as though worrying itself were the greater offense. "Come on, let me show you the property."

A pair of sweet, rambunctious dogs runs out from the wings to escort us to her all-terrain vehicle.

"Say hello to Treixadura and Fer. Hello, cuties!"

"Tresha what?"

"Treixadura and Fer Servadou," she explains, unhelpfully.

I stare blankly.

"The grapes? Spanish? No?" she offers.

"Sorry. Never heard of 'em."

She shrugs.

A couple of arthritic-walking chickens join the party. "Hey, little goobers," Jenni says, stroking their lustrous coats.

"You've got quite the menagerie, don't you?"

"And a parrot inside and I'm getting pigs next. Little piggies. I love it. All this land, and all these animals. I'm a country girl. I love being able to be free on the land like this, and breathe. That's why I moved here."

We hop in and drive. To the east, Bull Run Mountain, soft and shimmering in the heat haze, conjures a slumbering giant, lolling on the horizon as if it were a hammock. Catoctin Mountain lies opposite at a distance. Embosomed between them, the tiny village of Aldie nestles. Other than the planes that knife across the sky, unwelcome reminders of nearby Dulles Airport and the congested exurbs of northern Virginia, Washington, D.C., feels like a time zone away. As humid and thick as the air is, I can feel myself beginning to unclench and breathe, too.

"What is that, air?" I say, inhaling.

Jenni throws her head back in laughter. "Welcome to wine country, man."

It's sometimes the simplest of things, the silliest of things, that draw you to people, not their well-intentioned gestures or deepest thoughts. And so it is that I take an immediate liking to Jenni for following "wine country" with "man," for subverting the gentility of the one with the vernacular of the other. There's a subtle point here, too: Chrysalis, her vineyard, might be *in* equestrian country, but it is not *of* it.

Had I not turned sharply off John Mosby Highway, I would have continued to historic downtown Middleburg, skirting low-riding stone fences as I rose and dipped and wound my way through the arcadian countryside. Middleburg and Aldie are five minutes apart. They might as well be five hours. It is Middleburg that the rich and powerful flock to, Middleburg that is synonymous with the good life, Middleburg that is widely regarded as the village with a claim to history, all those battlefields of the Revolutionary and Civil wars scattered about the lush and rolling valley. Aldie is a small town; Middleburg plays at being a small town. It gestures toward simplicity and taking it slow, but revels in its members-only aura—a private club, lacking only bouncers to enforce its codes. The smell of old money, palpable as the smell of fresh-mown grass in summer, draws new money. And the presence of both, in turn, is an irresistible turn-on for those with no money. On nice weekends, particularly in the spring and fall, droves of Washingtonians set out for Middleburg to stroll its boutiques and buy its overpriced jams and sleep late in its inns and fantasize, if only for a couple of days, that some of Middleburg's charm and gentility has rubbed off on them.

Aldie is the opposite of a tourist haven. It is Middleburg's unlovely, unlettered sister. The town was established in 1765 and for a time was the fourth largest in Loudoun County. By the late nineteenth century, however, Middleburg was incorporated and Aldie descended into obscurity, only a Civil War battle punctuating its many meager decades of nonhistory. On principle alone, I would much rather find myself with a few hours to spend in Aldie than in Middleburg, preferring the hungry, unwashed outsider over the preening insider.

The SUV rumbles over the hilly, uneven earth toward the vineyards, a yapping field dog running alongside. Jenni comes to a sudden, playful stop, and the dog nearly leaps into her lap. "Hey there," she coos, stroking its fur. Then, like a mother grown impatient, she dispatches it: "Now, get out there and chase those deer!"

She cuts the motor and we jump out. For a long moment I stand staring at the perfect, parallel rows of grapes, the leafy vines straining upward toward the blazing sun like worshippers seeking a god.

"Pretty neat, huh?" Jenni asks, drinking in the tableau with me, beaming, then guiding me through the rows of vines with the unwavering focus of a general in the field. The ruddy skin, the long, clambering strides, the flinty impatience—it's as if some iconic pioneer woman, tough-minded and independent, capable of handling anything or anyone, has stepped out of the pages of a Willa Cather novel.

"Look at you little characters," she says, as we come upon a grape called Norton, the prize of her vineyard and the reason I've made the long drive out from the city. The grapes, still months from being plucked, are beginning to cluster on the vines.

"Come on, grow, Nortonians, grow!"

She draws her fingers through the tiny blue-black orbs, like a jeweler showing off the quality of the pearls. "That's history, right there. The native grape of America. Good old Norton. Born right here in Virginia, in Richmond."

Next to the names of the great European wines—Cabernet Sauvignon, Pinot Noir, Merlot, Chardonnay—the name Norton sounds jarring by comparison, and Jenni accentuates the effect by biting down on each syllable. The effect is to provide a kind of history lesson: elegant, sophisticated Europe; hard, pioneering America.

"I love it how in California they all think they're making American wine with the Zinfandel. Zinfandel! Zinfandel's from Hungary, for crying out loud. The Norton is *American*, it's one hundred percent American, it's ours. And the fact that it makes a phenomenal wine is just icing on the cake. Come on, let's go and taste some."

Inside the tasting room, the increasing depth and sophistication of Jenni's wine talk (malolactic fermentation, micro-oxygenation) leaves me feeling dazed and alienated, and after pouring a couple of her white wines for me to try, she leans across the counter and says, conspiratorially, "You wanna know something? For the longest time, wine gave me the willies. I didn't like it. I was drinking Boone's Farm and Strawberry Hill and wondering what all the fuss was, why everyone kept talking about wine. Honest to God's truth." She gives an odd little laugh, a sound that starts low, in the diaphragm, but finishes high and thin and reedy.

Few businesses are more paternalistic, more rooted in tradition, in habit, than winemaking, a livelihood that is typically handed down through the generations, and most often from father to son. Women are scarce; outsiders, even scarcer. New ideas are generally anathema. And here was Jenni, who—before purchasing the seventy-plus acres of her estate (she says, pouring a lighter-bodied red) and coming north to Jefferson country from Florida after selling her diagnostic software business at the height of the tech boom—had never owned a vineyard and never made wine. Nor was she related to anyone who did. Indeed, the very idea of winemaking as a calling, a way of life, was not something that could be said to have been in her blood.

She gives an exaggerated shrug of the shoulders, as if to suggest a combination of dumb luck and happenstance, or maybe divine providence, then tips a bottle of Norton Locksley Reserve into my glass.

I can smell the wine even before I jam my nose into the bowl of the glass. I give the inky liquid a swirl and a taste, and am back again at the dinner that brought me here, a party thrown together in the chaotic aftermath of a hurricane.

IT WAS AN early September night, the fifth night in a row we had spent without power, and all of the metropolitan D.C. area seemed to be in a state of suspended animation—sticky and silent. No lights, no stove, no TV, no radio, no stereo, no computer, no air conditioner. All the instruments of modernity rendered impotent by a violent thunderstorm that had pronounced its primacy over the city and then vanished. How much longer it would continue to disorder our lives, nobody, not even the electric company, knew. But that night I sat around drinking with friends into the early hours of the morning. The loss of our routinized, technological existence had become a kind of slipping of the veil, a time to forget all the doing and all the going, to reckon with the enduring power of elemental things.

"What's this stuff we're drinking, anyway?" somebody asked at one point.

My friend said it was the native grape of America, a grape called Norton.

My wife said, "I thought Concord was the native grape."

"OK: correction. The native grape that makes a good, drinkable wine."

"Hey," someone piped up, "don't knock Manischewitz."

Norton? All I could think of was Jackie Gleason's famously gravelly bellyache: "Hey, Nawwwwwwwwton!"

It didn't sound like the name of a wine, or anyway, a reputable wine; it sounded like something with cartoon animals on the label of the bottle. Real wines had French names that rolled off the tongue in an elegant procession of vowels.

I reached across a table cluttered with half-eaten plates and half-burned candles for the bottle and poured more wine into my glass. And just like that, with just that simple action, my damp stickiness had become a light, beading sweat.

Without air-conditioning, without ambient light, being on the inside felt no different from being on the outside, and the steady chirping of the crickets seemed an insistence of the supremacy of Mother Earth, of the ceaseless rhythms of nature. The dark was unending, all-encompassing. Examining my glass, I could scarcely make out the color of the wine. I held it out to the candlelight for closer inspection, but not only did the flame not illuminate the liquid, it seemed, if anything, to deepen and darken its color, as if the flickering light were intent on preserving its secrets. The wine was so opaque, it looked black, not red.

Whether it was the lateness of the hour, the subtle power of the wine, the sense of being at the mercy of the elements, my drunkenness, or all of these things working on me at once, I can't say, but it was as if what I was drinking was an embodiment of the moment, the mystery, a correlative to our primal condition. It was dark, it was earthy; there was something wild, something alive, in the glass.

I had seldom tasted this earthiness in California wines. I did taste it in European wines, particularly those from the Rhône, in France, and in the southern Italian and rustic Spanish wines I liked, but the Norton was bigger than most of those wines.

The conversation had moved on by this time, to talk of other meals, of movies, of how long we could live without our modern comforts, but I hadn't moved on. I was still thinking about the Norton. I reached again for the bottle.

Squinting, I scanned the fine print on the label for more information, much the way I used to read liner notes as I lay on the floor and listened to my father's old jazz records, in the hope that the words might illuminate some aspect of the music (in the hope, too, that this illumination would, in turn, illuminate some aspect of my father). No illumination, though I did fasten onto one detail: In 1873, at an exhibition in Vienna, a bottle of Norton was declared one of the great red wines in the world. I turned the bottle around to look at the front of the label: Chrysalis Vineyards. I had just begun writing a column about food and wine for a weekly paper in Washington, D.C., and, drunk though I was, I managed, somehow, to retain this piece of information. There was always another column to write. It might come in handy.

A day later, electricity returned to the city. And my encounter seemed, all of a sudden, a long-ago thing. How quickly my routinized life, my life of instruments, had reasserted its power over me.

STANDING ON the other side of the counter from Jenni in the tasting room, now, sharing the story of my encounter, gesticulating wildly with my hands, I catch myself, realizing the ridiculousness of what I have just done, of making myself vulnerable to a complete stranger, of professing to be profoundly moved by a thing I can hardly begin to describe.

"Oh," Jenni says, "my life changed when I first tasted a Norton."

The moment calls for a toast, some ratification of our discovered bond. She pours a glass for herself of the Locksley Reserve, swirls aggressively, sets the glass down, picks it up, swirls it again. We drink.

According to the protocol of a wine tasting, the taster is encouraged to offer up a few sensory thoughts. I think of all the words that connoisseurs come up with to describe their experience, cataloging and classifying smells with Dewey decimal–like precision, isolating the contents of a glass as if they were conducting a science experiment—berry, cherry, tar . . . I can't speak these words with a straight face, of course, but the fact is, none seem equal to the task at hand. Jenni's Locksley Reserve eludes easy classification.

As alert to my struggle to put the taste into words as she was, earlier, at my cluelessness at wine chemistry, Jenni smiles at my fumbling wine talk, as if my inability to express its character in a few neat phrases was a testament to the Norton's fundamental profundity, an it-ness that transcends the grasp of words. "Different, huh?"

This does the trick, dislodging the moment for me from the weight of expectation. "I mean, the thing is, it looks like a Cabernet or a Merlot. But then . . ."

"But then," Jenni jumps in to finish my sentence, "you tip it back and you taste the damn thing, and it's just—*whoaaaaaaaa.*"

Her eyes roll back into her head, which she flings back as if she were simulating whiplash, the operatic semaphore of the wine's effect concluding with a woozy side-to-side roll of her head.

Jenni's exuberance is infectious, and as she laughs at herself—laughs at the sheer joy of being silly, of being completely and utterly free—I find myself laughing right along with her.

But now she turns contemplative. She gives the wine another swirl, but gentler this time. She holds the glass out in front of her and offers a more thoughtful, analytical assessment: "It's unique, but agreeable . . . different, but attractive. It's kind of wild, yet the thing is that over time it does tone down while still keeping some of that power. You have to get to know it."

Is she talking about the wine? I wonder. *Or herself? Or both?* There is so much more I want to ask her. How she came to Virginia to make the Norton. How the grape, once so dominant, could simply disappear . . .

"Wow, long story. Long stories," she says. She has other business to attend to, other appointments to keep. "Next time." She extends her hand across the counter. "To continued conversation." And vanishes behind the tasting-room door.

. . .

SEVERAL DAYS LATER, back in my cubicle at the newspaper, I review my notes from the afternoon, hearing Jenni's voice all over again as I read the words on the page.

And then I close the notebook and put it atop the pile of all the other notebooks I keep and don't pick it up again for months.

I think I am putting it out of my mind. I think I am practicing self-preservation. I think I am being guided by the rational part of my being, the part that makes thoughtful decisions and puts up obstacles and is reluctant to become consumed by long, unwieldy projects (because I seldom attempt anything without becoming consumed by it), but another part of me, more instinctive, more animal—the part I have always believed drives everything that matters—cannot stop mulling it.

Finally, one day I give in and I get in the car and drive down to Richmond, to Norton's home, poring for days over documents, garden maps, court records, and newspaper clippings.

What, exactly, I am expecting to find among these papers, I am not certain. Where, exactly, these investigations will lead—if they will lead anywhere—I have no clue. All I know is that I am pursuing a new interest, because I have learned that it is not possible for me not to.

I still do not know that you have to give up control in order to learn a thing, that you have to go where you are taken, and that the only true knowledge is the knowledge that changes you. But I will learn that, too.

2

THE DOCTOR'S THOUGHTS that winter were as bleak and unrelenting as the season. Spring, with its prospect of planting and promise of renewal, had always done much to dispel his black moods, but as 1821 crossed into 1822, it seemed not just a long way off but in some measure inconceivable, an exotic country out of reach of a broken man.

Holed up at Magnolia Farm northwest of Richmond, Virginia, Daniel Norton's isolation deepened. His sense of paralysis deepened, too, so that he found himself caught once more between extremes, unable to rouse himself to follow through with the act that preoccupied him, yet unable to think of anything else. A man of science, a rationalist steeped in the imperatives of reason, he was at the mercy of the greater power of unreason, and it seemed to him that suicide, far from being a capitulation, would be a solution, a means of turning off the spigot of guilt and anguish and what-might-have-been that had left him gasping, yet still no closer to understanding the events of December 17, 1821.

On that day, the promised addition, his and Eliza's first baby, turned into subtraction by two. Labor had gone horribly awry, claiming mother and child.

"The unfortunate Dr. Norton," said his half-brother, John Jaquelin Ambler, summing up the doctor's circumstance for the *Richmond Daily Mercantile Advertiser,* "was at a single blow of destiny made a childless widower."

The catastrophe was compounded by his tendencies toward solitude and alienation, tendencies that lay dormant for the three years of married life he had enjoyed with Eliza. Having decamped with his wife from the city to the farm, to a quiet, ordered world of his own making, he was now all of a sudden at the mercy, again, of noisy, nosy society.

He became a figure of chatter and speculation. *Widower. Childless.* Better to be neglected or forgotten than to be pitied, he decided. The mere thought of making the rounds of the Richmond social scene exhausted him—the leisurely nights passed in drawing rooms and parlors, the young ladies gathering around the table for a game of loo, the women chattering about the visiting star of the English stage, Junius Brutus Booth, and his triumphal performance as Richard III, the men retiring to the porches to hold forth on the price of tobacco and the horses at Tree Hill. He had barely had patience for the pleasant exchanges required of polite society when he was not deranged by sadness and resentment; now, it seemed an enormous outlay of emotional capital to keep up appearances.

On January 24, a little more than a month after Eliza's death, he roused himself to take action. He sat down and, collecting himself enough to organize his thoughts, composed a letter to his sister—the first, he admitted with embarrassment, he had ever written to her.

> And if this poor acknowledgement of my fault is at all acceptable
> to you it will at least, lighten the great misery which I now
> endure—
>
> For the joy of the world has passed from me and I claim all the
> sympathy of my connections to support me, amidst the horror of
> the time that is to come. . . .
>
> Once I could watch the blooming hyacinth & dwell with
> rapture on the bursting petals of the rose, and then as I saw them
> wither, say thou art given to us for a season, & the time of thy
> flowering will come again; how charming are the works of nature,
> how divine the hand that formed them; then I drew closer to my
> bosom, my sweet girl, as the thought rushed upon my soul for I
> felt that, the bright eyes that beamed upon me with so much

fondness, must sometime fade & the whole form that I adored
perish like the flowers of the fields, that the morning would come
when there would be no light & the spring return without its
beauties. . . . [Now] the chilly hand of death has come in the blast
of the desert and severed for ever the twin buds of peace.

In his reverie of woe, Norton moved from addressing his sister to beseeching God:

All wise & gracious God, I bow with due submission to thy
decrees but I trust it is not against thy holy law, to mourn my
Wife, my all, my only tie to life; . . .—May I not answer to her
sweet call as it floats on the bosom of the air, may I not in my
dreams go close to the cold & silent grave and kiss those lips on
which I have dwelt so oft so happily. May I not at the mid hour of
the night converse with the dead and treasure up the admonitions
of an angel in Heaven. . . . The leaves of the tree that shadows her
grave will be still whilst I lay down in my sorrow & mourn her
forever.

He had arrived at Magnolia Farm, the biggest prize of his dowry, three
years earlier, full of hope for his marriage and his future and determined to
prove that he was his own man—that he was not dependent upon the Amblers, whose large and sprawling clan he had lived on the margins of ever
since his father had died when Norton was three, and his mother, Catherine, remarried. Norton retained little memory of the man, but his father's
absence as the years wore on became stronger, an absence that had come to
feel like a presence, and that lent Norton the air of an abandoned man—a
man forever in search of a missing piece of his puzzle.

John Hatley Norton had been a shipping merchant, with offices in England and Virginia, one of the industrial leaders of a state that was vital to
the economy of a young, developing nation. Prosperous as he was, however, he was neither as prominent nor as well connected as John Ambler,
the patriarch of one of Richmond's most famous families.

The Amblers had deep roots in Jamestown. Though by colonial standards they were regarded as latecomers, arriving from York, England, only sixty years prior to the Declaration of Independence, they remained on the island when the capital moved inland to Williamsburg, inducing many pioneer families to resettle. By the beginning of the nineteenth century, they had come to dominate financial transactions on the western end of the island. The accumulation of capital led to an accumulation of political power, which in turn led to a growing belief in the importance of public service. Business, politics, the military—it was widely understood that the Ambler man did not give himself to one of these fields, but rather that he devoted his time to learning to master all three. Accordingly, John Ambler volunteered as a "boy warrior" in the Revolutionary War and later served in the War of 1812, eventually earning the rank of lieutenant colonel. He also served in the Virginia House of Delegates and was a member of the grand jury that indicted Aaron Burr. At his plantation, Glen Ambler turned the booming demand for tobacco into a handsome profit.

Norton, his mother, Catherine, and the steadily growing Ambler family (she bore the colonel eight children in all) moved from Williamsburg to Richmond in 1806, settling a year later in an octagon-shaped edifice in Court End, a neighborhood north of the capitol that abuts Council Chamber Hill. Court End was more than a destination for lawyers. It was a destination for Amblers. In his memoir, *Virginia, Especially Richmond, in By-Gone Days*, Samuel Mordecai recalled that Ambler's married female cousins lived in the neighborhood and that a "distinguished circle they [all] formed." Among this circle was the most prominent legal mind of his generation—John Marshall, later the chief justice of the Supreme Court. He had married one of those cousins. All roads, it seemed, led to the Amblers.

It was a different world for the boy, an intensely social world, a world of privilege and wealth, of proximity to power.

Norton was raised alongside his stepfather's children, as if he were an Ambler too. But he was not an Ambler and never would be an Ambler, and in ways subtle and not, he came to internalize his status as an outsider, deepening his detachment and intensifying his loneliness. Studious and intense, with a fanciful cast of mind, he retreated into a world of books, learning poetry and studying philosophy, that time-honored preoccupation of lonely, sensitive young souls everywhere; in his case, it was both balm and affliction, because in his isolation he came to identify with the wayward Romantic figures he read about, their solitary adventures, their melancholic longing.

At eighteen, he fashioned an escape, going north to the University of Pennsylvania for medical school. Medicine was not a passion, but it would, he figured, provide a profession and a means of supporting himself apart from the Amblers.

Away from home and on his own for the first time, the world took on a new tint, acquired new depth and meaning. Possibilities opened up to him. He traveled to Europe, to Paris and Rome, trips that left such a lasting impression on him that even years later, in the throes of his melancholy, he could recall with precision and vividness the places he had been, the feelings they elicited. He envisioned a future for himself, a limitless future, in which he was no longer the brooding outsider but the doer, the man of action, making things happen.

In 1815, he graduated and returned home, determined to make something of himself—to elevate his profile in the rigorously stratified society of his native city.

Richmond was changing. The War of 1812 was over. Business was booming. Tobacco processing would not arrive for another generation, but the cessation of the war had opened up grain trade to Europe, and flour milling drove the economy, spurring a network of related industries, from machinery to ironworks to coopering. The next three years, the so-called Flush Years, witnessed a flurry of real estate speculation, birthing a massive, unsustainable bubble that eventually popped with the Panic of 1819. The city became a banking colossus, new neighborhoods popped up (some fully developed, some not), and a real middle class emerged for the first time. A sleepy town of rolling hills and deep ravines, of quaint, iron-fringed houses and gently undulating plantations, of lolling afternoons on wide porches and courtly dances at night in grand parlors, Richmond had emerged as a vital center, the unofficial capital of the South.

But some things had not changed. And coming home to Richmond meant coming home to assume his place among the Amblers. What choice did he have, after all? He was not a Northerner and never would be. He might not have felt a part of things at the Ambler estate, but it was a life he knew. And the ties that promised to bind him inextricably to the old life also promised connections that might prove useful in building his practice.

Now that he was settled at home, one of the first orders of business was to sit for his portrait, one of the rites of passage for Richmond's elite. He was twenty-one.

The picture, departing from the bland impassivity of most formal portraits, is startling in its directness. In a yellow waistcoat and muttonchops, he sits posed before an olive background, his body at a slight turn, his pale face in a subtle rightward tilt. His beady eyes are dark and imploring, fixing the viewer with an expression of insolence amplified by the attitude of his arms, which are crossed. A first impression would suggest that the sitter appears to be impatient with having to pose for a portrait when there are more interesting, more important things to do. But the picture also suggests another kind of impatience, an impatience with the codes and assumptions of a society he was ambivalent about rejoining.

In 1818, Norton attempted another escape. He wed Elizabeth Call, the daughter of Daniel Call, a Richmond lawyer, an ardent Federalist, and the brother-in-law of John Marshall. The three years of married life that followed constituted the most stable, tranquil period of the doctor's life.

A year later, he joined with another doctor, William Tazewell, establishing a practice at the corner of Ninth and Broad streets. They charged three dollars per visit; "advice" they dispensed for a dollar. Blistering pills cost seventy-five cents. Opiate pills were twenty-five cents.

Though as a doctor he enjoyed a measure of social standing, it was not lost on him that he was a working man, which marked him as a cut below the planter elites, accentuating the difference between him and the members of his adopted family. Worse, medicine was a repetitive bore, hardly worthy of his vast intellect or curiosity, a wan approximation of the life he had envisioned for himself at the University of Pennsylvania, a life that Mr. Jefferson (everyone in Virginia called Thomas Jefferson "Mr. Jefferson," a casual form of address that served to close the distance between the living legend and the common man) had shown was not merely possible but, for the young elite, imperative—a life of science and art, of philosophy and farming, of action and reflection.

It was the twenty-seven acres of land of Magnolia Farm that drew the greatest share of his concentration. In addition to the land, he had also received an allotment of eleven slaves and their children as part of his dowry, and with their help and with the help of the countless books and manuals he'd devoured, he had embarked on the ambitious project of turning the land into the serious experimental garden he had always envisioned.

Working with his hands had always had a way of allaying the agitations of his mind. The garden was a holy place, and gardening was spiritual work. All living things, he felt, were infinitely delicate, surprising, and miraculous. To grow and thrive was nothing less than a manifestation of the divine hand, yet he was convinced there was no great secret to bringing forth life from a seed: It was the constancy and care of the gardener, a devotion that was a kind of love.

Marriage to Eliza had moderated his inner conflicts, and her gentle disposition and good humor seemed to effect a balance between his two natures, the way an artist's chiaroscuro blurs the distinctions between darkness and light, softening them and easing their differences.

That winter, though, the darkness eclipsed the light, and he found himself on the precipice.

WHAT SAVED HIM? Not love, the oldest and surest salve for the soul. And not time, the proverbial healer of all wounds. No, what saved him was something simpler and smaller. What saved him was a grape.

His garden had always been the one place in the world he could count on, a place to repair to when life began to crowd him. But if it was a respite, it was a respite the way a small cabin studio adjacent to the house is a respite for an artist or musician—a place where the creative mind, freed by solitude, can run riot.

Like so many early Americans, the doctor was caught up in the frenzy of discovery of his new and lightly populated country, a rush to identify and classify the rich and varied bounty all around him, the fascinating species of fruits and vegetables and plants and trees. The possibility of creating new ones, of solving the innumerable riddles of the New World by applying Old World teaching to fresh problems, was more captivating still, and he had embarked upon a number of projects at Magnolia when he first arrived.

In the science of medicine, he was a professional; as a horticulturalist, he was an amateur. It is wise, in this instance, to dispense with a contemporary reading of the term and revert instead to the Latin root: to do a thing out of love. Like many other amateurs of the nineteenth century, his lack of training did not lead to feelings of insecurity and doubt; on the contrary, it released him from conventional wisdom and compelled him to find his own answers to things. He immersed himself in books, horticultural manuals, and botanical studies, educating himself, becoming an expert out of necessity—and by sheer force of will. He planted a wide variety of grapes, native and foreign alike, and an array of other fruits and vegetables, nurturing the land with the same ardor and attention he had lavished on Eliza.

Some of these grapes he grew for eating. Others he experimented on. These were his guinea pigs, assigned the role of testing the ideas and theories he was then reading about. One of his consuming ambitions involved the crossbreeding of varieties to produce a hardy, disease-resistant grape that would, in addition, make a supple, drinkable wine.

Grape cultivation is difficult, laborious, and not always rewarding work, dependent on a variety of factors (weather, soil conditions, insects, diseases) that are beyond a vintner's control. The only certainty is doubt. It is not for the easily dissuaded, nor for those who do not possess a deep and abiding connection with the natural world, who cannot live with and among its mysteries.

. . .

THE PROJECT the doctor had taken up, of crossing grape varieties in the hope of creating a durable, disease-resistant grape that might produce a soft and drinkable wine, was even less subject to control, even less certain.

In the field, his restless seeking found an outlet, a focus. He had conceived of Magnolia Farm as a kind of laboratory. Whatever he could get his hands on, he grew. Whatever new methods or practices he read about, he tried. (By the end of the 1820s, he would even begin grafting Spanish grapes, a variety of *Vitis vinifera*, onto native vines in the stretch of land between his house and the meadow. The practice would not become common in Virginia until the end of the nineteenth century, a means—the only means—of successfully growing *V. vinifera* in the state.)

Crossing varieties was an unusually ambitious undertaking for an amateur, and his success was so unfathomable—a strange and unlikely amalgamation of fate, chance, intuition, and risk—that for nearly two centuries his story has been called into doubt by some wine historians and horticulturists. Complicating matters is the fact that the doctor did not leave behind a daily or weekly chronicle of his activities in the field. All this adds to the rich air of mystery, obscuring, though not obliterating, the details of his discovery.

What do we know? A series of recent investigations by Dr. Cliff Ambers (a geologist by training, but in the spirit of Norton himself, an amateur horticulturist who operates an experimental vineyard at his home in Monroe, Virginia) suggests that as the doctor made his rounds in the garden one day, probably in the fall of 1821, he would have discovered that among all the innumerable darts he had thrown up at his target, one of them had somehow stuck. A low-lying cluster of grapes, with small, thick-skinned orbs that were blue-black in color, like a fresh bruise, would have caught his eye. Drawing his fingers through the cluster, examining the shape of the leaves, broad, floppy, and three-pointed, he would have been able to see that it was not a variety of the European grape, *V. vinifera*. But neither would it have resembled any other native variety he had seen, including *V. aestivalis,* which he himself had planted.

A lover and collector of wine, Norton was well acquainted with the noble European varietals and had been endowed with a palate discerning enough to appreciate the subtle differences among sometimes similar-seeming wines. He was well acquainted, too, with the many, repeated failures to produce a good table wine in the New World. The problem was that the European grapes were too delicate to withstand the humid summers and harsh winters of Virginia, while the native grape varieties produced such a musky, disagreeable liquid that, while it could be called wine—it was fermented—it could not be called drinkable. Winemakers refer to this insistently musky character as *foxiness.*

These new grapes would have impressed him at once with their promise. For one thing, they were healthy and strong—no small accomplishment, for many *vinifera* vines were unable to survive for long in the state. Not only that, but they lacked the foxiness that dogged every native grape he'd tried. They were sweet and juicy and flavorful.

Eager to arrive at some understanding of the origin of his discovery, his mind would have drifted back to one of his experiments in hybridization years earlier, when (as he later related, in a methodological account for *New American Orchardist*) he had emasculated a grape called Bland—a self-fertilizing species of *V. labrusca,* the "fox" grape—cutting away all the stamens with a pair of small, pointed scissors while the anthers were still unripe, leaving the style and stigmata uninjured. He had then dabbed it with the full-blown blossoms of another vine, probably a Pinot Meunier, a *vinifera* grape and a fuzzy cousin of Pinot Noir.

Accidents, mistakes, chance—in art, these are the shorthand terms accorded the arrival of an outside phenomenon that alters a plan and effects a new and welcome outcome. The doctor actively courted chance. Not wanting the plant to self-pollinate and complicate his attempt to create a new fruit, he had not protected the emasculated flower cluster with a bag, leaving it open to the possibility of further impregnation. He achieved his wish. Rogue *aestivalis* pollen, floating in the breeze at Magnolia Farm from any of several native varieties, penetrated the emasculated Bland and pollinated it.

What happened next is not entirely known. But the doctor was sufficiently intrigued by the grape to extend the experiment, planting cuttings of the new grape in the hope of producing enough clusters to make wine. He would have pulled those clusters of grapes from his wild vine and pressed them, producing a dark, opaque juice that he bottled and stashed in his cellar, to begin the process of fermentation, the great transformation from a sweet, grapey liquid into a refined drink.

Bottling the liquid was not a pronouncement of faith; it was simply testing a hypothesis, taking a supposition to its logical conclusion. When, many months later, he eased the cork out and poured the inky fluid into a glass, he would have had no reason to be optimistic about the output of his oddball grape, no reason to think that he had produced something other than an astringent grape juice. But not only was this wine drinkable, it was good. More important than what it was, though, was what it wasn't: It wasn't foxy. What the *vinifera* had done was to tame some of the foxiness inherent in the *aestivalis*—tame, but not defang. The native character came through but did not predominate.

Norton's knowledge of wines, coupled with his scientific inclination toward detachment, surely mitigated against snap judgments and unbridled enthusiasm about the prospects of his new grape. What was more, it was simply not possible to divine the real worth of such a crudely extracted liquid. And yet he could not help but be encouraged by what he tasted. Rough-hewn though it was, the wine seemed to him to possess some of the potential for the power and depth of a Bordeaux. And the mere fact that it was pleasant on the tongue, let alone promising, after two centuries of trial and error, but mostly error, in the colonies was significant.

How significant? That was the question. This was not Archimedes in his tub; not the utter elation of the joy of discovery. Of greater and more immediate significance was that, in the months to come, his odd grape began to assume the outlines of an obsession, one that would, in time, displace his other obsession.

He did not yet know that with this improbable act of creation he had succeeded in doing what nobody had been able to do in more than two hundred years of trying, not the colonists at Jamestown, not Jefferson— produce a wine on native ground that would not succumb to disease and was, above all, worth drinking. He did not yet know that he had cracked the code.

3

I F THE AMERICAN experiment had taken as long as the American
experiment in wine, there might never have been an America.

But if there had never been wine, or rather the promise of wine, there
also might never have been a fleet of ships dropping anchor at Jamestown
in 1607.

The English Crown was motivated by something more than mere discovery of territory heretofore unknown to the white man. It was motivated
by profit.

The monarchy had begun to tire of the monopoly the Iberian govern-
ments held over the wine trade. Elizabeth I had resumed relations with the
French by the end of the sixteenth century, but the queen chafed at the high
tariffs her neighbors to the south imposed on wine. Wine held great importance to the British. It was not a luxury, a beverage of leisurely contemplation, to the colonists or the English who sent them. No fermented or
distilled beverages were. Water was a dubious proposition in the seven-
teenth century; epidemics of cholera and dysentery were the bane of cities,
towns, and villages in Europe and America until well past the middle nineteenth century. Whiskey and ale and port could get you drunk, but they
possessed an incalculable benefit, too, inoculating drinkers to a degree
from the ravages of cholera and dysentery. Englishmen drank, on average,
forty gallons of alcohol a year. Drink was a preservative and, because of
this, a highly valuable commodity.

The members of Sir Walter Raleigh's 1584 North American expeditions glimpsed the verdant future site of the Roanoke colony, in present-day North Carolina, with its grapes growing in wild profusion. The English were not the first to "discover" the grape-rich area, however. A Spanish Jesuit missionary named Father Juan de la Carrera had sent a dispatch to his king, noting vineyards "so beautiful and so well plotted as any in Spain." (Inexplicably, by 1590 the Roanoke colony was gone—a victim, some historians believe, of a counterattack by angry, displaced Indians, but more likely assimilation.)

With rival empires lusting after the promise of its vines, the area was ripe for exploitation. It was simply a matter of time as to which kingdom got there first—and managed to hang on.

To the English, the New World represented a rare opportunity, holding out the promise of a self-sustaining source for wine that would liberate the country from the grip of its adversaries, while also giving it an opportunity to extend the empire. James I moved ahead vigorously with plans to voyage to the continent in 1606, recruiting investors, selling shares in the new venture on the London stock market, and chartering a trading company to set up a commercial colony in the New World. The voyage of the Virginia Company—named for Elizabeth, the so-called Virgin Queen—set sail in 1606 with 108 passengers divided among the three ships. Arriving four months later in the spring of 1607 at the mouth of a river emptying into Chesapeake Bay, they dubbed their destination Jamestown, after the King.

Enthusiasm was high. Company records note that Virginia "yeeldeth naturally great store" of grapevines "and of sundry sorts, which by culture will be brought to excellent perfection."

Captain John Smith, who led the expedition, echoed Sir Walter Raleigh's report. At Jamestown, he wrote, there were vines "in great abundance in many parts that climbe the toppes of the highest trees."

Of the colony's initial winemaking efforts, Smith boasted, "[O]f hedge grapes, we made neere 20 gallons of wine, which was neare as good as your French Brittish." He boldly ventured that if the grapes were "properly planted, dressed and ordered by skillful 'vinearoones' "—*vignerons,* the

French term for the workers who cultivate grapevines—"we might make a perfect grape and fruitful Vintage in short time."

Smith's optimism was unfounded. The colonists did not come close to making a perfect grape. As for the predicted "short time" until the vintage materialized, that was off, too. By about two centuries.

The Virginia Company's response to the colonists' first batch of wine amounted to a damning judgment of the venture. It implored the new governor of Virginia, Sir Thomas Gates, to "use the labour of your owne men in makinge wines"—drinkable wines, that is. In truth, the drinking habits of the settlers ought to have been incentive enough. Many of the thirsty pioneers had taken to slurping water from the muddy James River. "Our drinke," wrote one of the colonists, a man named George Percy, "[was] Cold water taken out of the River, which was at a floud verie salt, at low tide full of slime and filth, which was the destruction of many of our men."

The wine, believed to have been made from the Scuppernong grape, had the bouquet of a wet dog, and was reckoned to be "foxy," a highly untechnical designation, to be sure, but one that nonetheless paints a vivid and disagreeable word picture; it outlived its coiners, and remains the Jamestown colonists' most enduring contribution to American wine culture. Foxy wines have an insistent muskiness about them, a muskiness that crowds out the fruitiness of a wine and works against the chance of any kind of complexity. It is a characteristic of many native grapes, like *aestivalis,* and is seldom, if ever, found in the *vinifera* grapes that dominate Europe.

By 1618, the colonists had all but exhausted their available winemaking options. They had experimented with growing native grapes, including the Muscadine and the Catawba, but to little avail. Any number of theories were trotted out to justify the failure of the colonists to produce the wine that had been expected of them. The climate was poor. The soil was not good. They had not been outfitted with the proper equipment. What was more, there were deer everywhere, blithely munching the product of the colonists' backbreaking labors.

In 1619, the Virginia Company, rethinking its approach, went to the expense of bringing in eight vignerons from France, along with a variety of

French vine cuttings. Many of the imported *vinifera* vines died. Those that survived did not thrive and produced an exceedingly poor-quality wine.

The problem with native grapes was that they were a poor match for winemaking. The problem with European grapes was that they were a poor match for American soil and climate. The vines were ill-suited to the heat and humidity of Virginia and unable to adapt to the inevitable diseases and pests that preyed upon them. It ought to have been a mighty lesson learned. But the mistakes were repeated, over and over, for nearly two centuries.

The French have a term for the primacy of the role of the climate and the land in winemaking, called *terroir*. There is no practical equivalent in English. The word refers to the almost mystical combination of soil and air that, in the impassioned view of the French, for whom it is a kind of referendum on the national character, is imparted to every bottle of wine. *Terroir* cannot be forced or faked or imitated; it is innate, encoded within every bottle of wine as traits are encoded in DNA, a vast complex of characteristics that no vintner, no matter how skilled, can cover over—the irreducible stamp of a place and time. It differs from place to place, perhaps imperceptibly to the untrained, but in the end that modest difference is a mighty one, a great and enduring mystery of individuality. By the laws of *terroir*, you cannot simply uproot a vine, a vine that speaks of a particular place and time, and hope to transplant it successfully to another patch of the world.

The vignerons did not admit that their own vines were insufficient to the task. Their complaint was with the colonists, who, they alleged, treated them like slaves.

That same year, the Virginia Company also petitioned Jamestown legislators for a law that would make it mandatory for every household to plant and tend European vines. In 1619, at the first meeting of an English representative assembly in the colony, held in a Jamestown church—the first representative assembly in the New World—the burgesses passed Acte 12. All men who headed a household were required by law to grow European grapes:

> . . . every householder doe yearly plante and maintaine ten vines,
> untill they have attained to the arte and experience of dressing a
> Vineyard, either by their owne industry, or by the Instruction of
> some Vigneron. And that upon what penalty soever the
> Governour and Counsell of Estate shall thinke fitt to impose
> upone the neglecters of this acte.

The penalty was eventually decided: "on paine of death."

At the behest of the company, the vignerons were retained to instruct the colonists in the finer points of grape cultivation. But individual instruction was only a part of the program of education the company embarked on. It also supplied every household with an instructional manual on viticulture and silkworm cultivation—somewhat like equipping every room in a hotel with a Gideon Bible. As if these spurs were not enough, it exerted political pressure on the governor to impose price controls on wines from Spain and Portugal, so as to encourage the colonists to support their own industry.

The effectiveness of the mandate is perhaps best judged by a letter written by Governor Francis Wyatt three years after the law was passed:

> To plant a Colony by water drinkers was an inexcusable errour in
> those, who layd the first foundacion, and have made it a received
> custome, which until it be laide downe againe, there is small hope
> of health.

The experiment could not have been more disastrous. The Virginia Company's stock plunged precipitously back home. In Jamestown, families took to pitching their viticultural manuals into the fireplace, fuel for the long, cold winter. The manuals had proved useful, after all.

The Virginians turned to other beverages; by 1649, there were six brewhouses in the colony. Most had given up on growing grapes and making wine.

In 1658, an Act of Assembly took one last shot at spurring Virginia's wearied would-be winemakers. It offered ten thousand pounds of free to-bacco to the first household to produce "two tunne" of wine from its own vineyard. The prize went unclaimed.

UP AND DOWN the colonies, they tried. In 1662, Lord Baltimore had three hundred acres of vines planted in Maryland, and is said to have even-tually produced some wine that was purported to be comparable to red Burgundy. A decade later, the vineyard had collapsed, a victim of the harsh winter, and no doubt, of mildew, black rot, and (as yet unnamed) phyllox-era. William Penn tried, too, bringing French and Spanish vines to the colony on his first trip there. He even professed a belief that the future of American wine lay with native vines, writing, "It seems most reasonable to believe, that not only a thing groweth best, where it naturally grows; but will hardly be equalled by another species of the same kind, that doth not naturally grow there. But to solve the doubt, I intend, if God give me life, to try both, and hope the consequence will be as good wine as any Euro-pean countries of the same latitude do yield." Penn had intuited, correctly, that a knowledge of *terroir* was integral to the enterprise of cultivating a winemaking culture in the New World, but he did not back his words with actions. Pennsylvanians planted *vinifera*. And failed.

There were successes in Virginia, but they were small successes, per-sonal in nature. At his Green Springs estate, just west of Jamestown, Gov-ernor William Berkeley used trees as trellises to support an extensive network of vines. He claimed his wine was "as good as any that came out of Italy." The inventory for William Fauntleroy's cellar, in Rappahannock County, listed ninety gallons of rum, twenty-five gallons of lime juice, and twenty dozen bottles of local wine. The Huguenots arrived in Vir-ginia in 1700, and by the turn of the century were producing what they claimed was a "Noble, strong-bodied claret." No one, however, had found a method for producing good, consistent wine on a scale larger than the home cellar.

The colonists imported sherry, sack, claret, Canary, Malaga, and Tent from France and Italy, and Madeira from Portugal. The words of Hugh Jones, a clergyman who taught math and philosophy at the College of William and Mary in the early years of the eighteenth century, testify to the popularity of Madeira, a drink that "relieved the heat of summer and warmed the chilled blood and bitter colds of winter." The rest of the colonists, unable to afford the stiff tariffs on these imports, drank beer.

The intent of the Virginia Company had been to produce a self-sustaining wine colony, but in fact, the colonists were dependent to a startling degree on imports. In 1768, they exported to England a little more than thirteen tons of wine. Meanwhile, they imported nearly four hundred thousand gallons of rum from overseas, and nearly eighty thousand more from other North American colonies.

A century and a half into the colonial period, the wine experiment had long since been discarded as a project. It had eaten up a good deal of capital—social, political, physical, and psychological—reminding them of the limits of their new world. Many had turned their attention and efforts elsewhere, to other cultivation projects—tobacco, chiefly.

But there remained a few dreamers who held fast to a belief that with more experimentation would come more insight and that it was foolish to stop trying; if anything, it was important to keep trying. Scientific discoveries followed, more often than not, from a skein of spectacular failures—the moment of breakthrough made possible by the years of bumbling. In their work ethic and optimism, in their faith in the Enlightenment, these believers helped to lay the foundation of the American character.

In 1769, the House of Burgesses, now situated in Williamsburg, the seat of government, passed "An Act for the Encouraging of the Making of Wine."

Around this time, in an action that paralleled the importation of the vignerons a century earlier, the assembly also enlisted the assistance of a French winemaker named Andrew Estave. Estave came highly credentialed—in the words of his petition, he was a man who "hath a perfect Knowledge of the culture of vines, and the most approved Method of making Wine." The government challenged Estave: If he could produce ten hogsheads, or 630 gallons, of good wine within six years, it would sign over the deed to a property it had purchased in York County—a hundred acres, a house, and three slaves.

Estave, after studying the soil and cultivating grapes, was so confident of success that he set his own timetable, fearlessly predicting that he would produce "good merchantable Wine in four years from the seating and planting of the Vineyard."

By 1775, a defeated Estave had become interested in a new and different project: raising silkworms.

NO DREAMER was more hopeful of success—or better positioned to succeed—than Thomas Jefferson.

If anyone was going to solve the great riddle of wine in the New World, it was the restless and intense man of parts whose endless pursuit of knowledge had led him to author a life-script in which he played nearly every available part. He made the ordinary Renaissance man look like a layabout by comparison. An aesthete by breeding and by temperament, an intellectual, worldly and accomplished, Jefferson nevertheless liked to fancy himself a simple farmer. "I have often thought," he wrote once, "that if heaven had given me choice of my position and calling, it should have been on a rich spot of earth, well watered, and near a good market for the productions of the garden. No occupation is so delightful to me as the culture of the earth, and no culture comparable to that of the garden."

His devotion to gardening is well known, his oenophilia less so. But it is his oenophilia that shines the keener light on his character, for the measure of a great man is to be found more by his comparatively few failures than by his many triumphs; and Jefferson's failures to make wine and solve the problem of winemaking in the New World—one of the few enduring failures of his life—haunted him throughout his days.

Jefferson's love of wine began in college, at William and Mary, but flourished during the five years he spent as America's envoy to France from 1784 to 1789, years in which he seemed to have pursued an education in wine as ardently as he practiced diplomacy. He was blessed with an astute palate. In France, he noted in his diary that four vineyards were "of the first quality"—the same four vineyards that in the legendary 1855 classification would be declared "first growth" wines. "Good wine," he wrote to his friend John Jay, the foreign secretary, "is a daily necessity for me."

Serious collectors will no doubt recognize the strain of self-justification in this, of a passionate avocation dressed up in the plain guise of simple need. Jefferson had become an obsessive, and he knew no restraint when it came to his beloved wines. On the eve of his return to the States, in 1789, he shipped some "samples" of the best wines of France to Jay to "present to the President and yourself, in order that you may decide whether you would wish to have any." The shipments constituted an entire wine cellar: thirty-six bottles of Montrachet, thirty-six bottles of Champagne, forty-eight bottles of Meursault, sixty-five bottles of Frontignan, sixty bottles of Rochegude, and sixty bottles of Sancerre. During his first term as president, he spent nearly a third of his $25,000 income on wine—in today's terms, the equivalent of more than $75,000. Throughout his eight years in the White House, 1801 to 1809, he purchased more than twenty thousand bottles of wine.

Wine was more than mere drink to Jefferson; it was a pathway to enlightenment, an integral aspect of a healthy, temperate, and moral life. Whiskey drinking had become a bane in the colonies, and Jefferson believed that wine was a way out, a civilizing antidote. The problem was getting it. Importing wine in Jefferson's time was fraught with problems, among them the fact that shipping in poor weather boiled or froze the wine, and thieving boatmen, especially on the James and Potomac rivers, were prone to filching the highly prized bottles. What was more, there were no wine shops or wholesalers. What wines were drunk were often watered down or brandied. Jefferson himself engaged in these practices.

The answer was to cultivate a native wine grape. But it was an answer that, as the colonists and their descendants had demonstrated, posed an infinite number of questions in reply. Questions that had, to that point, proved unanswerable.

Jefferson embarked on this project—one that would consume his attentions, off and on, for more than fifty years, begun before his stationing in France—when he moved into the South Pavilion at Monticello (the great house was still then under construction), in 1772. Later the following year, he met and befriended Philip Mazzei, a Florentine noble whose self-styled Renaissance man proclivities—he was, variously, a merchant, surgeon, diplomat, pamphleteer, royal adviser, and horticulturalist—mirrored Jefferson's own. Mazzei had come to Virginia to make wine, and established a vineyard adjacent to Monticello, a project of great and abiding interest to his dabbling neighbor. He called the property Colle.

In a pattern that had by now become familiar, Mazzei summoned a team of vignerons, brought in from Tuscany, who planted thousands of vine cuttings from France, Spain, Italy, and Portugal. The past was not his past, he believed.

Jefferson, impressed, hired the vignerons, too. They planted thirty vines, including a number of native vines. With a reportorial eye and a fascination for the intricacies of process, Jefferson recorded the results of their labors, noting the methods of digging trenches, the optimal times for planting, and the importance of spacing the vines.

A month later, Jefferson took note of a "frost which destroyed almost every thing." It destroyed Mazzei's vines, too.

Mazzei called in reinforcements. That summer, he brought in six more vignerons from Tuscany. Trooping through the woods, they identified more than two hundred varieties of native grapes, six of which Mazzei chose for wine-making. Like so many others enticed by the promise of America, he could hardly contain his enthusiasm for the virgin land, later writing,

> I believe that in no other country are conditions so favorable to
> the culture of grapevines as there. I measured two vines, the
> stems of which were more than a yard and a half in circumference.
> July grape cuttings came up in such abundance that my men
> urged me to make wine. The first year, the various kinds that
> reached me in good condition produced shoots of such length that
> [one of my supernumeraries] remarked: "Master, don't write
> home about it, because nobody there would believe you and they
> would call you a liar."

Later that year, Mazzei put together an ambitious business plan—
"Proposal for Forming a Company of Partnership for the purpose of raising and making Wine, Oil, agruminous Plants, and Silk." The enterprise
that emerged from this proposal was the Virginia Wine Company. The
thirty-seven shareholders, ponying up at least fifty pounds sterling per
share, included Jefferson, George Washington, and George Mason. They
granted Mazzei full authority to produce the wines. The echo of the Virginia Company was perhaps unintentional, but the companies were similar.
Both were shrewd business schemes cloaked in high-minded ideals.

For three years, Mazzei attended to his vineyards with "great diligence,"
Jefferson wrote in a letter to a friend. Then came the war for American independence and the dispersal of Mazzei's men, and eventually Mazzei himself departed. Burnishing his vitae by taking on another identity, he assumed
a post in Europe as a commercial agent of Virginia. Some accounts of this
time single out the horses of Hessian prisoners of war quartered at Colle as
having destroyed the fields; Jefferson blamed the horses of a German general, General Riedesel, with trampling the vines.

Mazzei returned to Virginia after the war, but, unable to drum up local
interest, workers, or money, he gave up on the vineyard. In 1785, he left the
country for good.

MAZZEI'S LACK OF success did little to deter Jefferson. Nor did Virginia's long troubles with wine much trouble him. Jefferson never abandoned the hope that his native state would produce good wine.

Indeed, he pursued his dream more ardently than ever. During the
years he spent in France as American minister, wine seems to have come
second only to matters of state, and not always then. He drank widely and
spent profligately. But more than educating himself about Burgundy and
Bordeaux, he was amassing knowledge for the great project he would undertake one day at Monticello, the project that would succeed where Mazzei
had failed and redeem the promise of Colle. Under cover of official government business, he toured the great vineyards of Europe, visiting cellars,
taking notes on viticultural practices, and seeking out sources for the best

vines he could find—including Bordeaux, Burgundy, Champagne, Frontignac, Montrachet, Chambertin, Clos de Vougeot, some of the greatest wine-producing grapes of Europe—to plant at Monticello when he returned. He had retained Antonio Giannini, one of Mazzei's vignerons, and kept in contact with him via letters about the progress of the vineyard at Monticello. "How does my vineyard come on? Have there been grapes enough to make a trial of wine? If there should be, I should be glad to receive here a few bottles of the wine."

There was no wine, Giannini reported back. "[T]he vines are improving marvelously, but no wine has been made because each year the grapes are picked before they are ripe, which is very harmful to the vines. . . . The location is well adapted to a vineyard, as I have already told you."

Later that year, in a letter to Ferdinand Grand, a Frenchman, Jefferson expressed his belief that "tho' [North America has] some grapes as good as in France, yet we have by no means such a variety, nor so perfect a succession of them."

His endorsement of American vines was ultimately hollow—an outward declaration that did not square with his innermost desires. When it came to drinking wine, not expounding upon it, Jefferson was a *vinifera* man. He invariably chose Europe. (Later, as president, he served a few American wines in the White House, but native varietals were not served in great number by a president until Lincoln.)

He continued to solicit cuttings from friends and acquaintances overseas throughout his first retirement and during his time as vice president. Invariably, the vines budded, then died. "It was not," he wrote to a friend, Benjamin Hawkins, who had sent some cuttings, "for want of care." What, then? The climate? Winters in Virginia were rough, but he had been to France, and winters there were not much milder or more stable. The answer was elusive.

JEFFERSON MOVED into the White House in 1801, but the running of the country did not so preoccupy him that he neglected his pet project. This time he opted for a southwest planting, the better for the vines to face the sun. Suffering from deafness and tinnitus, he retreated as much as time permitted to his mansion. Among the six rows he planted were thirty vines from Burgundy and Champagne, sixty from Bordeaux, and ten from the Cape of Good Hope.

In 1807, with his second term coming to a close, Jefferson turned his attention in earnest to the vineyard—the one endeavor in which failure had been the rule in a great and storied life filled with successes. Retirement loomed, but not idleness, and he seemed more determined than ever to triumph, to subdue the forces of destruction and achieve dominion over them. The inability to produce wines of any satisfaction, let alone distinction, gnawed at him, and the instability of Europe led him to worry that his importation of wine was at risk.

If before he had engaged in tactical skirmishes in an attempt to achieve victory, now he embarked on war.

He undertook not just a southwest planting, but a northeast planting as well. In all, he had installed twenty-eight rows of grapes, some from Mazzei, some transplanted vines from the White House. There were Muscat grapes, Trebbiano grapes, San Giovetto (the grape of Chianti), Tokay, and Frontignac grapes, among others. He was confident of victory, full of newfound hope for the aggressive venture. This time he would get it right. As it had been with democracy, so it would be with wine: a fresh, sophisticated vision for the New World, brought forth, quite literally, from the roots and practices of the Old World. Here, in his own backyard, he would oversee the incubation of an industry that would one day rival the finest efforts of France and Italy.

And then, as before, all the vines turned up dead or dying.

Being the biggest undertaking of them all, the one he had invested so much money and time in, the defeat was that much more profound. What had happened? It was not, as he had written of his earlier experiments, for want of care. It could not simply be a matter of climate. It had to be, he reasoned, the grapes themselves.

It was a keen observation, but after months and months of loving, careful attention to some of the finest, noblest grapes in the world, after years of theorizing, and note taking, it must have been painful to be rewarded with something so paltry as an *insight*.

In 1809, two years after undertaking the extensive plantings of *vinifera* grapes, Jefferson reached out to Major John Adlum, a former Revolutionary War soldier and judge, for help. Adlum maintained a two-hundred-acre estate near Georgetown, and made wines from native grape varieties. Jefferson had tried one of his wines and found it promising; the company he had assembled at dinner, Jefferson wrote, could not distinguish it from a Burgundy.

The sentence after his praise for the almost-Burgundy testified to the evolution of his thought about wine and conveyed a full reckoning of his failure: "I think it would be well to push the culture of that grape, without losing our time & efforts in search of foreign vines, which it will take centuries to adapt to our soil & climate."

He believed—or rather, wanted to believe—that the grape of the future was the Scuppernong. Having tasted a wine made from the grape, he planted fifteen Scuppernong vines in his vineyard. In 1817, in a letter to Judge William Johnson in Washington, he touted a wine made in North Carolina from the grape: "Her Scuppernong wine, made on the south side of the Sound, would be distinguished on the best tables of Europe for its fine aroma, and chrystalline transparence." He continued to be supportive of the Scuppernong in another letter, writing, "That as good wines will be made in America as in Europe, the Scuppernong of North Carolina furnishes sufficient proof." His own Scuppernong was not nearly so successful. Nor, for that matter, had the vineyard at Monticello approached anything like abundance.

In a letter to Adlum, in 1823, three years before he died, Jefferson thanked his old friend for some bottles of wine he had sent, and begged off commenting about a book Adlum was writing on the culture of the vine: "It would be presumption in me to give any opinion, because it is a culture of which I have no knowledge either from practice or reading."

It was a humbling admission of defeat for a man who was not accustomed to failing, a wave of the white flag on the project that had consumed him and in which success ultimately eluded him. He had been one of the architects of democracy. He had been a governor, a statesman, secretary of state, vice president, and president. He had purchased the Louisiana Territory from the French, securing an important port in New Orleans and enriching the cultural life of the country beyond measure. He had signed off on the Lewis and Clark expedition, clearing the way for the acquisition of the Northwest. He had built Monticello, one of the most enduring monuments in the nation's history. Yet he had never produced so much as a jug of wine. He drank a lot of it and became a connoisseur. He spent a lot of his private income to acquire it. He devoted enormous resources of time and money to produce grapes, and spoke eloquently and passionately about America's capacity to develop a grape culture of its own. He became, for many, the first father of American wine. But for fifty years, he had tried and tried and tried to make wine, and he had come up empty. All his learning and all his study, all his travels and all his resources, all his passion for the subject and all his clear-headed reason had got him no further than the men who had first landed at Jamestown more than two hundred years earlier.

4

IF THE DOCTOR'S GRAPE was to have a life beyond him—if it was to fulfill its potential and produce the great American table wine—then it was imperative for him to spread the word of his discovery, to tout its singularity and importance. He did not have to go forth and market himself, hawking his product like some elixir salesman or prevailing upon skeptical members of the press. He had only to secure the blessing of one William Prince Jr.—provided he could persuade the great and powerful horticulturist of his grape's immense promise.

The Linnaean Botanic Garden and Nurseries of Long Island, founded and operated by the Prince family, was one of the preeminent nurseries of nineteenth-century America, a rich and extensive repository of plants, trees, and fruits, all tended with exquisite care and devotion. For a young agricultural nation, the population of gardens, hillsides, and valleys was a matter, not just of chauvinistic pride, but also of great practical necessity, and the Prince nursery was an incalculable resource; its catalogs were to early America what the Sears catalogs were to mid-twentieth-century America, consumer totems of surpassing importance.

William Prince Jr. was in the third generation of Princes in the nursery business. His grandfather had begun growing trees and shrubs before the signing of the Declaration of Independence, on a plot of land adjacent to a creek in the sleepy fishing village of Flushing. Almost from the start, it acquired a reputation as the first and last word in horticulture, and it exerted an enormous influence on what was grown, and how. The business grew quickly, increasing in size but also in stature, and it transformed itself in relatively short order from valuable resource to national treasure. The seven-year occupation of Long Island by the British during the Revolutionary War confirmed its importance to the colonies: The Redcoats ordered troops to guard it. Six months after becoming president, George Washington arrived at the nursery by barge, but pronounced himself unimpressed by its goods. He was an exception. Lewis and Clark, recognizing its worth as a center of science, shipped many of their botanical discoveries to Flushing for investigation and classification. Many others regarded it as a prime tourist attraction—in particular, many urban-addled Manhattanites, who frequently escaped the busy, bumptious city by taking a boat out to Flushing for the day.

Prince Jr. differed from his predecessors in staking out a much more ambitious, progressive agenda for the business. He envisioned the nursery as more than simply a purveyor of the known. Extending its aim, he turned it into a hothouse for experimentation, putting a special emphasis on the nurturing and cultivating of new native fruit and plant species, as well as those from Asia and Europe. He purchased a tract of land adjoining the nursery and created a second nursery. The invocation of Linnaeus in the nursery's name speaks to Prince's sense of history and mission.

He differed, too, in the finely developed aesthetic sense he brought to his work; he thought and felt like a poet. The gardens, to Prince Jr., were no mere commercial enterprise, but rather a spiritual endeavor; gardening itself, he felt, was akin to art or religion, something that reawakened the senses and reordered the spirit, something pure and true.

His son, William Robert Prince, with whom he collaborated on books, expresses this keen devotion to nature in a preface to a volume on roses they published in 1846:

> He who seeks for unerring truth, and has become sickened at the
> unmeaning forms and falsities of life, will find it in the charming
> realm of Flora, for there at least, as in the immutable paths of

astronomy and geology, he will find nature true to herself. In the
earlier days of the writer, it was his frequent response to friends,
when the sorrows of life formed the theme, that he 'ne'er knew a
sorrow, that he could not ramble among flowers and forget'; and
such indeed are the pure and unalloyed sensations that twine
around the heart and entrance the mind of the true votary of
Flora; sensations generated with our existence, the unadulterated
aspirations of the natural and uncontaminated mind, as it came
from the hand of its Maker; and which can only be neutralized,
blighted, or obliterated by the falsities of (so called) civilized
society. . . .

In their devotion to the ennobling glories of nature, and in their companion scorn for the falsities of society, it is possible to discern the rapturous strains of the transcendentalists.

Prince cultivated more than plants; he cultivated correspondents. He
was wise to recognize that, bound as he was to his long hours at the nursery and to life on his particular slip of Long Island, he was limited in his
knowledge and understanding of the terrain, so he encouraged contact
with the many amateur scientists scattered about the country who brought
him enthusiastic reports of new varieties. Rarely did a week go by that one
of these correspondents did not ask him to weigh in on unheard-of varieties of pears, apricots, or apples, the discovery of which they shared with
him as though they were passing on important news to a trusted friend.
Prince, more scientist than businessman, and more seeker, perhaps, than
either, remained open-minded to all these reporters, who represented possibilities to be discovered. He copied every report from the field into a journal for safekeeping and future reference.

Dr. Norton was one of these correspondents. He was keenly aware of
Prince's importance. A listing in one of the nursery's horticultural catalogs, and he might accomplish what months and months of dreary, self-
negating salesmanship up and down the colonies could not.

Prince, for his part, was not entirely lacking in motivation. He might
not have been desperate for Norton to happen along with his grape, but

Prince's eagerness was obvious. It was precisely the sort of project that he had envisioned for the nursery, a chance to nurture and develop a new variety or species, to create something of worth that did not previously exist, to turn promise into potential.

Prince made mention of the grape, christened Norton's Virginia Seedling, in his catalog of 1822.

Other native grape varieties carried single-word titles that evoked a hard, rugged land—Catawba, Scuppernong—or, if they paid homage to the men who discovered them, did so with matter-of-fact directness—Herbemont, for instance. "Norton's Virginia Seedling" sounded a characteristically nineteenth-century note. It was simple but lyrical, full of yearning but rooted, too, in a sense of place. Above all, it was personal—it seemed to convey that, because the person who had conceived it had consented to affix his name to it, you could trust it.

THE LISTING was a coup for Daniel Norton, but having long since tumbled down a mine shaft, having come to regard darkness as the natural order of things, he was unable to perceive that this crack in the gloom represented the possibility of a way out. On the cusp of triumph, he appeared to be a man in the throes of defeat. He believed in his grape, but about his own prospects for survival he was much less certain.

He remained secluded for much of the spring and summer at Magnolia, communing with Eliza, if only in his imagination—"[M]y only pleasure, for nearly two years," he later wrote, "has been to fancy you still miss me, that your death was but a dream"—and chancing little contact with family and friends, let alone others. "[B]ound as I am to this spot of affliction," he mused, how was it that he could "be otherwise than incapacitated for business, [could be] any thing but what I am, useless to myself and the world?"

He made an exception for his half-brother, John Jaquelin Ambler. The oldest of Norton's mother's eight children with the colonel, John Jaquelin turned twenty-one that year, seven years younger than the doctor. As the difference in their ages began to collapse, and as Norton grew older and more forgiving of the circumstances of lineage, the two grew closer. Norton turned to him often, regarding him as an intimate, someone with whom he could unburden himself of his deepest, most troubled thoughts.

Earlier that winter, he had scratched out a long, agonized letter while John Jaquelin was abroad.

> Spring you know is my favorite season and with all my heart I wish with the birds it had come, but I shall have to pass many dreary hours before the sweet season comes to my relief. I live to be sure, at this time, it may be said I barely live, for I enjoy nothing, my disposition has always been too dark and gloomy to bear the slightest shade of horrid winter . . . The actual state in which I exist [is] mysterious. I allow no passion to militate with the wishes of those with whom I am secluded, I stifle my thought, that has for its tendency, a separation from those who delight in my society.
>
> No dreams of power, no less of riches, no desire of place or station, has as yet tempted me to think of a change. I live careless of what surrounds me and dead to the incidents that daily present themselves for contemplation . . . Thought rich, but poor— wearing the smile of content, whilst torn with contending passions—little encouraged in my professional labors, when I feel it strong within me, that by a proper course I could rise in reputation. Circumstances have bowed me down to humble expectation, I once looked up to the splendor which wealth affords, and to the admiration which learning can inspire. All, all, I willingly sacrifice, to the gratitude I owe to those who respect, and who never cease to love me—I can never leave my best friends, old and in sorrow, I have been dutiful and affectionate, I have been mild and submissive to them, it would be tearing my heart asunder to quit them . . .

In August, he shed his cocoon. He canceled his appointments, took leave of his practice, boarded a horse-driven coach from Magnolia Farm, and headed north.

Leaving behind sodden, heat-stricken Richmond, with its drooping magnolias and parched plantations, was invigorating, but the distance he was seeking was more than physical; it was psychological, too. Distance from his problems, distance from the familiar, distance from routine.

He had not thought to impose on his travels anything so self-conscious as a *purpose* and had not set out for New York with an agenda. (Though it seems reasonable to suppose he might have visited the Prince Nurseries, no evidence exists to support it.) He was guided, rather, by a certain spiritual aimlessness, a desire to set his hungering soul loose in a strange land, to live "amongst the wilds and savages of our frontier country," and perhaps to recalibrate his ravaged senses amid the timeless rhythms of nature.

He was, he later wrote, "fully determined not to return for years." He returned in two months.

The next time he wrote to John Jaquelin was in October:

> My passing through the state of New York was pleasing and
> served in a great measure to dispel the gloom and melancholy that
> had fastened on me leading me little by little to perdition. I had
> my dear Brother looked to the grave with pleasure as a retreat
> from my misery. . . . No one knows the keen affliction I laboured
> under, the silent sorrow, that was gradually undermining the
> strength of my body and mind for more than a year. I never slept
> but for a few moments at a time, and then I would dream of
> Heaven, but to wake in Hell . . .

He closed his letter by recounting the story of being aboard a ship on Lake Ontario amid a storm. The lives of everyone on board were "in great danger." The trauma moved him to imagine not that his own life was about to end, but rather that he had switched places with his half-brother. "[F]or me to die was nothing, I had lived the happy part of my life but you in the bud & passions of youth, to perish on the waves . . . brought tears to my eyes, and had I practice the waves would have met the overflowing of my heart for you."

Recognizing in his tone the air of desperation he assured his half-brother had begun to dissipate, he begged John Jaquelin, "Do not let my letter disturb you, I think a little more time will make me reconciled to my fate, and I may again be interested in the affairs of life . . ." Then he elaborated upon one of those affairs. "[M]y little farm will amuse me this winter. I shall employ myself much in attempting to improve it and when you return you shall have grapes that will compare with those of France or Italy."

In the medical daybook that Norton kept in his office at Ninth and Broad, an informal, intermittent record of patients, ailments, and the various pills and powders he prescribed, there are no entries after October 30, 1823. The pages are blank. His mind was otherwise occupied.

IN JANUARY of 1824, Daniel Norton wrote his half-brother in Paris:

> . . . but for books, and attending to my flowers, I should be as mad
> as a March hoss, some will have me sing hymns, and some will
> have me marry, others sniff my moods and say I play cards and
> drink grog, some say I speak to men with red noses and black
> eyes, whilst others who have nothing else to say . . . in a word
> your poor brother has become an object of particular concern, to
> many people . . . I have red eyes, in consequence of being awake
> all night thinking on the nature of my own case. . . .
>
> I have all my life been as proud as Lucifer and as poor as a
> church mouse. My portrait, has never glittered, with the Prussian
> or Moroccan varnish, but dull and heavy as the hand of nature
> made it, amongst the gaudy crowd it has been seen only when
> sought for, I wish indeed I would fall upon some plan to add to
> the light of my [maintenance], that I might catch the wandering
> eye of beauty, or turn by actual insight the scale of importance in
> my farm . . .

I fear I am doomed to be a simple single Pill Garlick, forever
in competition with Doctor Caesar Hawkins, or Mullatto Dick,
who cures diseases without the use of Mercury, that is to say
Quack Seller. . . .

What a stupid employment of pen ink & paper to be allways
writing "to be well shaken before taken," take one of these
powders every two hours in a little sugar and water, "put the feet
in warm water at bed time & etc." The *savoyard* with his monkey
and red cape you passed just now in the streets of Paris, is a more
dignified personage than a Doctor in Richmond.

The intensity of his feelings notwithstanding, his grief had modulated
into something else, a more complex, more layered sense of melancholy.

He was, once more, preoccupied with the world around him.

Having secured the blessing of Prince, he now undertook to secure another, more important blessing.

He was not an Ambler and never would be, but what were they, after
all, next to the great man Jefferson? What did all their achievements
amount to, beside those of the famous Virginian? Here was his chance to
link himself to a greater, more exalted endeavor. To free himself of the
Amblers and their name. To turn himself into a dignified personage.

5

Y OU DON'T THINK Daniel Norton was *inspired* by Jefferson?"
Jenni asks me.

Only she's not asking. She's indignant. She cannot believe that I cannot
grasp what to her seems to be so patently obvious. I'm taken aback but
also fascinated by this exuberant remonstration of hers, so at odds with
the sunny manner she seems intent on projecting in her more guarded
moments.

"Come on, he was a *Virginian*. He was a part of the elite, part of that
world. And even if he was not at the center of that circle, OK, I don't see
how he couldn't have known what Jefferson was doing in the field and what
he talked about and wrote about."

We're hurtling down the highway in her mud-caked Saturn Outlook
one morning, on our way out to a couple of vineyards to see what the competition is up to and to talk Norton. The cabin of the SUV has become a
seminar room, and Jenni, the professor, is admonishing me to broaden my
inquiry, to reject easy conclusions, just as I used to do with my students. It's
fun to be on the other side, to be the receiver. Everyone I have talked to says
that Jenni is the one to ask about Norton the man and Norton the wine, that
she knows more than the books do, more even than many of the wine historians. She could be the doctor's biographer. She is certainly his curator, his
defender, his champion. Squinting into the sun pouring through the windshield, she turns down the radio and chides me for missing the larger impli-

cations when I argue that Jefferson failed—failed utterly—when it came to wine.

"I think that Jefferson's *failures,* if you want to use that word, OK, laid the groundwork for what Dr. Norton did. I frankly doubt you could have had the one without the other. I think very definitely there was a connection there."

It is possible, she seems to be saying, to look at something that is right there in front of your eyes and still not see it, possible to confront the facts and still miss an essential truth. Yes, Jefferson, a success in so much else, failed to establish the homegrown viticulture he dreamed of—to say nothing of his inability to produce a single drop of wine at Monticello in fifty years of trying. But to cling to that all-or-nothing view of Jefferson is to cling to an incomplete picture.

We seem to be reprising the age-old debates about Jefferson and slavery, with Jenni taking the long, commonsensical view that many scholars and historians do not, that a person is not an either/or proposition, but both, simultaneously. And neither, simultaneously.

"What you need to do is go and get your hands on Jefferson's *Garden Book.*"

THE MORE I talked to Jenni, the more I learned about Norton. Norton the grape and its crazy, complicated history. Norton the man and his motivations. But paradoxically, the less I seemed to know about Jenni.

I knew that Norton drove her and inspired her, but later, at night, thinking back over our conversations or reviewing my notes, I was at a loss to understand why.

It is a sort of badge of honor among journalists to poke and prod someone—the subject—until the truth emerges, but it is a trait that has always made me uneasy about the profession, and during those times I am up against it and unable to afford the luxury of self-righteousness, about myself. I find it to be not more honest but more dishonest.

As the toys and tools of our civilization have become ubiquitous, this need of ours to get to the bottom of things, to know a thing instantly and thereby to presume to possess it intimately, has become more pronounced, as if it were possible to drive doubt and uncertainty from the human sphere.

How much more interesting is the exchange of equals, the slow give-and-take, the real person unfolding over time. Not an interrogation, the surrendering of information, but the gradual peeling of the onion.

And isn't this the lesson of wine itself? Wine, which preceded the fancy instruments, which abided by different rhythms, slower rhythms, than our 24/7 culture. To learn about wine, as I was doing, was to appreciate more than varietals and pairings, more than vintages and estates. It was to appreciate the process, the elemental, irreducible cycle that is at the heart of nature and of life. Before there is something to drink, a seed has to be planted, then nurtured. Then the ripening of the vine and the budding of the fruit. Pressing, extraction, barreling. Finally, fermentation, the mysterious transformation of something sweet and grapey into something fine and subtle.

The needs of the vintner were nothing; wine happened on its own time.

JENNI HAD BID me to follow in her footsteps, to trace the path of her own obsession with the doctor and his discovery, and so it is that on a fine fall afternoon, I am paging through a yellowed copy of Thomas Jefferson's *Garden Book* in the Alderman Library at the University of Virginia.

Outside, the trees are ablaze with the colors of autumn, and sunlight slants through the tall windows, illuminating the table in long, irregular cones of gold. It's exactly the kind of day the school's pamphlets and videos hold out in offer to the students, a fulfillment of the arcadian ideal, the pursuit of noble knowledge in a gorgeous, sun-dappled idyll. Could anything be more seductive to a promising young mind? But discovery, real discovery, doesn't happen like this. Real discovery is haphazard. It proceeds in fits and starts, if it proceeds at all. It's a groping amid shadows, a desperate hunt up and down back alleys, a chasing of leads, most of them false. It's Sherlock Holmes as often as it's Socrates.

The *Garden Book* is largely a record of the day-to-day goings-on at Monticello, a hulking document that testifies to Jefferson's avid planting and his great persistence in the field in spite of the obstacles arrayed against him. But historians have also used it to read between the lines, to gain a better sense of Jefferson's routines and passions, and in this way, to come closer to understanding the man Joseph Ellis has called an American sphinx. Among its fascinations is the way it tracks the evolution of the life of Monticello, its drift from a kind of seat of government to a household in transition.

By the time Norton had made his discovery, Jefferson was a man in decline, frail and sickly. He died in 1826, his final years plagued with struggle and doubt and guilt. Profligate in his spending (on wine in particular), Jefferson had incurred enormous debts, and Martha, his daughter, stood to inherit them. There was, too, the looming problem of Monticello, which was not merely a mansion and architectural monument, but a many-legged operation, with about two hundred slaves performing the various tasks needed to keep it functioning.

With Jefferson ailing, the running of Monticello was left to his oldest grandson, Thomas Jefferson Randolph. This was the name that Jenni had directed me to look for.

My eye falls on a brief entry dated March 22, 1824.

On that date, cuttings of grapes from Dr. Norton had arrived at the counting house of a man named Bernard Peyton, Jefferson's Richmond agent. The doctor had not bothered to furnish him with instructions, Peyton noted, adding, "He tells me they were intended for Jefferson Randolph."

Randolph was close to Norton's age, though the two did not seem to know each another. Nor does Randolph appear to have shared his grandfather's enthusiasm for wine or viticulture, although it may simply have been that he was too preoccupied with keeping Monticello going, and had little time to devote to horticultural pursuits.

Whatever the reason, the doctor never heard back.

. . .

WHAT IF the cuttings had arrived earlier? What if Jefferson had been healthier?

It was not hard to imagine that Jefferson would have touted the grape to his friends and colleagues with the same ardency with which he had touted democracy and the virtues of self-sufficiency. It was not hard to imagine him planting the grape at Monticello and pouring the home-pressed wine he made from it at dinner, raising a glass at the table with his distinguished guests and declaring that here, with the emergence of this grape, and thanks to this obscure farmer-doctor, a new day had dawned in American viticulture. Not merely another grape in a long line of would-be saviors, but *the* grape.

I left Charlottesville that night pondering other what-ifs, other possibilities, only later realizing the importance of the entry in the *Garden Book* and why Jenni had sent me.

I had focused on what was obvious and on the surface: the nonresponse from Jefferson. *That's it?* I had thought. *This is what I've come all this way for?* I had missed the even more obvious fact that Norton had made the attempt in the first place, no small matter for someone so paralyzed—the will to action, after so many years of inaction, a triumph all its own. But more than that, I was struck, now, by his determination to get his grape into the hands of the one man in America who could understand what he had done, the one man who could recognize that after more than two hundred years the answer had at last been found, who alone could signal the arrival of a new era. What else could this be but an explicit acknowledgment of Jefferson's enormous influence on him? Did it matter that there was no answer? Daniel Norton had paid his debt.

Lesson learned, I wrote in my notebook that night. *Beware the first impression, the hasty judgment.*

6

H E WAS CLIMBING out of the mine shaft.

A man is what a man does, and Daniel Norton was again a doer. He had made himself a doer. He had willed himself to do.

If among the social circle of Richmond he was not liked or understood—a loner doctor playing with his plants, not unlike that other loner in town, the teenage Edgar Allan Poe, who holed himself up in the second-floor bedroom of the Allan House, at Fifth and Main, scribbling his strange and morbid verse—more and more that did not bother him. He had made a discovery about himself that was at least as important as his other discovery. He had discovered that the less he listened to the outside world and the more he kept his eyes to the ground and tended his vines, the better he was—stronger, more courageous, more fulfilled.

And that was not all: He had discovered, to his astonishment, that he cared about something.

Cultivation had become more than a passion—it had become a compulsion. He plunged himself into his work on the farm as if his life depended on it, which, he only now had come to realize, it did.

He poured his energy into his account book, a digest of the activity and experiments on the farm. He sketched the layout of his gardens. He pressed John Jaquelin for grapes from his travels abroad, and his half-brother complied, shipping "the best varieties of wine grapes from France and Italy." In all, by the late 1820s, there were more than eighteen varieties of grapes, all laid out in careful, lovingly tended rows.

In the garden, he did not brood—he did not think himself a man bookended by death, a thwarted man. Horticulture imposed an order on his unruly habits of mind. It was as though, by subduing the natural world, he produced in himself an equivalent sense of calm and control. More and more, he preferred the company of his plants to people. They needed him, and he needed them, too. They didn't know him by the tragedy of his circumstance, a man of rotten fortune—only by his gentle ministrations, his tender persistence. He had not taken very good care of himself. Indeed, he had let himself go—he looked as ragged and gray as if he had been on a bender—but he had been a loving mate to his plants. They thrived; they were more alive than he was. It was the gardener's obligation to impose order, not so much to tame the unruliness of nature nor even to manage it, but to harness its potential, give the wildness, the life force inherent in all creatures, an opportunity to properly develop.

Magnolia bloomed to life.

HIS LUCK TURNED, and suddenly. As suddenly, it seemed, as it had turned against him.

In 1830, the Princes published *A Treatise on the Vine,* the most important book to date in America on wine culture. Eight years earlier, the doctor had been favored with a kind, if brief, notice of his new discovery in the Prince catalog. Here, now, came validation of the grape's worth. And not least, of his own worth.

Introducing the doctor's hybrid as *Vitis nortoni,* a name that conferred upon the upstart grape the mantle of the official and acknowledged him as its progenitor, the Princes wrote, "This very distinct variety owes its origin to Doctor D. N. Norton of Virginia, whose assiduity and devoted attention to the culture of the vine for a period of years place him among the distinguished connoisseurs of the subject."

Speculating that the grape was a child of the Bland, a variety that Philip

Mazzei brought with him to Colle, and a Pinot Meunier, the authors went on to note its characteristics: its strong, vigorous vines, its ability to weather the brutal winters of the East, and its tendency to thrive in profusion. The grapes, they observed, "do not contain a great quantity of juice, but what they yield is of the richest quality; the skin is replete with a violet coloured matter, which imparts to the wine a shade equal to the Tinto Madeira, which last it resembles as well in taste as in appearance."

They concluded by quoting from Norton's own words about the grape: "For the purpose of making wine, this is hardly to be excelled by any foreign variety."

Astonishing! Had the doctor himself written the copy, he could not have produced a better, more powerful advertisement for his grape. Not only to be included in such an influential volume, but to have his discovery put on par with the best of Europe? And to have this company propagating and selling and shipping his vines throughout the country?

He could not have asked for anything more, but then a sweet-tempered twenty-three-year-old named Lucy Marshall Fisher walked into his life. Fisher was the niece of John Marshall, the former chief justice of the United States, and a cousin of Eliza's. She was well-connected, well-bred, and well-to-do, but of far greater importance to the solitary, uncompromising Norton was the fact that she was well suited to his dark and brooding nature; day to his night, sun to his moon. The doctor, in a cloud of love, dashed off a letter to John Jaquelin in February of 1831, informing him of his engagement and professing his faith in Lucy and his "future happiness." They married four months later: a proper, perfect June wedding.

Throughout his twenties and even into his thirties, Daniel Norton had waited in vain for his life to start, and now everything he had worked for and wished for arrived in a rush—as though Fortune had decided to repay him, all at once, for all it had taken from him, all at once. Lucy bore him five children. A new life, a new wife, and now a boisterous, bountiful household. The gloom was gone. The pallor that hung about the rooms, gone. The brooding, the anguish, the guilt—gone, all of them gone. No more the sad and lonely mausoleum. Magnolia was alive, fully, thrillingly alive.

He was back in the social whirl, albeit reluctantly. Marshall, the chief justice, had made several entreaties toward him, hoping to point the still-young Norton to a career worthy of his talents, a life in law or politics. These were respectable professions for men of the ruling class. In some ways, his new circumstance was not altogether different from his old circumstance, and reflecting on his apartness, his alienation, from the world of the elites, he had sounded a familiar refrain in his letter to his half-brother: "[Y]ou may well know the many difficulties I shall have to encounter with small fortune, with great pride, surrounded by rich and aspiring relations. . . ."

But things would be different this time. He was more clear-eyed than contemptuous. He was not the hot-tempered youth he had been. He had matured. Lucy and her love moderated his emotions. He was better equipped than he had been to survive the polite but withering judgments of social Richmond, and not just because he now had Lucy to lean on. He was better equipped because of his triumphs at Magnolia. No, it was not law. It might not be a "proper" use of his gifts. But he had done what no one who had trod the path before him had done. Not the Jamestown settlers. Not even Jefferson. Prince knew it, and soon enough, the rest of the world would, too.

I N 1833, the first reviews trickled in, and with them, a test of his resolve.

Given the weight that Prince's judgment carried, Daniel Norton had every reason to expect that whatever notices followed in its wake would be just as kind. This expectation, however, only set him up for disappointment, making the reality that much more perplexing and hurtful.

Gideon B. Smith, editor of the *American Farmer*, a pioneering agricultural paper based in Baltimore, passed judgment on a box of Norton grapes he had received from a reader in Pennsylvania. He found the taste to be harsh.

Whether Smith understood the grapes to be wine grapes, which are more astringent than table grapes, is not known. Nor is it known who sent him the grapes or whether in fact they were Norton's Virginia Seedling or misidentified. It did not matter, of course, once the verdict was printed.

The notice was picked up by another publication, the *Farmer's Register*. A doubling of bad news.

It was not enough, the doctor saw now, to have birthed the Seedling; it was incumbent upon him to shepherd its passage into the world. He responded swiftly—as swiftly as nineteenth-century communication would allow—and decisively, dispatching a small box by evening steamboat to the editors of the *Farmer's Register*. In it he had included two varieties of grape, Cunningham's Prince Edward, a native of Prince Edward County, Virginia, and his own Norton's Virginia Seedling. Referring to Smith's pronouncement, he challenged the editors: "[Y]ou are now to judge for yourself."

There was something new in his words, a confidence that months earlier would have been beyond his ability to summon: the unassailable assurance of a court-savvy attorney. "Both varieties are abundant and never failing in their crops," he wrote. "Any portion of the state will yield them to a certainty, and if the culture of these fruits is attended to, the United States in a few years will cease to import wine."

The editors' reply, printed just below the doctor's own boast, had the effect of inadvertent comedy, a dry undermining of the inflated. They began, "The grapes referred to above were received after five days had passed of the rainy weather in the latter part of September. Owing to this delay probably, many of the Norton grapes had rotted, or showed the commencement of decay, though the greater part were still sound."

The panel of tasters was "equally divided as to which possessed the better flavor, but all agreed that both kinds were excellent. The sweet of the Norton was the more unmixed and luscious—that of the Cunningham was flavored with enough of acid to make it (according to our individual opinion) still more agreeable to the taste."

The editors professed a keen interest in the culture of the grape, "not only as a new and profitable branch of agricultural enterprise and industry, but because we fully believe that the extensive production of pure and unadulterated wine in any country is one of the surest safeguards against drunkenness being a national, or prevailing, vice. But although the hope of the extended and general culture has often been held out by different persons, the best proof has not yet been furnished by the successful and profitable general results of the labors of any one individual."

Nothing in the purplish-black bunches of Norton suggested that proof had finally arrived.

It rankled. Three months later, the doctor fired back. If he seemed to swagger, well, why not? Who knew what he knew? Who had tilled the land as long as he had, or as assiduously?

> After the experimental culture of the grape for nearly twenty
> years, (for I commenced it when a boy at school,) I consider that I
> have at last arrived at the point so much desired, (that is, the
> discovery of a grape, or grapes, which afford abundant annual
> crops; and to the culture of which we may lend our labor and care,
> with the certainty of proper return, for all expenditures). All
> grapes, introduced into notice, either foreign or indigenous,
> except the two varieties above named, are subject to rot, mildew,
> and other casualties, in such a manner, that you can never rely
> upon any other return than an occasional small yield for the table.
> At great expense I have collected most of the varieties in a
> continuous line, from Rome to the upper Rhine, and these have all
> been discarded as worthless; having left me with an empty purse,
> as a requital, for many years hard labor.

Unlike foreign vines—how "illy they are formed to resist the agency of burning suns, and voracious insects," he noted—Norton's Virginia Seedling "has never been known to rot or mildew." He went on:

> The berries are so closely congregated on some bunches, as to
> indent one another; yet they all prove equally ripe at the same
> period of time. So replete are they with the saccharine principle,
> that if a bunch at full maturity be closely compressed in the hand,

it will continue to adhere even after the fingers are expanded; and
if a bunch is accidentally suffered to remain on the vine after the
first frosts of autumn, the berries become raisins, a circumstance I
have never known to take place with any other grape, indigenous
or exotic. I have a small cask of wine made from the Seedling last
year. It is luscious beyond any thing you can conceive. Some say it
resembles the Burgundy Madeira—others the Lachrima Christi
of Mount Vesuvius.

He concluded by addressing the matter of Gideon Smith, sounding like
a man who had opted to take the long view, who had no need to shout or
argue, because he knew that time would bear him out.

If I really supposed the circumstance could at all retard the
introduction of these two vines into culture . . . I would be at more
pains to combat his opinion. Relying however, upon the truth of
my assertions, and the strongest testimony to support them, I do
not hesitate again to say, that these two grapes properly
cultivated, will, at no distant period, be a nucleus whence will
emanate an advantage in our exports, scarcely to be calculated.

These battles of will were deeply frustrating to Norton, but they were
useful, too—intellectual exercises that forced him to frame and clarify his
thoughts and file the best, most cogent brief he could muster on behalf of
his Seedling. Never had he entered into these confrontations with the idea
of destroying an opponent. It was not personal with him. The only thing
that mattered was the grape. Give the Seedling an honest chance, the doctor believed, and it would not disappoint.

Not long after his response appeared in the *Farmer's Register,* the *Farmer
& Gardener,* a weekly publication out of Baltimore, lavished praise upon a
bottle of wine the doctor had made from the Seedling, in words that could
have been his own: "It is not our purpose to say, that this wine is as good or
better than *any* imported; but we do, in all candor affirm, that we consider

it a better article than one half of the newfangled liquors which we receive from Europe bearing the name of wine."

Here it was, the longed-for thing, to be a personage, a man of dignity, as his father had been, and his stepfather. And he had done it on his own terms, not in medicine or politics or law, and not by the patronage of the Amblers.

No more the simple, single Pill Garlick. He had emerged an authority.

WEST ACROSS the foothills of the Appalachians his Seedling spread, to Ohio, to Missouri, to Arkansas. A contagion. His Seedling's future as the foundation of American wine seemed assured. His own prospects were not so certain and much less bright.

As 1841 turned into 1842, Norton's health had deteriorated, and in mid-January he suffered a bout of dysentery. He died not long after.

The *Richmond Enquirer* eulogized the forty-seven-year-old doctor as "a gentleman of an enlarged mind, of fine literary taste, and celebrated for his knowledge of the vine, and his skill in horticulture. His disposition was amiable; his society most agreeable. The scope of his observation had been extensive—various in his reading, and original in his reflections. We bid him a last and affectionate Adieu!"

The doctor's final act of promotion—or of self-defense, perhaps—had been to give the Seedling a final, forceful push into history. Writing to William Kenrick, whose *The New American Orchardist* appeared in 1844, the doctor did not simply muster his dwindling resources to tout the virtues of his grape. He explained the source of his impregnation method; championed the Seedling's economic importance; issued the French a dare; and asserted the importance of *terroir* in American winemaking:

> Norton's Seedling stands unrivaled as a field and garden fruit in
> Virginia; crops always surprisingly abundant, and yielding wines,
> which, with proper care, will be found inferior to none of the
> imported drinks from Madeira or France. I obtained this variety

by artificial impregnation, after the manner of Knight. I consider
it capable of doubling the amount of our exports, when it is
properly attended to, throughout the Union; for there is not a
single state in our associated confederacy, which will not be found
propitious to its growth. Wherever the hickory and the oak are to
be found, there also you may expect to rear this fruit. In whatever
climate the Indian corns mature their seeds, the Norton's Seedling
grape will certainly retain a most astonishing yield to the
cultivator. In France, if its properties were understood, it would
supply the place of much of that useless trash, which just now so
unprofitably clothes her fair bosom; no casualty would then cause
any serious diminution in the vintage,—which circumstance
alone, independent of the improvement of her vines, would be, in
a national point of view, of incalculable benefit to that country.

He could not have conceived that the debate over the Seedling would
not remain a debate about worth. So long as people gave it a chance, he
knew he would be proven right. Nor could he have conceived that these
challenges were not his biggest ones.

His biggest challenge had yet to arrive, one that would render all
previous ones as significant as border skirmishes. It came not from editors sniffing at the quality of his wine. It came from an unforeseen rival,
a man named F. W. Lemosy, and it came, inconveniently, after Norton
had died.

In a letter to the *Horticulturalist, and Journal of Rural Art and Rural Taste*
in 1861, Lemosy claimed that his father, Dr. F. A. Lemosy, had discovered
the grape in 1835 or 1836, while shooting duck on Cedar Island, a small,
narrow plot of land in the James River, near Richmond:

During one of my father's rambles over this island, and while
eating wild grapes, he chanced to discover a grape much superior
to any other he had found there; so on his return home he carried
a few bunches to my mother, who, on eating them, recognized a

great resemblance to a grape much used for wine purposes in the south of France, the place of her nativity.

This grape thus became known to us, and brother and I called at Cedar Island every fall for many years thereafter to gather those grapes, and indulge our boyish propensities for fruit. About this time Dr. Norton (one of my father's companions) was establishing a small farm and vineyard near our city, and solicited all the information father could give him relative to the cultivation of the vine. It was during one of those conversations on the subject that father mentioned the existence of this wild grape on Cedar Island, and ventured the suggestion that it would make a good wine grape. . . .

After a few years Dr. Norton developed this grape, and produced a very fine wine; and as he took more interest in it than any one else, we universally called it Norton's Grape, and subsequently Norton's Seedling; by which name I speak of it to this day from mere habit.

The Lemosy story gained currency, even as the doctor's seedling continued to spread across the country.

It gained currency because Norton himself was no longer around to dispute the charge and because, even if the media of the nineteenth century had been a more coherent, more organized enterprise, so little documentation of Norton's work existed that anyone who might have turned to his papers in search of evidence would have found scant support. And even if there had been mounds of papers left behind to provide explicit proof of his triumph, the fact remained that Daniel Norton was a bit player in an obscure drama—a character actor, not a leading man.

There was another reason the Lemosy story did not die. In most instances, the word of one man against that of another amounts to a simple dispute, easily dismissed. But this one gained strength and momentum because it sounded like the truth; it conformed to conventional ways of thinking. Mendel's advances in genetics, in the new science of hybridization, did not become widely known until the early twentieth century. Norton had been working with these ideas for years, but without an understanding of his technique—which was not possible without an existing body of knowledge to explain his advances—it was hard for people to grasp what he had done, which was to introduce something different, something heretofore not seen. Far easier to presume that he had not done something new at all. Far easier to think cynically and to hypothesize that he had taken somebody else's discovery and passed it off as his own, as Lemosy insinuated, or, as rumor alleged, found it in the wild and claimed he had created a new variety.

The doctor's reputation was in a curious place in the second half of the nineteenth century. As the grape was planted and embraced, as its popularity spread and his dream of producing a native-grown table wine of suppleness and worth became reality, he receded further and further into the background, a figure of controversy, his achievement shrouded in mystery and doubt. If his name came up at all, it was to invoke the ongoing dispute over his claims of authenticity.

An 1883 catalog for the nursery Bush & Son & Meissner, a popular firm near St. Louis, wrote that the grape's origins could be traced to a "Dr. Lemosq." Liberty H. Bailey, the founding chair of the department of horticulture at Cornell University, referred to the Norton as an "epoch-making" grape in his book *Sketch of the Evolution of Our Native Fruits,* which appeared in 1898; he also credited its discovery to "Dr. F. A. Lemosq."

In 1908 U. P. Hedrick, in his *Grapes of New York* annual report, attempted to dispel the myths. Since Dr. Norton had sent this variety to Prince prior to 1830, he asserted, the Lemosy story "is evidently wrong as to dates and is suspicious as to facts." But the doctor's story did not persuade him either. He concluded that it was likely that the "true history of the Norton will never be known."

If T. V. Munson, an influential hybridist from Texas, read Hedrick's book, he seems to have been unpersuaded by it. He credited "Lemosque" in his *Foundations of American Grape Culture,* which arrived in 1909.

So there it was, the judgment of the experts: Daniel Norton's life work, his signal achievement, was a fiction, a creation myth in want of hard evidence.

Thus discredited, he faded into oblivion. His Seedling endured, and with it his name, and bottles of Norton's Virginia were poured throughout the Mid-Atlantic region and the West, heralding a new age in American wine. But the doctor's story was by then all but forgotten.

7

FOR WEEKS, Jenni had been planning to take a trip to visit her friends the Ambers, Drs. Cliff and Rebecca, and tour Cliff's experimental vineyard, Chateau Z, in back of their house in Monroe, Virginia, a couple of hours south of Aldie.

"Why don't you come on out to the house," she says over the phone one day, inviting me along. "Come on out, you can spend the night here, and then we'll hit the road good and early in the morning. Maybe hit some wineries on the way. A road trip, a good old-fashioned, take-our-time road trip."

I knew a lot of people when I was younger who just itched to do things on a dare, who didn't worry themselves about repercussions—didn't calculate the effect of their actions on their reputations—but rather flung themselves into circumstances, if only for the adventure of seeing where they would come out, on what side. Most of those people grew up, settled down, became conventional, turned boring. Or were revealed to have been boring all along, an inconvenient fact obscured (willfully, perhaps) by their youthful stunts. Jenni seemed to be doing them still. It was infectious. Road trip! I love it. The language of Spring Break. All that's missing, I tell her, is the "Duuuuuuude."

But she's already moved on, rationalizing the need to get away as if she herself needed a final, persuasive push: "I mean, jeez, what's the point of being in this business if you can't take your time once in a while and just sit back and smell the roses and have a glass of wine and just . . . re-lax. You know?"

It's as if some inner preacher were talking her down; down from long days, down from pushing too hard, too fast.

"Hell, wine teaches us this. If we'd only listen. It teaches us to take things as they come. In the vineyard, but also in the glass. Slow down, sip, savor."

Sermon over, something else takes possession of her now: the inner workaholic, the time-conscious CFO.

"Anyway, enough philosophizing," she says. "Good, you're in, I'm glad. Come on out. We'll have a blast."

THROUGH the tunnel, again.

Only a thin cone of moonlight pierces the dark, and my headlights are as effective as if I'd taken a couple of flickering flashlights out into a dense nighttime forest. I'm reduced to inching along the path as if I were stuck in rush hour on the Beltway.

It's August and dreary with humidity, the kind of night that inspires city folk like me to fantasize about decamping to the countryside. Except the countryside is not much more of a respite than the city. It's maybe three degrees cooler. Worst of all is the air, the obstinate air; it simply won't budge. Even at nine o'clock at night, my shirt is sticking to my chest as if I'd wallpapered it on.

The darkness lifts slightly as I pass through the tunnel and climb the steep rise toward Jenni's property. I curl around the shuttered tasting room, a small compound at the entrance of the vineyard, and now the house, a modern, multilevel construction, comes into view. A single light is on. I drive toward it, a moth to a bulb.

Jenni is waiting in the driveway as I put the car in park. "Hey, road tripper!" She extends her arm for a hug. I'm broad-shouldered, but I find myself being swallowed in her bearish embrace. It's a little like hugging an armoire.

Inside, the first thing she does, even before she bothers to take my bag, is to pour me a glass of wine: an Albariño, a crisp, fruity Spanish white.

"Here, take the edge off. It's brutal out there."

She pours another for herself, and only then do I notice that it's one of hers. We clink glasses. A toast: "To road trips!"

I swirl and sip. But Jenni is still swirling. Not a decorous swirl, the kind you see polite diners attempting with their stemware in elegant restaurants, nor the kind the wine-appreciation courses teach, a gentle circulation to activate the living elements in the glass. No: a vigorous agitation. The liquid circles the globe as if it had been jolted into action by electricity. This startles me, but then she gives a loud, honking snort, clearing her nose for the task now demanded of it, to isolate and identify the smells of the wine.

She jams her nose into the glass, then commences another swirl, more violent this time. Then jams her nose in again. Finally, she sips. With the wine in her mouth, and before she swallows, she makes a slight sucking sound, which looks and sounds crude, but which sends a rush of air over the palate that is supposed to stir up, once more, the active components of the liquid—a parallel of the violent swirl of the glass. Only now does she permit the wine to slide down her throat.

After all that, I feel a little ridiculous offering up the observation, by way of saying something, by way of showing my bona fides, that the wine is crisp and bright and fruity.

But Jenni is no wine snob. She nods approvingly and takes another sip. "Crisp and bright and fruity, and I mean, how refreshing on a day like this? Aww, man, you're dying over there, aren't you?" She studies my brow. "You look like you just ran a race."

"No kidding. It's horrible out there."

"Yeah, well, it's not much better in here," she says, aware, now, that it ought to be cooler, that something isn't right. "I think there's something wrong with the A/C. I'm burning up." I see it now: the tiny network of beads on her brow.

She has a thought: "Come on, let's take your bag downstairs, and get you set up, and we can settle in and drink in the rec room."

But no sooner have I picked up my overnight bag and flung it over my shoulder than she has another thought, and off down the hallway she storms to inspect the offending thermostat. I follow.

The house is enormous, full of rooms. Our footsteps resound as we walk, our voices echo. The white walls of the atrium seem to reach upward without end, and I find myself tilting my head back and gaping, as if I were wandering into the nave of a cathedral. It's an effort not to trip as I stare and wonder. Uncurtained windows capture the darkness in long, opaque panels. I think of Citizen Kane, Howard Hughes, Michael Jackson: eccentric loners in their massive, sprawling compounds.

"Fucking fuck." The thermostat reads seventy degrees. She fiddles with it, resets it, curses again.

The tiny beads have multiplied, massed along her brow like a deployment of troops. "I'm burning up here. Goddamn it!" She's more flushed than when she began. "Fuck it," she says, and leads me downstairs.

The den is measurably cooler and even slightly damp. An ideal temperature for a wine cellar, but nothing so grandiose has been devised for it. A couple of leather couches and a giant TV, which she rarely watches, a pool table, and a dozen unopened boxes of wine from the Tasting Room. The room feels unused, or underused. It also feels unfinished, and it is hard to shake the impression that it was established with great enthusiasm—a room to have fun and relax in!—and then abandoned, for lack of interest or time or company.

We sink into our seats, Jenni sighing as she does. It comes in through the nose and out the mouth, one great, long expulsion of breath. The sound catches us both by surprise and, startled, exchanging looks with me, she begins to laugh, not in embarrassment but in good humor, at the sheer, inadvertent comedy of it—a laugh that seems to admit what she herself will not: the enormous difficulty of sloughing off the tension and relaxing.

"All right, so where were we? To road trips!"

And the old vivaciousness is back. We clink again.

. . .

TWO GLASSES IN, I have learned more about Albariño—its history, its trellising system, its habits on the vine, its preferred climate, its ideal sugar levels, its peak point of extraction, its characteristics in the glass—than I ever thought I would be interested to know.

She decided to grow the grape after traveling to Spain in 1996, the first of three trips she made to the country after launching Chrysalis. She was struck by the commonalities of climate between Virginia and Spain, the long, hot summers in particular, and by the boldness of the Spanish wines, earthy and sensual. Of all the wines in the world, she says, what the Norton most reminded her of were the red wines of Spain: big, bold, earthy, full of character.

All roads with Jenni lead inevitably to the Norton. The Norton is the point of final convergence.

The mark of an obsessive is not just an unswerving commitment to a passion; it is the inability to move past that passion. Or to consider other passions.

But is that it? Is that the explanation for her attachment to the Norton?

Three glasses in, I figure we are both relaxed enough that it's safe to chance a little good, clean provocation, and so I decide to share some of my recent reading on Norton—my Norton homework—with her.

I know enough by now to know that the success of her vineyard doesn't rest entirely on the success of the one grape—she grows many other varieties and makes many other wines—but there can be no denying its centrality in her operation: She has devoted more acreage to Norton than any other winery in the world. On its face, this is a startling thing, in some ways an incredible thing, because in Virginia, the birthplace of the Norton, few other wineries are making wine from it, much less building their operations around it. And many scorn it.

One wag likened drinking Norton to sucking grape juice through a garden hose. The venerable R. W. "Johnny" Apple, writing in the *New York Times* nearly a decade ago, singled out Virginia's reds as being superior to its whites, but sniffed at a Norton he'd tasted at the time: "Rather off-putting," Apple wrote.

A tightening of her facial muscles, a bracing for confrontation—as if I'd just informed her what her friends had been saying behind her back.

"Yeah, well, whatever," she says, feigning nonchalance. She is hot again, and not temperature hot. "You know, we're all so goddamn hung up in this country on the C's, Chardonnay and Cabernet Sauvignon." She scooches forward on the couch. So much for relaxation. She is approaching the agitation of her swirl in the kitchen. "All these big, alcoholic fruit bombs from California. Well, you know, fuck, I would rather make the world's best Norton than the 450th-best Merlot. I would. What's the point of that? This is our grape. It's ours, OK, it comes from here. And it tastes of here. I mean, hello? *Terroir?* Isn't that what all the wine lovers and wine critics in the world prize in a wine? Yeah, it's a little wild, yeah, it's a little American, OK? It's *ours*. And if it's crafted well, it turns into an incredibly complex, interesting aged wine, like any other. You don't take a bottle of Château Latour home and drink it, you know, the next day. You'd rip your fucking tongue off. You have to let it lay down and improve."

I am enjoying this riff immensely, but it is late, and her intensity seems still, to be peaking. I try leavening the mood with a joke.

"Why," I ask, "do I have this image in my head of Don Quixote, tilting at windmills?"

"Who is that, Cervantes?" She is too riled to be so easily diverted. "You know, a lot of it has to do with conditioning. People know California, OK, and they know Europe. They don't know Virginia. They don't know Norton. They don't know anything about it. And they don't give it a chance. That's all I'm saying, is give it a chance. Here, let's kill it." She empties the bottle in our glasses.

"You're talking about the critics and consumers—but what about the wineries? Why aren't more of them giving it a chance?"

"Fuck if I know," she says. "Everybody sells out their Norton, so why the fuck don't people make more of them? I don't get it. The point is that they're all sort of Bordeaux-centric. It's not a fancy wine. It's. Just. Norton.

You know? It suffers from a reputation of being a local hick product or something like that. It's sort of like Scuppernong."

"I was just reading that Jefferson liked Scuppernong. He thought it might be the future of wine in America."

"Well, hell, a Scuppernong sparkling wine won the world's fair here in—I don't know, Louisiana or New Orleans or something, back in the nineteenth century. People were more open-minded. Look at what people were drinking then. All sorts of grape varieties, Herbemont and sparkling Catawba and Scuppernong and Norton. People were not sort of straitjacketed into that whole thing of, 'If a red wine doesn't taste like Cab Sauvignon, it can't be good.' It's very naive. And it's not a connoisseur's or an experienced consumer's consideration. It's an inexperienced, snobby . . ." She cuts herself off.

"You know what? First of all, if you took my old Nortons and you lined them up, blind, against a couple of Zinfandels and a couple of Bordeaux, they wouldn't be able to tell the difference. So it's all bullshit. As soon as they see it's Norton and that it's native—'Oh, it can't be good. It's one of those native grapes.' It's not in their vision. It's not on their radar screen. 'Yeah, I'm going to grow Cab Sauv, Merlot, and Chardonnay, just like everybody else in the world.' And they're market followers. And they're worried about—'Well, it's risky, what if somebody doesn't want to buy it.' Why don't you at least have it in the lineup? It isn't like you're only going to drink Norton. I'd go nuts if I only had Norton to drink. But—it's *our grape*. Why don't you add it to the lineup?"

Something about this exchange, the sitting on opposite couches, the volatile outpouring of pent-up emotion, suggests a session of therapy, and I notice that Jenni seems calmer, looser, more . . . relaxed. I haven't said anything or done anything, but I have listened, and sometimes listening is enough. The same role I play with my artist father, who often feels misunderstood and simply needs to be heard. Heard and affirmed.

The Albariño is gone, and Jenni begs off to go to bed. Enough for one night; more tomorrow.

She sets me up in the guest room, then heads upstairs.

"Good night, Quixote."

She smiles. Ruefully? No. More proudly than ruefully.

A solitary figure in a vast estate. A solitary figure in Virginia. A solitary figure in the world of wine.

THE NEXT MORNING, after a quick, Jenni-made breakfast of eggs ("fresh from my little chickies!") and toast, we load the mud-caked Outlook with our bags and hit the road.

It's early in the day, the sun is just inching up over the horizon, but the heat is already so unforgiving and inescapable it's like wearing an invisible wool sweater. "Fuck," she says. It comes out *Fuuuuuuuck*. An awe in there, a note of despair. How goddamn hot it is, how goddamn hotter it's going to be.

She pinches the opening of her cream-colored blouse and pulls, tenting it. Release, tent, release, tent.

"Hello, cuties!" Treixadura and Fer have emerged at the back wheels.

Jenni gives them each a good scratch on the scruff of the neck, and her forehead begins to rain. Tent, release, tent, release. She can't seem to stop. Her great, floppy sunhat provides little relief.

Inside the Outlook, she blasts the A/C, and within minutes, it's not just cool but cold, and within minutes of its being cold, I'm almost shivering. For a self-professed country girl, in tune with the rhythms of the land, the cycles of nature, she seems oddly to be caught off guard by the heat—seems oddly to seek immediate refuge in convenience. I'm fascinated by this, fascinated by her apparent contradictions, her extravagant extremes.

"You're cold? I love it! All right," she says dejectedly (mock-dejectedly?), "I'll turn it down."

We exit the property and find a small, side route, the road narrow and winding but lightly trafficked. Jenni has me unscrew the silver bullet of a thermos she has brought along and pour us each a cup of fresh, hot coffee. We hadn't had time to drink it all at breakfast. The cap for her, a mug for me. Another toast. "Cheers!"

"Oh, that's good," she says, almost gutturally, after her first gulp. It's the sort of rumble of appreciation that sometimes attends the first bite of luscious, smoky barbecue or a perfect oyster, an unself-conscious, wholly unbidden acknowledgment of a primal pleasure. It cheers me, to be in the presence of someone who takes such profound satisfaction from things, who recognizes good food and drink as a gift. As the old immigrant Jews used to say, Landsman!

Another gulp, another rumble.

"That's good. I've gotta have my coffee. It's not even the amount so much. You know how people are always saying, 'Well, I have to get my two cups, I have to get my three cups'? I think, for me, it's also the warmth of it. The warmth of it, plus the caffeine, of course. Plus, you know, the whole routine—the sip, the savor, just like with wine. Taking the time out for it."

"The ritual."

"The ritual, right, exactly. And you know, it's interesting, because it's a fairly recent thing in this country, that sense of a ritual with coffee. I didn't grow up with it. You didn't grow up with it. It's the young kids today, the ones hanging out in Starbucks all the time. They're the ones who have it. They're hooked on coffee, so many of them, and that's a really, really good thing if we're talking about the future of wine in this country."

"How's that?"

"Well, because it's a way of training the palate. Training the palate to accept and appreciate bitter. That's new for us as a country. You look at Europeans, they know bitter, they don't have to have everything sweet, the way we do. They drink coffee at a young age, they drink wine at a young age. They have cultures that revolve around coffee and wine. Hmm, you think there might be a correlation there—do you think, maybe? Hmmmm."

We speed along 17 in refrigerated obliviousness. The sun bears down on the windshield, and I find myself squinting at times even through sunglasses. But the blasting cool renders impotent the blasting heat. I feel only the slightest sensation of warmth on my uncovered arms.

Jenni's conversion from neophyte to connoisseur is a good story, and she tells it with great relish, gesturing with her large, strong hands as she talks. Soon enough, she's sweating again. "Fuck," she says, and turns up the A/C one more notch. I settle back in my seat with crossed arms, relishing the details.

She was a teenager in Miami in the late 1960s, a city riven by immigration, drugs, violence. *Look* magazine, in a cover story, had declared it "The Drug Capital of the World." At Palmetto High, "everybody smoked pot." The entire school seemed to be high all the time. Wine? "Ugh."

The "lightbulb moment," as she calls it, came on Christmas Eve, 1977, on the Miracle Mile in Coral Gables, when she walked into a Big Daddy's Liquor Store. This was it, the "last-ditch effort," wine's last chance to win her. She paid $11 for a bottle of 1971 Château Léoville–Las Cases. She brought it back home for a big Christmas dinner, popped the cork, poured a glass, and drank.

And drank. And drank again. *Fuck*, she thought. *This is fabulous.*

She got it. In the way of a reader who discovers Faulkner and is seized by a desire to read not just all of Faulkner, but all of *everything*, she began exploring her options with the hunger and avidity of the newly converted. Convinced, like most converts, that she was in a rush to make up for lost time, lost knowledge. Whatever she could get her hands on, whether it was in grocery stores or wine shops or liquor stores. Every bottle was potentially a great bottle, a discovery that would lead her to other discoveries, a door through which she would pass through to the next room. Hell, even a bad bottle was useful, because it was a chance to learn what was not good, what did not work, what she did not like.

The next leap forward in her wine education came when she sprang for her first case of wine, a 1974 Limited Cask Inglenook. By 1978, she had become a collector. Get it? She had more than gotten it. She was hooked now.

She was no expert, but already she had perceived something important about the wine world, something she immediately saw herself at odds with, a strain of elitism that she could not reconcile with the sense of joy, the deep, sensual pleasure she experienced on drinking something good or great.

"Wine is one of the wonders of the world," she says, intoning the words with awe and reverence. "And here you have these attitudes, these snooty attitudes, that just won't go away." She adopts a mocking French accent, the haughtily uptight maître d' of innumerable movie comedies: " 'Eef you don't know what zees ees, you should not be drinking eet.' Fuckin' frogs. Oops! Did I just say that?" She covers her mouth halfheartedly. And roars.

Beyond the windows of the Outlook, the countryside, lazy and still and undisturbed, whips by in quick, shimmering tableaux. In spite of our speed, in spite of our high-tech conveyance, these images always lead me to wonder if what we are passing through is anything like what earlier generations passed through—to wonder if "the sublime," as Jefferson famously referred to Virginia, would be at all recognizable to him today. Still the sublime, in other words, or only the intermittently pretty?

Over highways and country lanes, through shaded woods and sun-blasted small towns, the Outlook barrels on. And Jenni barrels on, too, the words tumbling out of her, pungently articulated opinions and tender-hearted reflections, fierce and raunchy denunciations and thoughtful, sentimental musings. Jenni's inimitable take on the world, on nature, on man, on wine.

Chrysalis, she tells me, is the thirteenth business she has run. Her twelfth was the most successful, a business built on all the businesses that had preceded it, a company she ran in the late 1980s out of Clearwater, Florida. What she and her partners offered the customer was a tool to achieve greater technological self-sufficiency, a piece of software that enabled PC users to diagnose their own hardware problems, thus circumventing costly computer repair shops and technical-support centers. The company grew bigger and richer, and she and her partners pushed it to become bigger and richer still. There were stumbles. By 1990, the company was half a million in debt. But that was a temporary setback, and over the next few years the company was turning a tidy profit. In 1995, it sold for $40 million.

I know that two years later, she will have given it all up to come to Virginia and grow Norton, and I am like one of those Victorian readers waiting breathlessly on Dickens and his next chapter, enthralled by the pacing and the suspense, the tantalizing, almost painful, sense of the thing withheld. Here it comes, the next installment of the story, the next revelation in her improbable personal saga. At which point her cell phone rings. Her son.

"Boy, I'll tell ya," she says a minute or two later, shaking her head. "You never stop being a parent. You never forget. Do you have kids?"

"Not yet, no. But soon—my wife's pregnant. She's due early next year."

"Your first! Well, you're gonna learn. That's wonderful, by the way. Congratulations."

"Thanks. You have two kids?"

"I have six."

The information is offered up as matter-of-factly as the information that, upon closing her business, she'd amassed a personal net worth of $19 million. Each fact was like a feather; it was not the entire plumage, but how many brilliant feathers!

For months now, ever since I'd learned that my wife and I would be having a baby, I have been asking my friends and colleagues for their advice or their insight, and I've been astonished to hear the many profound and wonderful things they have shared with me—privileged, heretofore unseen glimpses into their hearts and minds. ("One of the great gifts of children," an editor friend of mine said, "is that when you're sixty-five, you won't feel alone in the world.") Because we are already talking about children, I figure it is only natural to ask Jenni, too.

We are off talking about our fathers, about the passage of time, about lessons learned too late and . . .

"I fathered those children," Jenni says, turning toward me. "I did not give birth to them."

Her eyes become glassy as we talk about her six children, and, tentatively, gropingly, about her change. I am eager to hear more, to be able to connect the dots, the now wildly disconnected dots, but then somewhere around Monroe the cold, automated voice of the Outlook's GPS intrudes upon us: "Make a legal U-turn."

"Where in the hell are we?" Jenni asks, unfolding a map on the steering wheel, smoothing its wrinkles, and squinting at the network of lines.

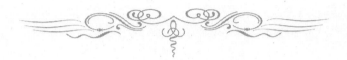

PART TWO

8

H ERMANN, MISSOURI, lies on the southern bank of a bend in the
Missouri River, an hour and a half drive west from St. Louis. More
properly, it lies at the intersection of imagination and practical necessity, a
city that was dreamed into being, then hammered into reality almost overnight. To paraphrase the writer A. J. Liebling's famous boast: No city that
sprang up so quickly is as rigorously conceptualized, and no city as rigorously conceptualized sprang up so quickly.

As I drive across the glittering Missouri River on a warm spring afternoon in my rental car, the spires of churches on hilltops and the slanted
rooftops of old houses put me in mind of an old European village, and I can
feel the desire of all history-loving travelers welling up within me; the willful desire to believe that a place that has come alive in the fertile fields of
our minds still carries on as energetically as it once did. To believe, that is,
that the past has not passed.

Hermannites are a friendly and unfancy people. They look you in the
eye. Level gazes, open faces. They speak slowly and surely. No one's toting a BlackBerry or iPhone or Palm Pilot—none of the toys that urbanites
in the East like me have come to regard as indispensable to living, that keep
us captive to their ability to deliver up-to-the-minute, potentially life-
altering (but much more typically, utterly trivial) bulletins. These desul-
tory first impressions fill me with the momentary hope that I have somehow
managed to erase the time-space continuum, that driving from the airport

at St. Louis, I have driven into the nineteenth century, that the Hermann of today is the same as the Hermann of yesteryear. But that hope quickly fades. Twenty-first-century Hermann feels less like a city than a quaint small town, a B-and-B getaway, a chance for city folk from St. Louis and Kansas City to abandon their busy lives for a long, leisurely weekend.

As a purpose-minded interloper in the midst of a purposeless oasis, I feel somewhat out of place among these good-time seekers. It is not the quaint Hermann present that I have come for, but the faded Hermann past. Navigating the wide, lightly trafficked streets of the historic downtown, studying the sturdy-looking facades of old buildings for clues to the town that was, I think about Jenni. It was Jenni, after all, who had sent me, Jenni who in our innumerable tutorials had held out Missouri as some kind of ancient, irreducible text, to be studied and studied again. And Hermann was the relevant chapter. "If you want to understand this thing, I mean really understand how things developed," she said, "you have to get out there."

And this was another lesson I had learned from her: When one door leads to another door, which leads to yet another door, you don't question why there are so many doors; you enter, and go where the doors take you.

STREET NAMES echo in stately succession as I pilot the rental through the heart of old downtown: Gutenberg, Mozart, Schiller.

I realize it's not much of an indication, perhaps, that the past I am hoping to find is not gone and buried, but neither is it Elm, Spruce, and Maple, and such are my lowered expectations that this incantation of Teutonic cultural heroes makes my heart beat just a little faster, and I nearly run a stop sign.

The mission of the German Settlement Society of Philadelphia, which conceived the town in 1837, had been to create a city for the massive influx of German immigrants then coming into the West, a city that was "characteristically German in every way." Here, eighty miles west of St. Louis, stood the prospect of a new Rhineland, right down to the precipitous river bluffs and the graceful, rolling hills. The layout would be clean and impeccable, the vistas clear and wide, the architecture stately and sound.

There is a German word that means more than melancholy and speaks to the predicament of these game but unmoored settlers: *heimweh*, a sense of homesickness so pervasive, so profound, it is akin to the longing for something that has been lost forever. The immigrants, for all their wild hope in the future, must also have felt an enormous and unfillable hole in their lives. In a characteristic bit of nineteenth-century German expression, that ache was transmuted, in Hermann, into aching art, the sorrow over the past subsumed into a place that was both homage and promise, less a city than an idea of a city.

A new Old World, a genuine fabrication.

I TRY TO PICTURE it as I head out toward the vineyards, past the dollhouses and the stately churches—the Hermann that was. Or, as my shuttle bus driver had put it, "the Napa before there was really a Napa."

He was ferrying me to the rental car office outside the St. Louis airport when, catching my eye in the rearview mirror, and with a slight lift of his head, he asked what I was in town for.

Not St. Louis, I replied. Hermann. It was late at night; we were the only ones on board.

"Ah, so you're heading out to the vineyards," he guessed correctly.

He proceeded to unspool a lengthy, comprehensive, and heavily contextualized history of the town that, besides demonstrating his impressive grasp of local lore, suggested he had once been a teacher—and that a classroom was perhaps a less rewarding audience for his off-the-cuff lectures than a stranger who was new to town and open to experience. I didn't yet know that many St. Louisans and nearly every Hermannite could deliver much the same information-dense history, as if they had all taken the same seminar.

"Well, we got about eighty vineyards in the state right now," my driver began, as if this were a tour bus and I were waiting to be dazzled with data.

"Not bad," I replied.

"Well, not bad," he shot back, "if you consider what we had to do to get this thing back up and running again after Prohibition shut everything down, shut down the whole industry. But now put that up against the 120 or so that you had going a hundred years ago. A hundred years ago! Think about that. If you wanted to talk about wine in America, and you lived in the nineteenth century, you pretty much had to talk about Missouri."

"So I've been reading."

At this, the driver again caught my eye via the mirror, and, sensing a fellow history buff on board, continued his recitation with increased confidence as the shuttle bus hurtled across a darkened landscape of arched, crisscrossing highways.

"For a long time, this was the number-one wine-producing state in the country at the time of the Civil War. Number one. Not California—Missouri. The *Weinstrasse*, they called it, because of all the wineries. The Wine Road. And Hermann was at the center of the wine road. Hermann was *it*."

"And now?"

"Now? Nothing now. Well, not nothing, but you know what I mean: nothing like what it was. Outside of the Midwest—and even that's a debatable point as far as I'm concerned—who knows anything about Missouri wine?"

Until I met Jenni, I told him, I was ignorant of the idea that there was such a thing as Missouri wine, let alone Hermann wine.

"Well, see, there you go."

What I didn't have the guts to admit to such a proud and knowledgeable native was that, no matter how many times I have read or heard that the state once led the nation in wine production, it was still astonishing to comprehend, like one of those apocryphal-sounding stories that happen to be true but which we stubbornly refuse to accept. Missouri wine? Many, many things come to mind when I think of Missouri—Mark Twain and Calvin Trillin, the great Mississippi and the Gateway Arch, smoky, tangy barbecue and beer, oceans and oceans of German-style lager. But wine is not one of them.

The story of Hermann, in particular, feels like some tall tale, an outsize, truth-stretching story of the Old West, something Twain himself might have conjured, especially if he had been born, not in Hannibal, but eighty miles south. It even comes complete with a rousing and unexpected climax:

In 1873, at the Universal Exhibition in Vienna, a bottle of Norton from Hermann took home a gold medal, ratifying it as one of the best red wines in the world.

THE PICTURE won't come. Nor is it any easier to conjure after several days of touring the vineyards and drinking the wines and talking with some of the winery owners.

Especially not after talking with the winery owners, the majority of whom would prefer to talk of what is, not what was. The present—the great, eternal now. They might occasionally allude to the past in their marketing, but no more than that—no more than the briefest of acknowledgments. They steadfastly refuse to look back, as if some Orphean fear of vanishing—Poof!—haunted their dreams. Their websites are testaments to the good life, alluring invitations to come out and spend a few days, lounge around, and drink wine.

Hermann is peaceful, it's relaxing, it's restorative. A pretty palimpsest.

The street names remain, the legends remain. And not much of anything else.

The tourists drain their bottles of wine and kill the hours in the hot tub, while I search the erasures and attempt to reconstruct what was.

9

BETWEEN 1827 AND 1856, more than 150 works of emigration
literature appeared in Germany, none more influential than the
volume produced by a former lawyer, onetime lieutenant in the Twenty-
eighth Prussian Infantry Regiment during the Napoleonic Wars, and justice of the peace named Gottfried Duden. He titled it *Report on a Journey to
the Western States of North America.*

The *Report* was a continuation of the themes of his previous study,
*Concerning the Significant Differences of the States and the Ambitions of
Human Nature,* an exploration of German politics in the aftermath of the
Napoleonic Wars, published in 1822, that reflected upon the uneasy rela-
tionship between the state and the individual. Germany in the 1820s and
1830s was not a unified state but a loose network of principalities, each
presided over by a separate prince, duke, or bishop. It was a nation struggling to remake itself and find its purpose in the wake of Napoléon's recent, brutal rule, and to Duden and other liberal nationalists, it had never
looked more oppressive.

The advent of mechanized looms was putting German weavers out of
work, potato blights and failing flax crops were causing starvation, high
taxes to support armies and the lives of the wealthy were undermining the
economy, and the government was exercising greater control over religious
worship. As the once sustaining family farms were dying out, the cities

became crowded, chaotic, inhospitable places. The problem of overpopulation was particularly vexing to Duden because it meant there was far too much competition for far too little.

Revolution was inevitable, but all such attempts at retaking the country had failed, and the increasing unrest, and the frenzied talk of further such uprisings, had only encouraged the country's rulers to crack down on the citizenry. Political activity was forbidden. To utter the word *freedom* was to risk reprisal from police.

Convinced that the state would never change, Duden looked elsewhere for solutions. He turned to America, and with the thorough, methodical approach of a lawyer girding himself for a long and involved trial, he made a case study of the young country, read the existing literature, examined the geography, the cost of land, and the methods of transportation. Finally, in 1824, he set sail for America with a friend, Ludwig Eversmann.

Their target was Missouri, which, of all the locations Duden had explored via books and maps, came closest to fulfilling his utopian ideal. Gentle in climate, abundant in natural resources, replete with sources of sustenance (the forests were filled with wild turkey, rabbit, and deer), and possessed of sometimes breathtaking beauty, from the undulant hills and green-carpeted valleys to the great rivers, the Missouri and the Mississippi, the state seemed to him to be the best possible alternative for a German in need of a fresh start, the closest thing to the homeland, indeed, a kind of New World counterpart, a new Fatherland.

They arrived in the recently incorporated city of St. Louis, where they met Nathan Boone, who was a government surveyor and the son of Daniel Boone, and embarked on a tour of the Missouri River valley. They eventually settled fifty miles north of the mouth of the Missouri, near present-day Dutzow. Duden bought 170 acres and lived in a cabin for nearly three years. He hired help to do the dirty work of clearing the land and harvesting the crops. Focusing his attention on the mission at hand, that of determining whether an ordinary German could survive and profit from the new land, he set about exploring the wilderness with a reportorial eye.

Six years before de Tocqueville published his ruminations on America (Duden in his next book, *Europe and Germany*, would take issue with the French political theorist's work, believing *Democracy in America* to be full of contradictions), there was Duden, prowling the countryside, talking to his neighbors, lighting out on hunting expeditions, and traveling. He toured Kentucky, Ohio, Indiana, Maryland, and Pennsylvania, all the while setting down his impressions of the new nation, whose social structure was so different from the institutional hierarchies that held sway in Europe. The American, he believed, represented a new kind of man, an agrarian who lived in tune with nature.

The thirty-six letters that comprise the book's argument touch on a broad range of topics: political parties, lawyers, education, commerce and trade, and slavery. He abhorred it morally, but historically speaking, he reminded skeptical readers back home, "among most of the nations of the world, slavery has been a part of the legal order." He even discussed birding: "Actually one misses only the nightingale. The rest of America's songbirds can compete very well with those of Europe." Wine was not a pressing concern for Duden, but he duly noted the abundance of grapes and the encouraging prospects for winemaking. "There are several kinds of grapevines here," he wrote, "and some hills are so densely covered by them that wagonloads of grapes can be gathered in a short time. The grapes of some varieties are sweet and palatable but furnish little juice. In the fertile river valleys they are mostly sour. I do not doubt that culture would produce the desired improvement. I have drunk juice from them that was quite enjoyable."

The book was many things at once, perhaps too many things at once. Duden, a single-minded pragmatist in his desire to assess the worth of a possible new home for his countrymen, one that could sustain them and keep them, could not always curb the yearning Romantic within himself. In one letter he wrote breathlessly, "I do not conceal the fact from you that the entire life of the inhabitants of these regions seemed to me like a dream at first. Even now, after I have had three months to examine conditions more closely, it seems to me almost a fantasy when I consider what nature offers man here." The sober, legal mind in him could offer sage counsel in one passage—". . . I must advise against moving here by oneself and without careful consideration. Success depends completely on the way emigration is carried out; and without special preparation or adequate guidance, everyone will be exposed to chance more than he might expect"—and then give way to the eager optimist: "No land on this earth offers more to German emigrants than the western part of the United States."

His stirring conclusion amounted to a bright and shiny invitation for many desperate Germans to pack their bags and venture west:

> How many consequences of despair would be prevented if the transition to a life in America would only be made a little easier for the Germans. It would offer to the fathers the surest relief from worry; it would assure the most rewarding sphere of influence to the drive to engage in enterprise and praiseworthy activity. . . . In a single generation the German states would themselves be restored to the health and strength of which they have long been deprived by counteracting those unspeakably harmful effects of overpopulation. At the same time they would see a new colony blossom [sic] beyond the ocean that in grateful loyalty would never cease calling down the blessings of heaven upon the mother country and as a second home would receive the late arrivals.

The success of the book could hardly have been calculated. Emigration societies, inspired by Duden's *Report* and by other popular examples of promotional literature, sprang up in Germany, and amid feverish talk of a new *Vaterland*, a massive tide of immigrants crashed down upon Missouri in the 1830s and 1840s.

From the beginning, there were grumbles. Duden had been overly confident about the ability of cultured, citified Germans to adapt to the life of the farmer, and he had minimized the challenges inherent in the landscape of the West, particularly the Indians. In letter after letter, the new arrivals spilled their anger and frustration, railing about the hyperbole in his *Report*. Many damned the book as "Duden's Eden."

An entire literature rose up to excoriate Duden's conclusions. An attorney pilloried him in a popular magazine, laying out the great difficulties many of the pilgrims had encountered as a result of following his fanciful pen. A literary journal ran a series of articles denouncing the book, one calling it "shallow, fantastic, and exaggerated." Nicholas Hesse, a minor government official in Prussia who had resettled with his wife and six daughters in Osage County, returned to Germany after less than two years, complaining of homesickness, a lack of community, and the hard labor of the farm, all of which he recounted in a book that was intended to suppress Duden fever: "The longing for relatives, friends, and old acquaintances often brought a melancholy that could not be cured by any medicine."

But these refutations, no matter how fierce, and no matter how valid or vivid their counterclaims, did little to dam the stream of immigration. And just as many accounts attested to the plenty on the other side of the Atlantic, so Germans continued to flock to the West in search of relief from want.

Many farmers in Germany worked for the nobility, earning little or no pay, and had to content themselves with a single hog for an entire winter; opening a letter from a loved one, they could read of the wondrous lives of their brethren who had emigrated to Missouri, who owned—some of them, anyway—forty acres of land and log houses and who enjoyed the luxury of eating meat every single day. Nearly 450,000 people left Germany in the 1840s, and more than a half million between 1850 and 1854: farmers and noblemen, artisans and merchants. Missouri was a panacea, and it did not matter if the cure was not as absolute as promised, so long as it brought about some measure of improvement in their dire condition.

DUDEN HAD urged his readers to take "special preparation" for the journey to America by organizing in groups, and so it was that many of his middle-class followers arrived in the wilderness of the West as members of one of the various settlement "societies" that had sprouted in Germany, their numbers and their missions a form of protection against the unknowns of a strange new land.

The Berlin Society, which established Dutzow, in Warren County, in the 1830s, numbered among its moneyed members some men of minor nobility; most lived a lord-of-the-manor existence. Johann Wilhelm Bock, a landowner in Germany, fancied himself "Baron von Bock" and was famous for holding parties at his clubhouse. The baron's was the only household for miles with a piano.

Another society, the Giessen Emigration Society, envisioned a day when all Germans would be gathered under its wing, and the United States would eventually recognize a German-speaking state. Friedrich Munch, the Protestant minister who founded the society with his lawyer friend, Paul Follen, was a rough-bearded man with a searching, almost scrutinizing expression and a mind that was set afire by his many Romantic impulses. He later went on to make wine at the Mount Pleasant Winery in Augusta, Missouri, and later still established himself as an outspoken abolitionist. His 1834 poem "Auswanderungslied" ("Emigration Song"), reflecting the utopian mood of the time, locates the land of Duden as the land of hope, inviting all who long for escape to follow him to the New World and

> build cabins on the Missouri,
> Where the sun of freedom shines . . .

That year, the group's five hundred members arrived in St. Louis. Munch and Follen had imposed few conditions on joining, and the society attracted members from nearly every religious group and occupation. They did not lack for idealism, or faith, or a singular determination to make it. What they lacked was much less ineffable: the practical knowledge that a pioneer might be expected to possess. Most knew considerably more about philosophy and culture than they did about farming. Or about finance. The organization mismanaged its money, and many members scattered and returned home. Some committed suicide.

A phrase came about to describe these incongruous Dudenites, these ill-fitting pilgrims determined to make a go of it and civilize the wilds of the West: the Latin Farmers. It was a disparagement, spit by the rough-hewn have-nots at the putative haves.

PERHAPS the most successful of these member-supported societies was the German Settlement Society of Philadelphia, the organization that created Hermann from scratch. If it succeeded where others failed, it was because it understood that the utopian dream must be preceded by quotidian reality, a mastery of the innumerable logistical details that enable a vision to come to fruition.

About eighty miles west of St. Louis, near the confluence of the Missouri River and its tributary the Gasconade, just a few miles from where Duden himself had settled, deputies for the society bought eleven thousand acres of wilderness. They christened the town Hermann in honor of the Teutonic prince and warrior whose bold, defiant stand near Minden, in AD 17, freed Germany from the tyranny of Roman rule.

It was 1837; a spirit of starting afresh was alive in the land, a promise of new modes of being, of new ways of thinking. In his American Scholar lecture to the Harvard chapter of the Phi Beta Kappa Society, Emerson promised: "We will walk on our own feet: We will work with our own hands; we will speak our own minds. . . . A nation of men will for the first time exist, because each believes himself inspired by the Divine Soul which also inspires all men."

The settlers—nine adults, eight children—arrived in Hermann on the last steamboat of the season, in the midst of a cold, brutal winter. Neither the forbidding weather nor the arduousness of their long journey from Europe could diminish their enthusiasm. William Godfrey Bek, in his 1907 book, *The German Settlement Society of Philadelphia,* marks the moment in a rhapsody of prose:

"Land! land!" they cried, like anxious mariners after a dreary journey. New hope, new expectations, filled them all. A giant stride had been made towards the coveted goal. Here was, at last, a tangible proof of the sincerity of the undertaking. The dormant ones became aroused, the faithful stimulated and encouraged. The organization had gained a new lease on life. The world beheld that the Germans were, indeed, in earnest, and that their perseverance was about to be crowned with glorious success.

In their report to the home office—based in Philadelphia, not Germany—the deputies had remarked upon Hermann's natural beauty, noting, "The few fruit trees found in this region have a good growth. Vineyards will probably flourish when more of the land has been cleared." Some of the grapevine trunks were thirty-six inches in diameter.

This echoed what Duden had written, and inasmuch as it proved that not everything that had issued from his pen was an exaggeration, it was a promising report. Less promising, however, was the immediate realization, shortly after arrival, that the land in and around Hermann, steep and rugged, was ill-suited to most other agricultural purposes, and that wine was to be not one among many pursuits, but for all intents and purposes, the one and only.

The first experiments were disastrous. As it had been for the settlers at Jamestown, so it was for the settlers at Hermann. They planted cuttings of European vines in the limestone bluffs overlooking the Missouri River, only to watch them wither and die. They might have given up, except that they had no luxury of an alternative. So they tried again.

The settlers who persisted had come largely from northern Germany, not from the wine country to the south. Grape cultivation was not a trade they had been weaned on. This was a hindrance, but not entirely. In some ways, it was a help, because they were not beholden to long-held notions of what constituted a proper wine industry or proper wines. They were not beholden to old ideas—or any ideas, for that matter. All that interested the Hermann settlers was what worked. Defeated by *vinifera*, they quickly turned to native varieties, among them the Isabella and Catawba. They might have been Romantics, but in the field, at least, they behaved like realists.

Grape growing took off. Intent on encouraging this nascent industry, in 1844 the city trustees of Hermann put up town lots for sale at fifty dollars per lot, interest-free, for five years (they later extended the offer to ten years). It had the intended effect; in short order, there were almost one hundred acres of vineyard in town. A year later, Hermann's winegrowers formed an organization to offer deferred-interest loans to vintners who lacked the means to purchase something so tenuous as a vineyard. Within a year, more than fifty thousand new vines had been planted. The industry boomed.

By 1847, just a decade after the colony was founded, there were twenty-eight winegrowers in Hermann, and they accounted for 584 gallons of wine. The following year, the town was producing approximately 10,000 gallons.

This success, so unexpected, called for a celebration, a rousing marker of growth and progress—a *Weinfest*. A six-pound cannon boomed its welcome over the festival grounds, and visitors converged on Hermann from all over the state, some well-heeled curiosity seekers journeying south from St. Louis by steamboat. In a letter, a young minister captured the spirit of revelry, a small town giddy with its great good fortune:

> Toward evening the procession to the festival began. In a long
> parade the citizens of Hermann and vicinity walked down the
> streets. At the head of the parade was a wagon pulled by four
> horses, which bore "Bacchus" seated on a large cask decorated
> with wreaths, grapevines and flowers. He held a goblet in his
> hand, acting the drunkard. Musicians followed the big "Bacchus"
> wagon and then came the citizens.

The most important development of 1848, however, was neither a public spectacle nor a statistical milestone. It occurred in silence, on the margins, the work of an unlikely practitioner, a baker from the Rhine named

Jacob Rommel, who two years earlier had obtained a vine cutting from a friend in town, Hans Widersprecher, who himself had obtained his slip from a contact in Cincinnati. Catawba and Isabella had provided the foundation for the budding industry, and were responsible for the bulk of those gallons, but the future of wine in Hermann, and indeed in all of Missouri, arrived that winter when Rommel pressed and bottled the first Norton.

10

THE GRAPE GROWERS of Hermann could not have foreseen what was coming, the explosion of the grape in the vineyards, its dominance of the industry. The Norton did not engender fantasies.

George Husmann, writing many years later in *The Cultivation of the Native Grape and Manufacture of American Wine*, a hugely influential wine manual, described his first encounter with a "small, insignificant looking grape":

> The vine seemed a rough customer, and its fruit very insignificant
> when compared with the large bunch and berry of the Catawba,
> but we soon observed that it kept its foliage bright and green when
> that of the Catawba became sickly and dropped; and also, that no
> rot or mildew damaged the fruit, when that of the Catawba was
> nearly destroyed by it.

It is not hard to imagine that, in the story of the unlovely Norton, Husmann saw a familiar narrative, one that paralleled the epic journey of his ancestors and even traced the arc of his own unlikely evolution from nobody to somebody, from rough matter to man of refinement.

The youngest of four children, Husmann was a puny, sickly boy. Doctors put him on a milk diet to strengthen his bones. He stayed out of school until he was eight.

His father, Martin Husmann, had purchased stock in the German Settlement Society of Philadelphia in 1836, and the following year, several members of the family, inspired by Duden's journey, left Hanover, Germany, for America, "this distant country [that] had charmed and inflamed our youthful imaginations," as George Husmann later wrote, memorializing the exodus. They arrived in Missouri in 1838. A riverboat, the *Clementine,* dropped anchor in the new village, where a "motley" crowd of townsfolk greeted them. "Coming from all parts of Germany and even Switzerland, many of them in the costumes of their native province and speaking its own peculiar dialect, we could hardly understand them." Disdain greeted them, too. "Our captain would not land at the upper landing, claiming that he could not do so, but in reality because the steamboat people had an aversion to the 'Dutch Town,' as they called it, and often did not land at all."

The family settled on two hundred acres four miles east of Hermann. Martin Husmann ran a strict household, insisting on discipline and demanding obedience to his laws. A former church organist, he convened meetings every Sunday on the farm, a precursor to the organized church services that would come later, with the arrival of the town's first church. He was also among the first grape growers in town and worked hard to promote the industry. A visitor from Germany, Jacob Naumann, was so taken by his industriousness and by the astonishing versatility he displayed that he coined a phrase in his diary to characterize him: "the superior immigrant." He set a superior example, a sometimes impossible example. At night, he sent his children to sleep with a family prayer; in the morning he roused them from their sometimes snow-covered beds at four, thundering about the perils of laziness and sloth. "Children, get up!" he would shout. "We have overslept ourselves."

The exigencies of a wilderness existence demanded that everyone earn his keep, even a young boy. Husmann drove oxen during plowing and sold his mother's cheese and butter in town. Learning was prized in the Husmann household, but there simply wasn't the luxury of time to permit him to go to school. His older half-brother, Fritz, became his school. Fritz tutored him in German, English, and French. Together they read and discussed the classics of German literature.

In 1840, when Fritz left to study at a medical college in Philadelphia, Husmann was devastated. In his autobiography, he recalled the moment of departure on the dock as the steamer prepared to glide down the river:

> I could not leave him the last few hours. "George," he said, "follow your studies of English and German diligently . . . you are now far advanced enough to understand the beauties of the best authors. . . . Cultivate a taste for reading . . . love good books as your best friends, but shun all that do not tend to make you better, wiser and happier." . . . When the departing steamer took him from our sight, I looked at his handkerchief waving a farewell, until it became only a speck in the distance, and felt that I had parted from the dearest friend I had on earth.

It was a portent of hardships to come, of the convulsions that would disorder their methodical life on the farm. That November, his mother died of "brain fever"—likely meningitis. The following summer, his sister Johanna, who despaired of the "dull routine" of the pastoral life, left Hermann to live with relatives in Philadelphia. Fritz passed his medical exams with high honors in 1843, but his triumph was short-lived. Two years later, he fell victim to the typhoid epidemic. Then, in 1847, the deciding blow: Martin Husmann was crushed to death in the machinery of his mill.

This was it; George's moment of self-definition was at hand. He would either shrink from the challenge before him or rise to embrace it, either remain what he had been or set about to refashion himself for the new, enormous demands of a new, uncertain life.

Husmann was now twenty. An old twenty. He was alone in the world.

In Hannibal, eighty miles north, the rascally titan of American letters, Mark Twain, was watching the glittering palaces known as steamboats glide down from St. Louis and belch their black smoke high above the Mississippi, learning the way of boys and men, dreaming his big, impossible dreams.

Husmann's own childhood was over. His dreams appeared to be finished, too. He was no longer the frail, sickly boy he had been but neither was he fully a man. What was he, then? A boy-man. A dutiful son and brother. A follower of orders. That life was over, but what would the new life bring? Assuming it would bring anything. It was terrifying, the prospect of not knowing. But just as terrifying was the prospect of knowing exactly, of the realization that he was trapped, that there was no way out. Having operated the mill for his father, the idea of staying on to work there seemed to him intolerable. Nor could he bear the thought of continuing to live on the farm. Too many memories. Too many reminders of the past.

His other sister, Josephine, had recently wed Carl Teubner, a well-educated, well-traveled man with an avowed interest in grape culture who had been among the early Hermannites to enjoy success in the field. Teubner lived on two hundred acres high above the Missouri River. On it, he had planted eight thousand fruit trees and vines from some of the best nurseries in Cincinnati.

Husmann moved in with his sister and brother-in-law, embarking on a two-year apprenticeship under Teubner that changed the way he thought of himself, changed the way he looked at grape growing, and eventually changed the future of wine in the West. More than applying himself to his task, more than learning his craft, Husmann "imbibed the love for . . . the noble grape . . . which has clung to me during good and bad fortune all my life." He had grown up around grapes and grape culture all his life, but he had been too young to appreciate what a gift he had been bequeathed. Now, on his own for the first time, intent on reconstructing a life for himself, he learned to see grape growing as a calling, not just as a means of survival, but as a means of sustenance. There was something about the field, something giving and deep and salvific, that nurtured him back to sturdiness and health and returned him to himself. His favorite poem, "The Garden," by Andrew Marvell, is a buoyant expression of tended land as a retreat and restoration, a small patch of heaven on earth where men return to seek their best, truest selves:

> *What wondrous life is this I lead!*
> *Ripe apples drop about my head;*
> *The luscious clusters of the vine*

Upon my mouth do crush their wine;
The nectarine and curious peach
Into my hands themselves do reach;
Stumbling on melons as I pass,
Insnared with flowers, I fall on grass.
Meanwhile the mind, from pleasure less,
Withdraws into its happiness:
The mind, that ocean where each kind
Does straight its own resemblance find;
Yet it creates, transcending these,
Far other worlds, and other seas;
Annihilating all that's made
To a green thought in a green shade.

Teubner died in 1851, and Husmann returned home to take over the nursery. Winemaking in Hermann was still largely an amateur affair, and despite their first flush of success, the town's grape growers were remarkably limited in their knowledge of winemaking procedures. Contaminated barrels were not uncommon, and many cellars were not optimized for wine. Few knew to measure the sugar in the grapes prior to fermentation, a standard winemaking practice. And these were the conditions that could be controlled.

Frosts and rot continued to plague the town's harvests. Many of Hermann's wines were spoiled, although that did not stop some vintners from trying to turn a profit by selling the wines to local inns.

Husmann took it upon himself to master the whys and wherefores of viticulture, to penetrate to the heart of its seeming mysteries. Holing up with the horticultural manuals Teubner had left him, he read late into the night by lamplight—turning to books for aid and support, as his brother had enjoined him; willing himself to master new worlds, as his father had demonstrated, over and over and over again. He studied the time-honored methods on how to process wines, conducted tests of native grape varieties, and taught himself the techniques of layering and grafting.

Had he not undertaken to educate himself and save the industry, by which he was also saving a town and its people (a logical leap that doubtless would have made him uneasy, because the simple fact of the matter was that his immersion was, first, a means of saving himself), the Norton might not have survived its infancy in Hermann. The grape, difficult to propagate, needs a high degree of attention and nurturing in the field and in the cellar, and without his knowledge of grafting and layering, the grape growers of Hermann might have given up on it before it bore them results.

Husmann began writing about winemaking for local journals, eager to disseminate his hard-earned knowledge and help the legions of other self-taught vintners. His name and fame spread. He had turned himself into an authority, and having done so, he eventually assumed the aura of a guru, a shaman of wine, the man an entire industry turned to for help, for insight. The Norton might not have been the answer to all things, and he was loath to burden it with the weight of responsibility. His deep reading in viticulture had taught him that it was foolish to anoint a single grapevine a savior in the field; location and climate were too fickle, and being fickle, too determinant of success—but it was, often enough, the answer to most things.

His faith in the Norton's future was strong. But beliefs are like values or ideals—meaningless, that is, until you are challenged to defend them and forced to fight for their honor. The time had come to find out just how committed he was to this faith, how fervent his belief in this grape. Would he be willing to stake his growing reputation on it?

THE EMERGENCE of Husmann, Hermann, and the Norton were not universally welcomed developments. Ohio had styled itself as the locus of wine in the West, and even had its own "father of American grape culture"—the eccentric multimillionaire Nicholas Longworth.

The eventual success of his well-connected son, the popular Ohio congressman Nicholas Longworth, who became speaker of the House under Hoover and Franklin Roosevelt and married the president's daughter, Alice

Roosevelt, tends to frame and thereby diminish Longworth Sr.'s story, but his was arguably the more interesting, more colorful life. A short, owl-faced man drawn to ill-fitting suits that lent him a disheveled, distractible air, he served up an unreliable image to the world, concealing a will to domination that marked his many pursuits as banker, real estate baron, and art collector.

In *History of Wine in America*, Thomas Pinney identifies the planting of a vineyard at what is now the intersection of Main and Third streets in Cincinnati by a Frenchman, Francis Menissier, in the late eighteenth century, as the beginning of wine culture in the Midwest. Menissier managed to grow *vinifera*, but he was unable later to persuade Congress to grant him a parcel of land to grow more vines and continue his work. His success with *vinifera*, however, did attract the notice of Longworth, who had moved from New Jersey to Cincinnati in 1804 and who immediately established his reputation in his adopted city, becoming a prominent banker and merchant. His talent for property speculation, in particular, made him one of the richest men in the country. At one time, he and John Jacob Astor were the two largest contributors of taxes to the U.S. Treasury. His passion was horticulture, and he began to spend some of his considerable fortune dabbling in the field and making wine.

"Old Longworth," as he often referred to himself, set out on a massive data-collecting enterprise to determine the best wine-producing grape in the land. He planted more than 120 native grapes in his Cincinnati vineyards, set high on the south-facing banks of the Ohio, and recorded the results. But his experiments to the contrary, Longworth was not a scientific seeker like Husmann. He was not particularly interested in viticulture, which was ultimately a subservient endeavor, one that required heeding the wishes of nature and compromising accordingly. Nor was he particularly interested in variety, in putting together a broad portfolio of reds and whites that would demonstrate his firm's range and style. What he was interested in, primarily, was building a successful, thriving business, and he had undertaken his extensive plantings as a means of winnowing out the weak in order to find the strong and thus master the vagaries of nature. It was a vineyard version of survival of the fittest.

Only the fittest, he reasoned, was worth his time and investment; only the fittest was worth his constructing an entire industry around a single grape.

The best of the bunch was the Catawba, which, because it had won his competition, therefore represented the best hope for American winemaking. There was still the foul, musky taste to contend with, the foxiness intrinsic to all native grapes, but Longworth minimized the power of this component by separating the skins from the juice prior to fermentation, and creating a white Catawba. It sold decently throughout the 1830s among the growing population of German immigrants who were settling in the Ohio Valley, who regarded table wine as a necessity at dinner, but it was unable to gain traction among the general population—mainly white Anglo-Saxon Protestants, who had no such traditions. His breakthrough came in 1842, entirely by accident.

A batch of Catawba had been mistakenly submitted for a second fermentation, resulting in a sparkling wine that possessed so little foxiness as to seem to him almost a different variety of grape. Importing winemakers from Champagne, he attempted to replicate the *méthode champenoise*, a laborious and expensive process, perhaps the most laborious and expensive in the world of wine, the reward of which is the unmistakably fizzy drink that is universally embraced as the embodiment of elegance, refinement, and good times. Bottles kept exploding on him—in one year, he lost 42,000 of them—but eventually he achieved mastery, or enough mastery, anyway, to profit from his discovery.

The WASPs at home drank it. So did affluent Easterners who disdained any wine that didn't come from Europe. Longfellow was so taken by it, he was moved to pen a poem, "Ode to Catawba Wine":

> . . . *For the richest and best*
> *Is the wine of the West,*
> *That grows by the Beautiful River,*
> *Whose sweet perfume*
> *Fills all the room*
> *With a benison on the giver . . .*

Across the Atlantic, Longworth's sparkling Catawba was regarded as not merely a worthy alternative but a serious rival to Champagne. Some believed it superior. In the *Illustrated London News*, Charles Mackay assured his readers that it "transcends the Champagne of France." Robert Browning referred to it (though, unlike Longfellow, he was not inspired to translate his fandom into verse).

Longworth was producing more than a hundred thousand bottles a year, advertising in national publications and inspiring countless others (some serious, most simply chasing a rumor of money) to try their hand at this thing called wine. A vineyard explosion was on.

In 1857, the *Cincinnati Commercial* canonized Longworth as "the founder of wine culture in America, author of sparkling Catawba, the munificent and judicious patron of Art."

IN CHAMPIONING Catawba, Longworth was not only championing his authority and his product; he was also championing Ohio, which he believed to be the true seat of American wine. No American grape had yet emerged to rival the great burgundies and clarets of Europe, but in *Culture of the Grape and Manufacture of Wine*, a journal published in 1846, Longworth predicted, "The day is not distant, when the Ohio River will rival the Rhine, in the quantity and quality of its wine. I give the Catawba the preference over all other grapes, for a general crop, for wine." He went on to assess the worth of a number of other native grapes, giving low marks to the Norton:

> . . . far inferior as a table grape, to the Herbemont, Ohio, Lenoir, Elsinborough, and Missouri, which it resembles in the size of its fruit. It has a pulp. I am trying it this season on a small scale, for wine. The grapes were very ripe, and the wine has much body, and is of a dark claret color, though pressed as soon as gathered. I do not admire the flavor of the wine. Writers tell us to the contrary, but grapes may be too ripe to make good wine; and I

incline to the opinion that this was the case with my Norton's
seedling. The grapes were pressed as soon as gathered, yet the
wine was nearly black. A certain proof that a fermentation had
taken place in the fruit, before gathered. It was increasing the
saccharine principle, at the expense of the aroma and flavor.

Years later, Longworth's partner, John Zimmerman, wrote to the *Her-
manner Wochenblatt*, one of the town's newspapers, urging the grape growers of Hermann to redirect their operations and sell juice, not wine.
"Winemaking is different from grape growing," Zimmerman opined, "and
the Hermann growers do not understand the work. The problem can be
avoided if we are allowed to purchase the juice as soon as the grapes are
pressed." He compounded his condescension by advising them to abandon
the Norton, which had become the foundation of their vineyards, because
it was simply not conducive to "the mission of making a mass-produced
wine." The superior grape, he wrote, is Catawba.

Zimmerman had a point. Like most potentially good or great wines, the
Norton needs aging, the mellowing and softening that comes from years
and years in the cellar and then in the bottle, to fulfill its promise. That
process takes time and money, neither of which most beginning vintners
can afford.

Longworth was a respected name, the most respected in the business.
Everyone sought his judgment. But the letter rankled. Cincinnati was not
Hermann. He couldn't possibly know what they knew about their own soil,
their own vines, their own yields.

In 1852, the Catawba was attacked by diseases, and throughout the
West, the hardy, pest-resistant Norton emerged as an alternative among
those who had not already embraced its uses.

Longworth consented to give it another try. Previously he had found
the grape wanting, but now he regarded it as almost beneath contempt. He
could not have been blunter in his evaluation: The Norton, he declared,
was "worthless."

For an industry so young and, despite its early successes, so insecure, the effect was stunning. A sneak attack on the vineyards of Hermann could not have done as much damage as Longworth's dismissal.

Years later Husmann described this "fiat" from the "father of American grape culture" as very nearly the "death-blow" of the Norton. Longworth's opinion was, for many in Hermann, "conclusive evidence," and although they had grown fond of the Norton and had come to rely on its vigor in the vineyard, they soon "abandoned it." After all, they were mere dabblers, dilettantes of the soil and cellar; what expertise could they lay claim to when it came to winemaking? What learning did they possess about the culture of the grape? They were immigrants, recent arrivals, outsiders. Nothing like the great and revered Nicholas Longworth.

A SMALL COTERIE of loyalists, Husmann among them, persisted in the belief that the Norton was not merely not worthless, but worthy of investment. Longworth's rebuke did not dissuade them; if anything, it encouraged them to redouble their efforts on the Norton's behalf—to try to make better wine from it and to work harder to promote it.

Husmann performed double duty, working from within to exhort the winemakers of Hermann to make use of his wide learning and employ the best available techniques to produce good wine, while championing the Norton from without in articles, treatises, and eventually books. In 1854, Husmann was elected the first president of the Hermann winegrowers association. His first book, a treatise on grape culture, written in German, came out in 1857, attracting the notice of the country's leading horticulturalists. A year later, he helped to found the Missouri Pomological Society. All the while, his nursery continued to thrive and expand, so much so that he sought out a partner, Charles Manwaring, of Geneva, New York. In short order, theirs became the largest, most profitable business in Gasconade County, and Husmann and Manwaring two of its wealthiest citizens.

No one at the time seems to have been particularly bothered by his cheerleading. Husmann, to his credit, appears to have done everything possible to maintain his sense of balance, never allowing himself to come across as a shill for the industry nor using the power of his pulpit to dictate the terms of grape growing in the town. But it remained true that his grow-ing fame put pressure on the winemakers to produce great wine, and it could not have escaped anyone's notice that his reputation was on the line with every bottle that was shipped. And who would not want to purchase grapes from the nursery of a man of such influence and importance, a man who knew what worked and what didn't? He had become both the indus-try's watchdog and its biographer, both its scold and its spokesman.

HERMANN WAS ON the verge of passing Cincinnati and New York State as the preeminent wine producer in America, Husmann was on the verge of passing Longworth as the preeminent figure of American viticulture, and Norton was on the verge of passing Catawba as the preeminent wine in the country when the Civil War broke out, in 1861, blunting their collec-tive momentum. Husmann served an eighteen-month stint in the Union army as a lieutenant and returned to his nursery in 1863, having been mus-tered out of active duty. That same year, he traveled to Washington, D.C., with the Missouri Radical Republicans to meet with President Lincoln and demand the emancipation of the slaves. Lincoln received them cordially but refused to alter his stance.

Husmann returned to a jumpy town, in some ways an unrecognizable town. Confederate forces briefly occupied Hermann in 1864, and the threat of rebel raids set residents on edge. Most in Missouri had favored secession, had voted for Stephen Douglas in 1860, and had no qualms about owning slaves. Yet the state also sent nearly three times as many men to fight for the North as for the South. Hermann was not nearly so schizophrenic. It was an unabashed bastion of abolitionist sentiment. Many in town were outspoken in their views on slavery and developed reputations as radi-cals, Husmann among them. As immigrants, they found themselves un-able to reconcile the lofty ideals of America, which had inspired them to leave their homes and begin their lives anew, with some of its degraded realities.

One irony of his growing fame was that Husmann had unwittingly turned himself into a prime target of Confederate forces. "I had the distinguished honour," he wrote, "to be on the 'black list' of the rebels with about a dozen other inhabitants who had taken a prominent part on the Union side, in consequence of which we could not expect any mercy." There was plenty of work to be done at the nursery, but not plenty of workers. With so many men enlisted in the Union cause, labor had proved hard to come by, and for long stretches of time the vineyards of the *Weinstrasse* lay dormant, silent, and untended. Husmann, author, horticulturalist, intellectual, spent his days on the run, scurrying among the shadows, "scouting after guerillas [sic] and fighting the rebels."

Manwaring was killed by bushwhackers in 1864, and throughout the final years of the war, the specter of capture or death haunted Husmann. When General Marmaduke's 2,500 troops romped through Hermann, camping on Husmann's farm, they destroyed thousands of vines and emptied his entire stock of cider and wine—in all, a loss of $10,000—but he survived.

Hermann emerged intact too. Throughout the occupation, it refused to surrender its identity, holding horticultural fairs and even going so far as to construct an octagonal wine exhibit hall.

The wine continued to flow, and so, after the war, did Husmann's prose. Determined to chronicle every development and every breakthrough—determined, it seemed, to match the output of the vineyards with his words—he began churning out articles and books, including his first work in English, a monograph on viticulture in the West.

To the *Horticulturalist, and Journal of Rural Art and Rural Taste,* a leading periodical of the day, he contributed an article in 1865 called "Grape Culture at the West—Our Leading Varieties," an account of the "very fair returns" in the fields of Hermann. The fairest of those returns belonged to the Norton, which was fetching $5 per gallon, twice the price of the Catawba and at least $2 more than the Concord. Having shown great promise in its infancy, in its adulthood it now looked to have arrived:

> To make a dark red wine of the character of the best Port or
> Burgundy has long been the aim and object of our wine growers,

and for this purpose this noble grape stands as yet without a rival. Add to this its adaptability to any soil, be it the rich alluvial bottoms of our rivers or the sterile southern slopes, its healthiness, hardiness and luxuriant growth, and we need not be surprised that the demand for the plants is far in advance of the supply. . . . It is truly invaluable. . . .

The next year saw the publication of *The Cultivation of the Native Grape and Manufacture of American Wine* and with the Norton, his gamble, performing so well, a chance for Husmann to seek redress for an old grievance.

In a tone by turns mocking and messianic, and so full of brimstone that it recalled the exhortations of his late father, he revisited his old debate with his rival to the north, Longworth, and declared victory. The Norton, "that despised and condemned grape," had proven its worth,

> . . . equal, if not superior to, the best Burgundy and Port; a wine of which good judges, heavy importers of the best European wines too, will tell you that it has not its equal among all the foreign red wines; which has already saved the lives of thousands of suffering children, men, and women, and therefore one of the greatest blessings an all-merciful God has ever bestowed upon suffering humanity. This despised grape is now the rage, and 500,000 of the plants could have been sold from this place alone the last fall, if they could have been obtained. Need I name it? It is the Norton's Virginia. Truly, "great oaks from little acorns grow!" and I boldly prophecy to-day that the time is not far distant when thousands upon thousands of our hillsides will be covered with its luxuriant foliage, and its purple juice become one of the exports to Europe; provided, always, that we do not grow so fond of it as to drink it all. I think that this is pre-eminently a Missouri grape. Here it seems to have found the soil in which it flourishes best. I have seen it in Ohio, but it does not look there as if it was the same grape. And why should it? They drove it from

them and discarded it in its youth; we fostered it, and do you not think, dear reader, there sometimes is gratitude in plants as well as in men? Other States may plant it and succeed with it, too, to a certain extent, but it will cling with the truest devotion to those localities where it was cared for in its youth.

Husmann could be forgiven his rhetorical fancy, his I-told-you-so gloating, his odd forays into philosophy. The triumph of the despised Norton was the triumph of the despised who had planted it, nurtured it, and pressed it, the Hermann pioneers, the motley immigrants and their lowly "Dutch Town."

More validation came three years later, and from the least likely source imaginable.

In 1863, the year of his death, Longworth himself had applied to Husmann for Norton cuttings, and now William J. Flagg, Longworth's son-in-law and the winery manager at his Cincinnati estate, came out with a book, *Three Seasons in European Vineyards*, in which he recounted a cellar tasting of wines from one of the oldest and grandest French estates, Château Latour. Longworth had never given the grape his blessing, but now his son-in-law asserted, with pride, "I turned away from Latour with more hope and faith than ever in the Norton's Virginia Seedling."

Europe. There it was again. Norton himself had made the comparison, then Husmann, and now Flagg had, too. A wine that could rival the best of Europe. It was not wishful thinking. The dream for nearly two and a half centuries—abandoned, taken up, abandoned again, taken up again—had not died. It was alive. It was real.

11

Because Michael Poeschel had started from nothing and *with* nothing, he had not expected much of himself when he began making wine, in 1847, on property he had purchased west of Hermann, between Cole's Creek and the town center—an area that eventually became known as *Weintahle,* or Wine Valley. He was a wool-spinner from Altenburg, Saxony, the eldest of three brothers, who, prior to his arrival at the Hermann colony in 1839, knew nothing of grapes or wine or grape culture. But his first success encouraged him, and he aimed higher. Each subsequent accomplishment, in turn, spurred him to further boldness, as if part of the attraction for pushing himself was to see how much bigger he could still become, how much higher the gods would let this passionate amateur, this unlettered immigrant, fly.

The answer came in 1873: Very big. Very high.

And it came because of an equally unlikely asset, a grape dismissed in Baltimore and despised in Cincinnati, a grape in cultivation at the hands of ignorant upstarts in a tiny country town, Hermann, for only thirty years—a historical blip by the standards of European winemaking, where the thick, gnarled roots of the great wine-producing grapes, Cabernet Sauvignon, Pinot Noir, Merlot, reach deep into the earth and where the aristocratic houses can boast of hundreds upon hundreds of years of longevity and standards. Hardly enough time, in other words, for a wine to age and mature and develop the grace notes that connote real worth.

And yet.

POESCHEL'S WERE among the first Hermann wines shipped to nearby markets, in small quantities (about a thousand gallons). Catawba and Isabella formed the bulk of production. In the early, experimental years, the vast majority of wines that poured forth from Hermann were more promising than good, and the potential greatness of the industry, which it was possible to taste in a few of the wines, had a way of coloring judgments, imbuing the actual with more worth, more weight. About Poeschel's wines, however, it was not hard to project what they might become.

If not yet distinguished, they were nevertheless solid, honest embodiments of the winemaker's craft, a correlative of the integrity and skill of the industrious Germans in the new colony and, along with the wines of Teubner and Franz Langendoerfer, an erstwhile shoemaker (Husmann later referred to them as "fathers of grape culture here"), notable for their quality and consistency, no small accomplishment. Poeschel's vineyard was small, about an acre, but as one observer of the time noted,

> [T]he rows of posts seemed to consist of nothing but a wall of
> grapes and among them not a single rotten berry was to be
> found. . . . The product of the vintage of this small vineyard was a
> very expensive but good Catawba, which, when it is treated right,
> resembles Rhinewine very closely, and was at times in great
> demand and brought a good price.

An early homage was paid him at the town's initial *Weinfest*, in 1848, when revelers, continuing the party started the night before, made the twenty-mile pilgrimage through the center of town to Poeschel's vineyard.

The following year, the *Western Journal,* an English-language periodical based in St. Louis, noted the developments in Hermann—"So quietly
has this new settlement proceeded with its enterprise . . . that we question if
one in a hundred of our own citizens is at this day, aware of the fact, that
wine has ever been produced at Hermann, although some of the vineyards
are in full view from the steamboats, which daily pass the romantic bluffs
on which the vines are growing." And so the editors invited Poeschel to
share some words (German words, alas, which they took the liberty to
translate) with their readers.

"Three years ago," he recounted, "I commenced my little plantation,
planting about 1000 rootlings [yearlings] on 7/8 of an acre, raised them all
on Espaliers, and they grew wonderfully . . . In 1847, I earned from my
little vineyard nearly $700 in grapes, and $400 from wood . . . In 1848 I
made wine to the amount of 1600 dollars, 400 dollars of wood (slips and
yearlings)."

He went on to describe his methodology with such artlessness and directness as to inspire a novice to try his hand at the task.

> My mode of pressing is very simple. I wash my grapes, then let
> them stand twenty-four hours, press them in my wooden press;
> when pressed let the juice run into a suitable cask, let it then stand
> quietly until the fermentation is over, for which a cool place is
> best. For this the bunghole should be covered with a wet rag.
> After the fermentation has continued nine or ten days, pour the
> liquid over softly in prepared casks, let it stand slightly closed
> until a second fermentation is over, which requires about three
> days, and then shut it tight till February or March, when the
> young wine is drinkable. If you want to improve it further, let it
> lay undisturbed until April, then bottle it.
>
> I am from the northern part of Germany, therefore had no
> knowledge of the culture of the grape before I came to Hermann;
> the same is true of the settlers of this section of the country; they
> are from all parts of Germany.

News of the Norton had yet to reach him ("The only grape that will make good wine here, as far as our experience tells us, is the Catawba"), but already he was certain that the future lay in native grapes. "Foreign wine will not do here; the plants freeze in winter, and dry up in summer. . . . Our wine was readily sold at $2 per gallon in St. Louis and elsewhere this spring, and I think the world will be our market after a short while, though not at the same prices; but we will strive to diminish importation of foreign wines. The grape has never failed here, as long as this settlement exists."

He concluded by offering the would-be winemaker a bit of advice: "Have you love for your wine, let it lay undisturbed till April, then bottle it."

By the outbreak of the war, demand for his wines was high enough and the output of his vineyards strong enough that establishing a full-blown operation was no longer the foolish proposition it had seemed when he had first entertained the idea. Too old for military service—he was fifty-two at the time—he threw himself into the project of turning his vineyards into a full-fledged winery with the urgency of a man who knows life is short and time is wasting. He persuaded John Scherer, another German, to leave De-troit to become his partner. On a large hill that formed the southern bound-ary of Hermann, the two men set up shop.

It was no estate. Indeed, to a visitor who had toured the great and noble châteaus of Europe, the notion that this humble compound in the wilds of the West would dare to call itself a winery was laughable, although no more laughable, perhaps, than the idea that civilization could be brought to a land overrun with so-called savages and rough-hewn settlers. The main building, a great house at the front of the property, was a two-and-a-half-story brick edifice of exceptional craftsmanship, with intricate ornamenta-tion, that summoned the image of a community hall in a German village. It went up in 1869, and Poeschel and his expanding family (he and his wife eventually had six children) lived above its offices. The sprawl of build-ings—a pressing room, a bottling house, a barrel shop—suggested a small farming collective. John Michael Vlach, in his 2003 book, *Barns*, claims status for the winery as a kind of glorified farm, writing, "The storage buildings and the cellars clearly are barns by another name. A hay barn is a large structure in which hay is stored. But a large building in which vats of wine are aged is called a winery even though it is in form and function little different than a barn."

What Poeschel & Scherer lacked in form, it made up for in function. It might not have pleased Poeschel to know that his estate would one day be referred to as a compound of "barns," and certainly the word lacks all trace of romance, but it is oddly fitting, suggestive of the raw, animal power that undergirded the operation, the up-from-the-ground force. A visitor from the Missouri State Horticultural Society noted the process in an 1864 report to colleagues: "The grapes are crushed between two wooden rollers, and the juice extracted by a screw press of the capacity of 500 gallons per twenty-four hours. The wine as it runs from the press is conducted by pipes through the vaulted roof of the cellar underneath into casks." From this method of brute efficiency, he fashioned wines of uncommon grace and depth. The wines that best demonstrated what his young firm might yet become were two reds, the Norton and another, remarkably similar wine, called Cynthiana, made from a grape believed to have been discovered in the wild, in Arkansas. The Princes had brought the grape to wider attention in the 1850s, three decades after commending the Norton. The nursery shipped cuttings to Husmann in 1858.

Across the state, the no-longer-young men of the war, having slogged back home to their farms and villages, groped to rebuild their lives. It was the era of Reconstruction, a self-important-sounding word—a brave face of a word—for a period of failed governmental promises and limited opportunities, of thwarted aims and lingering resentments. In Hermann, though, things were different. Promise abounded, ideas flourished, plans moved forward. The wine industry resumed its work as though no disruption had taken place, least of all something so traumatic and divisive as the most devastating war of the century.

The energy seemed to flow from a single source. Every industry has its colossus, the firm that emerges from a crowded field to dominate the competition. On the *Weinstrasse*, that colossus was Poeschel & Scherer, the most successful of the estimated 120 wineries.

By 1870, Missouri led the nation in wine production. Of the more than 320,000 gallons produced in the state, Gasconade County accounted for approximately 200,000. And of those, Poeschel & Scherer was responsible for perhaps 50,000.

The company was bigger than everybody else, but wine is not diamonds or pearls. Size is not everything. It is not even most things. The fact was, Poeschel & Scherer was also better than everybody else.

That was true, not just for Hermann, but for America, too. And for one brilliant five-year stretch, starting in 1873, with the improbable performance of a bottle of Poeschel's Norton at the Universal Exhibition in Vienna, it would be true for the world, as well.

12

~~~~~~~~~~

H E STOOD OUT. He always stood out.

Of all the wine critics who arrived at the behest of Emperor Franz Joseph in Vienna in May of 1873 at the Universal Exhibition to pronounce judgment upon the greatest collection of wines ever assembled, Henry Vizetelly was the most influential, the most accomplished, the most provocative.

So singular a personality was he, so flamboyant and unpredictable, given to regarding life as grand, improvisatory theater, that wherever he went, the air stirred in his wake—news was made, and controversy inevitably followed. He atomized a room.

If it seemed unlikely that his stint as a juror on the panel at the Weltausstellung would create a scandal—wine calms the senses and rarely causes the blood to boil—it was just as hard, given his long record of affronts, to suppose that something would *not* happen, some incident that would cause the normally placid waters of a wine tasting to ripple.

By the time he arrived at the grand rotunda, Vizetelly had already established his reputation throughout Europe as a man of irrepressible daring and unorthodox action. Tall and thin, tending toward gauntness, with a beard that protruded from his chin like a scythe, he did not cut an especially compelling figure, and his charisma was not immediately obvious. It was in his eyes, alive and dark and mischievous, in which it was possible to discern the flickerings of a new scheme or concoction. His great gift was

for the well-considered provocation, perfectly timed. Like all great provo-
cateurs, of course, he would have rejected so tidy and dismissive a label and
said simply that he saw things that others did not or could not. To say that
he stirred the pot—that enduring and reflexive put-down of iconoclasts
everywhere, regardless of medium—was to comment on the result, not on
the motivation, which was, after all, a refusal to be bound by convention, a
disdain for orthodoxy and hierarchy.

He was fifty-two, just past the midpoint of a long and remarkable career
as engraver, journalist, publisher, author, foreign correspondent, and now
wine critic—a storybook of a life that was as rollicking as the epic serial-
izations he printed in his penny newspapers in London, from the ambitious
and impudent youth who dominates its early chapters to the sad and dramatic close, in the late 1880s, with the hero in aged defiance, going to jail
on obscenity charges.

At eighteen, he had announced his presence on Fleet Street by pulling off an act of rare effrontery at Queen Victoria's coronation, in 1838.
Attending the event as a credentialed illustrator for the *London Observer*, Vizetelly walked alongside a train of proper, plume-hatted ladies as
they made their way to the Abbey of Westminster, chronicling the event
with an immediacy and intimacy no ink-stained wretch had ever thought
to do.

At twenty-nine, he had published his first book, *Four Months Among the
Gold Finders in Alta California: Being the Diary of an Expedition from San
Francisco to the Gold Districts,* under the pen name J. Tyrwhitt Brooks. A
candid eyewitness report of Gold Rush fever, the chronicle became a best-
seller. It was republished in numerous editions, translated into several lan-
guages, and for decades thereafter trusted as a historical source. Only later,
after he had gotten rich off of it and enjoyed a good long laugh at the depths
of human greed and gullibility, did he reveal that he had perpetrated one of
the greatest literary hoaxes of the century. He had never left England and
had written the thing in a matter of weeks.

Over the next three decades, Vizetelly turned himself into one of the
most respected men of Fleet Street, running the *Illustrated Times* of Lon-

don with vigor and mischief, supplying etchings and sketches that brought the city's teeming streets to life no less vividly than the stories of his friends Dickens and Thackeray (a contributor). As a correspondent, sometimes with his preteen son in tow, he filed rambling, candid dispatches from France about Napoléon III's policies.

The adventures of his youth and the exploits of his middle age were mere precursors for the late-career Vizetelly who emerged in the decade after the Weltausstellung—foreshadowings of a controversy that was perhaps inevitable, and a fitting farewell to a strange and extraordinary career. Having as a teenager provoked the tut-tutting of a London ruling class committed to upholding the decorous standards of the early Victorian era, now, as an older man, he inflamed it with his decision to publish, among others, Zola in English. To some Londoners, Zola's brand of naturalism went beyond acceptable realism and bordered on pornography. Some thought it crossed the border, and defiantly, scandalously, so. Predictably, the books were a sensation. Zola's *La Terre* went into multiple printings, Vizetelly responded by coming out with an equally racy edition of Flaubert, and the debate about propriety spilled over from the taverns and offices into the newspapers and eventually into the courtroom. Vizetelly spent three months in jail, and was never the same again, his end hastened by his troubles with the "National Vigilants," the antifreedom fundamentalists of the day.

Bracketed thus, his opinions of the wines at the Weltausstellung, and again in Paris, three years later, constitute a short passage in a relatively calm and uneventful chapter of his life, hardly to rival the drama that precedes and succeeds it.

THE WELTAUSSTELLUNG spanned two months in late spring at Prater Park, a onetime hunting ground of royalty and aristocrats northeast of the city, surrounded by the Danube River and Canal. The rulers of the Austro-Hungarian Empire had conceived of the extravaganza as an act of foreign policy in the form of a grand and triumphant show. The country had been at war with France and at odds with Prussia in the previous decade and as a result had lost much of its land and power, but its economy was returning, and it was intent on showcasing its changing image in Europe, erasing its perception of instability and positioning itself as a center of trade between the East and West. Of the twenty-eight galleries that had been created to display goods, the biggest and grandest—the one that crystallized the ambitions of the empire—was the rotunda, a tour de force of nineteenth-century technology, structurally perfect, dazzling to behold, and capped by a grand dome that was three times larger than that of St. Paul's in London and more than twice as large as that of St. Peter's in Rome.

These lofty hopes were never realized. The fair was, in so many ways, a disaster. The opening ceremonies began in a cold drizzle of rain on an unfinished site. Days after the opening ceremony, the Vienna stock market crashed, plunging the country into a depression and bringing on steep unemployment. Then there was an outbreak of cholera.

More damaging to the fair itself was the fact that the exhibits were so poorly thought out. About half of the space had been set aside for Vienna's own exhibits. France had just lost the Franco-Prussian War and had neither the time nor inclination to put together a comprehensive exhibit. The United States had not understood the importance of the fair until it was too late; it had no exhibit at all.

It did, however, send wine, as did every other wine-producing nation on the globe. The Weltausstellung may have lacked for visitors; it may have lacked the deep resonance the emperor sought. But it did not lack for wine. There were, Vizetelly wrote later in his report to the British Parliament, "twenty thousand specimens of fermented drinks" that "taxed incessantly the palates, heads and stomachs of some thirty jurors and experts." The only rule that guided them in the often unruly process was that "not only were the individual intrinsic qualities of the different wines to be taken into account, but considerations of country and even of district were to have due weight. To have instituted anything approaching a comparison between the wines of different countries, and have decided on their relative merits, would have been impossible, and was of course not attempted."

Wine was a sideline for Vizetelly, a passionate avocation—one interest among many in the life of an autodidact with a rapacious curiosity and an unslakable thirst for adventure. Indeed, he had been writing about wine only since 1869 when, deep into a stint as Paris correspondent for the *Illustrated London News* (which he had since sold), the *Pall Mall Gazette* asked him to contribute a series of articles on the French vintage.

Had he been a less confident man, his meager experience might have tempered the urge to pass judgment on the finely wrought work of men who had labored all their lives to reach perfection in their two or three varietals; but Vizetelly went at wine as he went at everything else in his life, throwing himself into it as if it were a new lover to woo and win—as if it were the only thing that mattered in the world. His series complete, he took up residence outside of Paris to resume his "studies" of the "more famous wines of the world," and "every succeeding autumn for the next six years toured the celebrated vineyards in Champagne, the center and south of France, along the Rhine and Moselle and in the Palatinate," tasting, taking notes, asking questions.

He was not content, however, to be a mere student of wine, and so he pushed himself to become a connoisseur, poring over the literature, learning the styles, mastering the regions. There was no point to do anything if you couldn't write about it, and so it was inevitable that he would look to translate his thoughts into prose and package them. Why not? What qualified anyone to be a critic, other than pronouncing yourself a critic and writing critiques? Did he know anything about being a foreign correspondent before he became a foreign correspondent? Or being a publisher of a newspaper? He became a publisher when he published. Reading the literature, touring the vineyards—these things, he knew, could only take you so far. First you do, then you learn.

Writing about wine necessitated a voice, and that he already had— a forceful, authoritative, confident voice. The voice of the intrepid foreign correspondent, whose dispatches, evoking the sweat of battle and conveying an eagle-eyed clarity that sees through and above everything, must earn the reader's trust and convey the ring of truth. It was simply a matter of feeding his ideas through the mill of that voice and giving the thoughts the shape and heft of something durable and lasting. Begin thinking in the voice, and let the voice guide the thoughts.

He bypassed an apprenticeship by sheer force of will and, with a swiftness that might have seemed sudden had it been anyone else, became an expert. Writing with authority, he became an authority.

BY THE TIME of the Weltausstellung, Norton had been in production in America only since 1848. Twenty-five years. Michael Poeschel's winery had been a serious, large-scale commercial enterprise only since 1861. Twelve years. What were these numbers, compared with the great vineyards of France and Italy? A blinking of an eye.

It's not only that good wines get better with age, softening in the barrel and mellowing in the cellar. The vines that produce them get better with age, too. The repeated stresses of hot and cold over the seasons, over the years, decades, and centuries, concentrate the flavors of the grapes, improving their character, making them more complex, more subtle. What could be packed into twelve years? What could the young, unstressed vines give to the fruit in so short a span? What character could a winemaker hope to coax from these grapes?

To the Europeans, it was either a case of hubris or delusion that any American winery would compare its bottles to such an esteemed group, unless the idea was to hope, somehow, that merely by entering the judging, the prestige of being among the noble houses would rub off on them— mixing among their betters in hopes of raising their status.

There was also the matter of the grapes themselves. It was not merely a matter of age. Not merely a matter of experience and skill and centuries upon centuries of craftsmanship, the handed-down knowledge of the generations. Anyone could see that *vinifera* produced the only wine worth drinking. The ancient Greeks knew it, and so did the men of the Renaissance, who had subjected every inch of their world to endless trial and error. *Vinifera* had stood the test of time many, many times over. Why couldn't the Americans see that? The ignorance—nay, the arrogance— of youth. Even allowing for the possibility that the Americans were possessed of some skill and knowledge in the cellar, in extracting and blending and balancing the juice, the fact remained that American wine- makers who produced wine from *aestivalis* were starting at an extreme disadvantage.

Vizetelly's tastes jibed with those of his more experienced colleagues in many areas, particularly in his love of Champagne and Bordeaux. The dif- ference was that his range was wider, his tastes more catholic. Aware though he was of the prevailing attitudes of his fellow judges, he was not circumscribed by them. Experience didn't matter; age didn't matter; repu- tation didn't matter. Quality mattered. Only quality. Had he sneered or snickered at the thought of a winery in full-scale production for only twelve years deigning to enter the competition, he would have been guilty of hy- pocrisy. He had become an expert on wine in four.

EXHIBITIONS tended to favor established names; they were occasions for large firms to discover their worth in judgments handed down by well-known jurors eager to demonstrate their importance and influence. It was simply chance that the Weltausstellung became a meeting ground for a new critic and a new winery to become acquainted. Their needs were mutual. In Vizetelly, Poeschel & Scherer found an honest assessor. In Poeschel & Scherer, Vizetelly found a promising varietal to single out and champion.

It was Vizetelly who compiled the report on the wines of the United States at the Weltausstellung, and the thoroughness and liveliness of his subsequent chronicle for the British Parliament suggests that he was in charge of the judging of these wines as well.

What is remarkable about the report is what it chooses to allot space to—what it expands upon and what it stints. For every region Vizetelly describes, he dispenses quickly with the particulars of the wineries that took home honors, and with the relative strengths of their winning varietals, devoting the bulk of his account to ruminations upon the past and predictions for the future. He is not hung up on hardware. History is what animates him, the story in its context, the present moment set off within the frame of the past.

That Poeschel & Scherer broke free from a congested and competitive pack of twenty thousand bottles to claim a medal of merit, one of only three wineries in America to do so, is of less importance to him than that the Norton is a wine of potential greatness and that Missouri has announced itself as a region to be reckoned with. Noting a "marked difference" between those wines "vintaged in California and those produced in other States, a circumstance due to the fact that European vines are almost exclusively cultivated in the former province, while in Missouri, Ohio, New York and other States, the indigenous varieties alone are grown," he declared an enormous preference for the latter:

> The finest American red wines were those yielded by the vines
> known as Norton's Virginia, and the Cynthiana. The former
> produces a well-blended, full-bodied, deep-colored, aromatic,
> and somewhat astringent wine, only needing finesse to equal a
> first-rate Burgundy; the second, probably the finer of the two,
> being a darker, less astringent, and more delicate growth. . . .
>
> The wines known as Norton's Virginia, Concord, and Clinton
> form to-day the basis of the Missouri vineyards, which promise to
> become not merely the most prolific vineyards of the States but
> also those yielding the best wines. Herman [sic] is the centre of
> viticulture in Missouri, but grapes are also grown and much wine
> made around Boonville in Cooper County, and Augusta in St.
> Charles County, also in Hannibal on the Mississippi and in the
> vicinity of St. Joseph on the Missouri, there being hardly a county
> in this favoured State, which enjoys the advantages of longer
> seasons, a warmer climate, and more suitable soil than other
> regions, but has some flourishing vineyard.

He showed himself to be a student of American winemaking, writing with insight and understanding of the problem that had dogged winemakers for more than two hundred years, that of subduing the foxiness of American grapes:

> When the wine is made from the grapes of the labrusca group, the principal difficulty that has to be contended with is to prevent too much of the strong musky flavour of the fruit from entering the wine, and which is accomplished by removing the first juice expressed from the grapes and not allowing it to ferment on the lees. In this manner the dark red grapes yield a white wine, the flavour of which is not nearly so powerful as it would have been had this precaution not been taken. The extensive introduction of the Norton's Virginia and Delaware varieties which are without this defect, has done much, however, to obviate the inconvenience.

Whether his understanding of the epic difficulty of the Americans in coaxing wine from native grapes had any bearing on his estimation of the Norton from Poeschel & Scherer is hard to know. It seems unlikely. As with the great estates of Europe, all that mattered to Vizetelly was performance. What does seem likely is that his awareness of these difficulties, of this long and tortured history, deepened his appreciation of the accomplishment, casting the success of the Norton in high relief.

Tempting as it was to regard it as an underdog, the Little Engine That Could, the Norton was also the result of an exhaustive period of trial and error, the literal fruit of centuries of exasperation in the field and cellar. Like the author who is declared an overnight success, only to reveal a stash of manuscripts that never made it past his desk, the Norton was not without a past. Twelve years? Twenty-five years? It had been 266 years since the colonists landed at Jamestown, the start of the winemaking enterprise in the New World.

Vizetelly did not touch on these earliest beginnings, but his report does convey the impression of a country that has finally rounded the corner, and the intrepid critic is only too happy to be the first to forecast a brilliant future. On the strength of Missouri, which is to say, on the strength of the Norton, America was, he wrote, "destined to become . . . one of the great wine-producing regions of the world."

POESCHEL & SCHERER won another medal for its Norton, at the Universal Exhibition in Paris in 1878, where Vizetelly was again a judge. And the run of honors did not stop there.

An outfit calling itself the Monticello Wine Co., founded in 1873, claimed a silver medal in Paris and two first-class medals at an international exhibition in New Orleans, in 1884–1885, for a Norton it packaged as Virginia Claret. In describing the wine as a claret and invoking the name of the famous mansion, the company, a collective of grape growers, evidently decided it was wiser to market Thomas Jefferson than Daniel Norton. Thus was the tie between the doctor and his grape, already frayed by the myth perpetuated by Dr. Lemosy's son, further damaged. These PR decisions were obvious appeals to the European market, but they also were intended to lend a young business a little gravitas: The Monticello Wine Co. had just been founded at the time Vizetelly was presiding at the Weltausstellung.

In 1900, at the Paris Exposition, came another honor: a Frenchman named Émile Dubois, who had relocated to Tallahassee and planted over 150 varieties of grapes, won a silver medal for his Norton and Cynthiana wines.

Significant as these successes were, benchmarks against which to measure the evolution of the Norton, of Missouri, and of America, the medals amounted to baby steps, historically speaking. A good beginning, but a beginning nonetheless.

Under ordinary circumstances, the arrival of the Norton and with it the emergence of winemaking in America would have amounted to a nice little sidebar, a promising development for Europeans to keep a paternalistic eye on.

But the wine world was in a panic, and America's epochal failure at growing grapes was not the only context against which the Norton's unforeseen successes were being assessed. They were being viewed against an even darker backdrop: the unforeseen epidemic that was destroying France's vineyards and threatening to wipe out European winemaking.

13

P HYLLOXERA IS a big Greek-derived word for the tiny thing it describes. Its four singsongy syllables refer to a yellow, aphidlike bug so small, as to be virtually undetectable to the unaided eye. Its invisibility is precisely what makes it so insidious. If allowed to enter a vineyard, it burrows into the roots of vines, destroying the grapes at their source, in the same way that a smart tackler aims to cut a shifty running back at the knees. The aphid is merciless, and even more so because it is so hard to stop once it has gotten a purchase on a vine in the field, multiplying and spreading like a contagion.

By the time of the Weltausstellung, phylloxera had been on the attack for nearly ten years, and had taken on the dimensions of an epidemic in France.

The siege had begun in the mid-1860s, on the southern coast of France, in the Languedoc region, and gradually moved inland. The famed region of Bordeaux initially remained uninfected, but fear of the coming plague had created a panic. Fully one third of the French made their living from the production of wine and wine accounted for one sixth of the country's tax revenue. In destroying the vineyards, the aphid was destroying more than an economy. It was destroying a tradition, an identity. Wine was not just what the French made. It was who they were.

It was years before scientists isolated the cause—the importation of

American vines a generation earlier—and in their fear and desperation, many decided that the scourge had been divinely inspired, a punishment by God.

The unseen attacker unnerved them, made them doubt their good intentions, made them wonder what they had done to deserve such a cruel, vindictive fate. What great wrong had they committed? What did God want of them?

At least with a military takeover, you saw your enemy. French vintners were in quarantine, in lockdown. And they had no idea why.

BUREAUCRACY intervened, as bureaucracy typically does, just in time to give the people the impression that something was being done to put a stop to the problem, but not in time to actually stop it. Commissions were formed to investigate. In 1868, with the siege advancing, a group of citizens in Hérault, in Montpellier, in the heart of the Languedoc, enlisted the help of five scientists to investigate. One of them was a man named Jules-Émile Planchon, who previously had been an assistant to Sir William Hooker at Kew Gardens, in London, and had corresponded with Darwin about hybrid infertility in the 1860s, while the great naturalist was researching *The Variation of Animals and Plants Under Domestication*.

With magnifying glasses and notepads, the Hérault commission began its inquiry at the vineyard of the Marquis de Lagoy, near Saint-Rémy. Where once there had stood a lush, vine-covered yard, now there was, one member noted, "a veritable cemetery." The manager of the vineyard lamented, "It is terrible, it advances like an army."

After many weeks of study, the Hérault commissioners were divided as to the best and most efficient way of curbing the plague, but in its report to the Academy of Sciences in Paris late that summer, it did identify a new species, *Rhizaphis vastatrix*, "root aphid devastator" (though it is now called *Daktulosphaira vitifoliae*, "finger-ball of vine leaf"). "Devastator" aptly desribes the almost bulletproof resistance of the aphid to ordinary disease-killing measures. No means of counterattack could destroy it, and the French, in their desperation, tested all manner of methods, including petroleum, heavy oil, coal tar, black soap, arsenical acid, phenic (carbolic) acid, salts of copper, and an infusion of tobacco, mustard, aloes, and walnut leaves.

In November 1869, the Société des Agriculteurs de France gathered at Beaune, in Burgundy, the wine capital of France. Planchon was in attendance. He speculated that there might be a natural predator of phylloxera, a natural means by which to eradicate the bug. Also in attendance was a man named Léo Laliman, a wine collector, who had been importing the American varieties Scuppernong and Catawba for about twenty years. Laliman, like many Frenchmen, had little regard for American wines, but he believed, as some did, that they were well suited for grafting onto French rootstocks in order to strengthen them.

Over the next couple of years, Planchon became convinced that the aphid had come from America. He prophesied that it was a threat to "all the vineyards of the world." Believing that the bug posed a greater danger to countries in which it was a stranger than to those in which it was a native, he warned vintners in Burgundy and Champagne to be wary of importing foreign vines. The national phylloxera commission, the Central Commission, in 1871 urged vintners to follow the radical example of those in the Hérault and Gironde—uprooting the vines and disinfecting the soil by burning the surface. In 1872, the prefect of the Hérault made this practice mandatory. He also banned the importation of foreign vines.

Vintner has a noble ring. It stands for many today as the embodiment of the Romantic life, a simple and pure existence spent in the field, bringing forth a delicate and complex elixir from grapes. It is easy to forget that most vintners were peasants, uneducated and stubborn in their ways, which were, after all, the ways of their ancestors, the ways that had sustained them for centuries. Many ignored these decrees, trusting in their senses. And trusting also in God. They believed that the bug would not reach them, that just because it had wiped out a vineyard nearby, it would not necessarily wipe them out, too. This obstinacy, coupled with a reluctance to dig up the healthy vines that neighbored those that had been destroyed, only encouraged the epidemic.

As the crisis deepened, the desperation mounted. Some saw supplication as the only hope, and placing vials of holy water from the shrine at Lourdes beside the ravaged vines was proposed. Parishioners made pilgrimages to the vineyards, lacing the air with incense and praying to God to release them from the serenity of the decree. Louis Pasteur advocated using a disease of silkworms he had isolated. He, at least, had a background in science. Snake-oil cures proliferated. Insecticides were tried. The French government dangled a massive reward for any citizen who could come up with a solution; it received almost seven hundred proposals. Planchon was not impressed. The reward triggered "an avalanche of grotesque *elucubrations* which would be laughable if they were not a humiliating symptom of the failings of our national education."

In hopes of pinpointing a cause, from which he might eventually divine a cure, Planchon traveled to America.

In Webster, Missouri, just outside of St. Louis, he met with a man named J. J. Kelly and inspected his fields. There was Catawba, and it looked as bad "as anything in the south of France." Next to it, however, was Norton, and it was flourishing—proof, Planchon thought, of the inherent resistance of American vines to phylloxera. In his notebook, he recorded his tasting notes of Norton wine: "Red, complicated enough wine, the bouquet recalled Burgundy of secondary quality. Pleasant nevertheless." (Planchon was not much enamored of America, lamenting its preference for distilled liquor and beer over wine, its predilection for drinking cold water, and its habit of churning out ice cream that was "much inferior to that in France.")

Planchon was reluctant to recommend the wholesale replacement of French vines—"the wealth and glory of France"—with American vines, and his surmise proved correct. Two to three years after the first planting of Concord in the Midi, the vines died. It was Jamestown and Jefferson all over again, only in reverse: American grapes were ill suited to the land, as poor a fit for Europe as European grapes were for America. In their great panic, it was as though the French had forgotten the wisdom, the immutable truth, of their beloved *terroir*.

Some, including Laliman, believed that the answer lay in grafting French vines onto American rootstocks. While the crisis had been caused, most likely, by the importation of American vines, these American plants also happened to be naturally resistant to the disease, and it was this technique, urged by Planchon and others, including a number of American scientists (among them two Missourians, the entomologist Charles Riley and the viticulturalist Hermann Jaeger, the first vintner in the West to spray for fungal diseases), that would evetually do the trick, curbing the advance of the plague. The process allowed the French to keep their vines and their varietals while taking advantage of the hardiness of the American rootstock. But for a time, many were encouraged to keep trying.

In 1874, a report to the Academy of France noted that the cuttings and roots of many varieties of American vines had been distributed to grape growers, underscoring the point that they were "not only for experiment, but actually with a view to cultivate them for their fruit; hence it may be surmised, with some certainty, that a considerable trade in this new staple of importation from the United States may be looked forward to for the future . . ."

That same year, the French Academy of Sciences had commissioned a study of American grape varieties designed to put Laliman's contentions to the test. Not only did it identify which varieties were capable of withstanding phylloxera, but it also analyzed the grapes as potential wine producers, testing to determine which succeeded best in the cellar and which offered the best hope of aging and softening.

The result was a judgment of American grapes that was startling for its absence of rancor. Startling, also, for its openness to American variety:

> They all recommend themselves by their vigor and fecundity,
> some, at the same time, by the quality of their grapes. The
> "Clinton," "Warren," and "Cunningham," make good ordinary

wines; the "Taylor," "Jacquez," and, above all, "Norton's
Virginia," produce wines of the first quality.

The thirty members of the International Congress of Viticulture, in
Montpellier, convened to conduct a test, too. George Husmann had shipped
180,000 cuttings of vines from Hermann, along with two boxes of American wine. The wines, fifteen varieties in all, came from Poeschel & Scherer,
fresh off its triumph at the Weltausstellung.

A member of the committee, noting the expertise of his compatriots—
"they were about the best connoisseurs of France"—later shared with
Husmann the group's enthusiastic appraisal of the American wines: "Norton's Virginia and Cynthiana, as red wines; Martha, Goethe, and above
all, Hermann [an offspring of Norton] and Rulander, were highly
praised."

He added that "the general opinion is, that after we have restocked our
vineyards with American vines, we will not regard the loss of our own
very much."

Husmann, writing in the *Tenth Annual Report of the State Board of Agriculture of the State of Missouri* that year, exulted in the committee's findings.
"If this is already the verdict abroad," he wrote, "should it not stimulate us
to renewed exertions, and fill us with bright hopes for the future? Let us
look forward to that good time, which is soon to come, of ready sales and
good prices for first-class products. . . ."

IT SEEMED an absurdity. A straining of belief, of logic, of common
sense.

For nothing quite signaled the utter desperation of the French—neither
the fervent apostrophes to God nor the endless pilgrimages to the vineyards—as clearly as this embrace of American grapes.

That proud, fiercely chauvinistic France was willing to abandon its
Pinot Noir, its Chardonnay, its Merlot, its Cabernet Sauvignon—willing
to toss out centuries of tradition; willing to start over and construct a new

history—was unthinkable. But that it would turn without apology to the vines of America to make up for the epic loss of its own? Young vines. Historyless vines. And that it would speak of this unprecedented act with the blithe casualness of one exchanging a summer wardrobe for a winter one? *We will not regard the loss of our own very much.* This was more than a bowing to imperatives, the adoption of the practical posture that extreme times call for extreme measures. This was—*sacre bleu!*—the beginning of thinking like an American: *Don't look back; keep moving.*

It was premature and not a little reckless to suggest that a changing of the guard was coming, that America was about to overtake France for supremacy in wine, but already the whispers had begun that the old hierarchies were about to tumble. The American experiment was not yet a century old, the peculiar institution had just been abolished, and the country was still quaking from a bloody Civil War that had shaken the self-image of the fledgling nation as a bastion of new and improved ideas. But American wine—which, since the country's inception, had been derided by foreign visitors and aesthetes for its foxiness, a quality that had frustrated and embarrassed a wine-obsessed Thomas Jefferson—had clearly arrived.

And an American type had clearly arrived, too. In the novel, there was Twain's crudely vernacular first person; in poetry, Whitman's ragged, exuberant lines; in music, the emergence of an exciting new sound that improbably set the formal harmonies of European balladry with percussive African rhythms. All were met initially with disapprobation or derision, dismissed as coarse, barbaric expressions, beyond the bounds of taste, of what was acceptable. Norton, departing from familiar models, was their counterpart in wine: earthy, bold, and wild on the tongue, sometimes overlooked and often misunderstood, a mélange of *aestivalis* and *vinifera,* of Europe and America, that was, ultimately, nothing so much as itself.

A new century loomed—"the American century," an era of unprecedented American economic, political, and cultural might—and it was not hard to imagine that American wine would be a force, too. Europe had every right to be pessimistic, just as America had every right to be optimistic. Never had the prospects for wine in the Old World looked darker. And never had its future in the New World looked brighter.

In his book *Judgment of Paris,* George Taber argues that the historic blind tasting, in 1976, of California wines and French wines by some of France's leading wine critics, was the event that heralded America's emergence as a winemaking nation. But more than a century earlier, American wine did not need the acceptance of Europe to signal that it had arrived. It had something better: the acquiescence of Europe.

14

I N MONTPELLIER, FRANCE, a curious monument hunkers in a
lush garden at the region's leading agricultural college.

Two figures are depicted in the sculptural homage to a man named
Gustave Foëx, a French professor and one of the *dramatis personae* of the
phylloxera crisis: a young woman and an old woman. The young woman is
strong and fit; the old woman wrinkled, haggard. The young woman appears to be cradling the old woman. Comforting her. It is an allegory:
America succoring France.

Or so I concluded the first time I looked at it, given to seeing the piece
as a symbolic interpretation of a particular moment in time, when France
was ailing and America was ascendant, when it seemed a distinct possibility that America would assume a position of prominence in the world of
wine. A public acknowledgment of gratitude to America, a bold admission
of weakness and vulnerability.

That moment in time was brief. When, in 1870, the American entomologist Charles Riley, a Missourian, confirmed Planchon's theory that
the aphid was the cause and not an effect of the blight, the French turned to
grafting, revitalizing their vineyards by splicing imported aphid-resistant
American rootstocks onto existing *vinifera* vines. The rescue mission succeeded, ending the epidemic and rendering that period a historical aberra-
tion. By the turn of the century, the vineyards of France, with the help of
American grafts, were largely alive and flourishing again. And the Not-

THE WILD VINE ✧ 135

ton, the would-be savior and potential future of the Languedoc? It had no future at all. The French needed quickly rooting vines, and the Norton was notoriously slow to root. Nor did the grape respond well to the highly calcareous lime-based soils typical of French wine-growing regions.

It was as if some kind of transference had taken place, some vital charge of energy conveyed from one country to the other.

And that's when it dawned on me to return to the piece, if only in my mind's eye: the young woman in the sculpture is not merely comforting the old woman. She is kissing her. Resuscitating her. It is impossible to understand the sculpture, impossible to understand that moment in time, without understanding that life-giving kiss.

France rose again, and America fell back down to earth. The Norton's swift rise was answered by a swift fall. In a generation, all the promise and excitement of American wine and of the Norton's limitless future had come to seem like a phantom. Missouri had gone bust, the native grape was no longer being grown, and the dream of a distinctly American wine culture was all but dead. It was as if, having reached the height of its renown, the Norton had vanished from the public stage in an act of deliberate leave-taking—pulled a Garbo.

What happened?

IN HERMANN, at the Gasconade County Historical Society's office of Archives and Records, a small, tidy research library on Schiller Street, a fastidiously put-together woman with round glasses, a short white crop of hair, and a schoolmarmish manner—yes, she once was a principal, Lois Puchta tells me evenly—retrieves several thick binders for me to pore through.

Lois's husband's ancestors comprised seven of the first seventeen settlers to arrive in Hermann, and her husband's family operated Adam Puchta Winery, the oldest winery in town to have stayed in one family (her son, Tim, runs the vineyard today). She knows her history, she knows her wine, and she figures to be a good guide for filling in some of the gaps in my knowledge, beginning with the medal of merit in Vienna.

The medal seemed to me a thing of great significance, and yet I kept coming up empty in my efforts to discover more about it. I knew by now that the available literature on the Norton was not extensive, but the years between the Weltausstellung and Prohibition—between the pinnacle of its history and its near-death—ought to have been different, a rich, event-filled epoch in the crazy, fortune-tossed life of the great American wine. Shouldn't this have been a period when more was written about it, not less, because interest had grown and demand, presumably, had increased? Shouldn't the Norton have built upon its successes?

I had been looking for months in libraries and online, and had found only a few documents. And those that I did find confounded me—not for what they said; for what they didn't say.

In the golden age of Norton, the short, twenty-year period from roughly 1870 to 1890, the wine was nearly as prized for its medicinal qualities as it was for its complexity and sophistication in the glass.

The *American Cyclopaedia, a Popular Dictionary of General Knowledge,* published in 1883, lauded it as the "best medicinal wine of America. It is dark red, almost black, very heavy, astringent, and of strong flavor, some-what resembling the flavor of green coffee. It is a remedy against bowel complaints, chronic diarrhoeas, and summer complaints in children and . . . a preventive of intermittent fevers and other malarious diseases . . ." It added, almost as an afterthought, "[It] has already been appreciated in Europe as one of the best red wines of the world." *The Detroit Lancet, a Monthly Exponent of Rational Medicine,* recorded a meeting of doctors in 1884 to discuss "prevailing diseases." One of the physicians informed his colleagues that he advised patients suffering from dysentery—coinciden-tally, the condition that led Dr. Daniel Norton to his death—to "drink plenty of Virginia Seedling Wine, which is an astringent."

It was the Puritan aesthetic, or rather, the Puritan anti-aesthetic: a product is good insofar as it improves a person—the sheer pleasure to be had from imbibing be damned.

At the time, I regarded these odd bits as distractions from what I was looking for—mere marginalia, when what I needed was to get my hands on the document or documents that would prove definitively how important the Norton was. How much the wine made by Poeschel & Scherer had mattered.

Now that I have come to Archives and Records, now that I have journeyed to the source, a naive hope stirs within me—a hope that all will be revealed. Surely some trove of documents awaits me, some cache of papers, pamphlets, diary entries with the goods I'm craving. There's just one problem, and not a little one. Hermann did not print an English language newspaper until 1875, two years after the Weltausstellung.

"Do you read German?" Lois asks.

I groan audibly: it's like being asked by the librarian, when I was a procrastinating kid of a student, how many weeks I had to write my report on aborigines in Australia. (Weeks? Try *hours*.)

Lois volunteers that her German is pretty good, and so I mark the articles I want, articles from that landmark year that include mentions of Poeschel & Scherer, and she pulls up the microfilm. Ten minutes later, I hear her reciting, rather loudly, in German, and I get up from the long table where I am reading and rush over to stand by her side, to be there and see history unfold in front of me.

"What's it say?" I ask excitedly.

She translates her translation. "Something about a cart that went through town."

"That's it?"

"That's it."

AT A LIBRARY in St. Louis, I check out a dozen boxes of microfilm of a publication called *Anzeiger des Westens* (Bulletin of the West), an important cultural resource for Germans in St. Louis from the middle of the nineteenth century to the early part of the twentieth century. I had already learned a couple of interesting facts about it. Its owner was a rabid anti-Semite, and Twain had worked for its English-language edition as a teenager in the 1850s, setting type.

I thread the film through the projector, scroll the pages, squint at the smeary surface of the screen, and immediately understand that I am deluding myself in coming here. It is bad enough to try to make sense of the tiny type, but I am trying to make sense of tiny type in German. I stay a while, nonetheless, hoping to get lucky, hoping that I will stumble upon something I have no business finding. Or hoping that what I am looking for will up and announce itself through the smear and I can take the passage home to a specialist and get it translated, or take it back to Lois. But I don't see any mention of Poeschel & Scherer or the Vienna Exhibition, and eventually give up. All the squinting has given me a headache.

I DO get to see the medal, at least. It sits in a glass case at the German School Museum in Hermann, across from Archives and Records. A nice man named Steve Mueller is kind enough to open the case and let me hold it and attempt the sort of crude reproduction we used to do in school, placing a piece of notebook paper over the surface and rubbing a pencil back and forth over it, in the hope of recording the embossments. I don't have much luck.

The raised lettering is not raised enough, having been worn down to barely perceptible characters over the past century and a quarter. All I get are a bunch of thick pencil lines. It stands for me as an emblem of my inquiry, the disappearance of the actual, the erasure of history.

WHY WASN'T more made of the accomplishment of Poeschel & Scherer with their Norton?

I had a hard time believing that the absence of an English-language paper in Hermann was solely to blame.

Small towns are not often the best source of perspective on things, lacking the long view that can put a moment into its proper context, and a clipping I unearthed, later, about Poeschel & Scherer after the fact— after the Weltausstellung—was not particularly satisfying. It would have been no more satisfying had it appeared earlier and in English. The article made no mention of the Norton and reminded me of the kind of item you tend to find in a community newspaper about a local kid who has recently graduated college and taken up a career in the city in computer sales.

There was no mention at all, small or otherwise, in the big English-language newspapers in St. Louis, nor even in the German-language papers there. And if St. Louis could not be bothered to pay attention to the international doings of a company eighty miles from home, is it any wonder that the big cities around the country could not either?

But still, why? The question nagged at me.

And something else nagged at me, too, something that made me wonder if the two were somehow related, if these naggings in any way explained each other.

Reading through the records in Hermann, the two-paragraph news clippings, the old ledgers detailing varieties and prices, the second- and third-hand accounts of the past, wine seemed to be of less importance in the specific than in the general. Wine was the town's industry and thus its identity, and running through every line of copy was an enormous local pride in the notion that Hermannites, having started with nothing, turned that nothing into something. Many articles talked of tonnage, of output. The development of the industry, the growth of production. I saw more mentions of the fact that Poeschel & Scherer had become the second-biggest winemaker in the country than I did of the medal at the Weltausstellung for a bottle of Norton.

The American preoccupation with size, the animating idea that bigger is better.

But shouldn't the judgments at Vienna in 1873 and Paris in 1878 have stood as proof that better is bigger? Or at least that better is better (and bigger, merely bigger)?

And shouldn't they have swept the land, the news spreading from state to state with the same swiftness and excitement as the cuttings of the Norton had, two generations earlier?

. . .

IT WAS ONLY AFTER I'd returned from Missouri that I remembered something Jenni had said, in passing, many months earlier.

Just as the events of 1873 seemed of greater significance now, with the benefit of more than a century of distance, so did Jenni's remark, having found its proper context, take on a deeper resonance.

I flipped through my notebooks, looking for the relevant passage, the exact words, which now seemed absolutely necessary, like a missing piece of evidence, but that at the time, I had not bothered to underline or put an asterisk beside. And I thought, *This is what happens. Events rush by, and in that rush it's hard to know what matters and what doesn't, what to keep and what to discard. Only later does the picture come into focus. Only later does the insignificant become significant, the margins gravitate toward the center.*

Six notebooks in, I found it. We were in the Outlook on our way back from the trip to Drs. Cliff and Rebecca Ambers. We were getting hungry, and I had mentioned to Jenni that there was a good taqueria that we could hit if she didn't mind going slightly out of our way. The outer edges of Northern Virginia were filled with taco joints because they were now filled with Latinos, recent arrivals from El Salvador, Guatemala, and central Mexico. Cuisine follows culture.

We had been talking about Norton and about the Weltausstellung, and Jenni had said—well, *blurted* was more like it: "Imagine if you had a couple of Latino businessmen win some big award somewhere. Do you think anybody'd care? Hell, no. Why? Because they're immigrants."

How had I missed that? Had I been so preoccupied with Jenni and her past that, despite my interest in absorbing everything I needed to know, I had missed something illuminating about the Norton and *its* past? Or had I simply not been alert to all the multitude of possibilities before me? It would not have been the first time.

A sloppy notebook has a way of collapsing time. I had moved onto a new line of thought—"musings on wine," I'd written—and so it was hard for me to know just how much time had passed from the time she had connected the dots between the Latino immigrants of the twenty-first century and the German immigrants of the nineteenth century. But on the next page, there was this: "Who was drinking wine at the time? The elites, they were drinking wines from France and the rest of Europe. Most Americans at that time didn't drink wine. They drank booze. So who was drinking Norton and all these other American wines? Yeah, okay, you had Ulysses Grant drinking it at the White House, and he liked it. But it was immigrants, mostly."

After which there was this, from me: *"If a tree falls in the woods, and there's nobody there to hear it . . ."*

15

I N HERMANN, popular lore has it that Prohibition killed the wine industry. "Then came Prohibition," is the oft-repeated phrase, a grim punch line offered up by the town's many amateur historians, the deus ex machina of a colorful immigrant story of ingenuity, resourcefulness, and success. "All those awards and all those medals, the industry was going strong, and things couldn't have been better. And then came Prohibition," Hermannites say with a shrug and a sigh. They might as well be saying, "And then along came the angel of death . . ."

But the truth is more complicated than that. Grand, overarching theories, much like simple, good vs. evil narratives, make for a good story, easily digestible, but seldom one that captures reality in all its messy strangeness. And it was messy strangeness I was after, because it was what I had come to expect and to trust in. Messy strangeness was not a residue of the story of the Norton; more and more, it seemed, messy strangeness *was* the story.

The truth was, the Norton's downfall was being plotted even as the medals were piling up and its long-term future seemed assured, not unlike the tragic and untimely end that awaits a great thoroughbred who is pushed to exceed his levels of endurance and talent, and whose destruction is sowed by his success—ruin being the reward of the gods for ignoring history, tradition, and fate.

Husmann had sensed as much, even as he was celebrating the French embrace of his favorite grape. In "The Future of Grape-Growing in the West," included in the *Tenth Annual Report of the State Board of Agriculture of the State of Missouri* for 1874, the same report in which he reported the response to Hermann's wines in Montpellier, he wrote, "Grape growing in the West, and especially in our State, promising and lucrative as it was in its infancy, is at present under a cloud. The markets are flooded and glutted with cheap wines and low priced grapes, so low, indeed, that they will hardly pay the grower, and it has become a question of vital importance, which every grape-grower anxiously asks, 'Will grape-growing and wine-making pay in the future?'"

He attributed the "depression" in the market to a number of factors, including a lack of professionalism on the part of some of the state's wine-makers, some of whom, he argued, had believed they could tend to grapes as they could corn. Having devoted himself to the study and introduction of new techniques and processes, he had grown increasingly tired of the amateurism he saw. Worst was the cultivation of too narrow a variety of grapes. Concord and Norton had so dominated production that they dis-couraged the cultivation of other grapes. Valuable though they were, they were not suited to every taste.

"The Concord as a market grape does not carry well," Husmann con-cluded. "It has too tender a skin, and although of fair quality, clogs the palate too soon, while the Norton is no market grape at all."

The doting father had looked at the brilliant child and with a merciless-ness that was all the more startling for being so blithe, sized up his one ir-redeemable flaw. *No market grape at all.* The Norton had surpassed expectations: it had won the admiration of the French and garnered the at-tention of the world. But it was not a marketplace performer; it did not travel well. A critical success, but not yet a commercial one.

What accounted for this hard, unsentimental view? The wine depres-sion had underscored the tenuousness of the industry and magnified its weaknesses. Much had been accomplished—much more, certainly, than anyone a generation earlier could have anticipated. But Husmann saw the potential for more. Missouri was just a start; the Norton was just a start; the Weltausstellung was just a start. Now was not the time for the state's winemakers to revel in the glory. Now was the time to raise standards, become more professional, work harder, learn more, and get better. Not just bigger; better. He was willing to put in the time and study necessary to grow and develop and improve. Was everybody else? He had his doubts. Provided they could lift themselves out of the depression, could they continue to build on their impressive gains? Could they make good on the immense promise he had foreseen for the state?

He had always been skeptical of the idea that any one grape could carry an entire industry. For one thing, it left winemakers at the mercy of diseases; one unchecked pestilence could erase decades of progress. But it was clear to him, more and more, that the Norton could not be the only American wine grape.

BY THIS TIME, Husmann was comfortably ensconced in the next phase of his career, a wise old head collecting appointments, presidencies, and professorships, an establishment sage. He'd left Hermann in 1866 and had settled in nearby Bluffton, becoming president of the Bluffton Wine Company. In 1870, he was appointed to the Board of Curators of the University of Missouri. Several years later, he was named to the State Board of Agriculture. The University of Missouri appointed him a professor of Pomology and Forestry. It was a life made for contemplation, for the transfer of knowledge to a younger generation, for surveying the scene from a distance and sharing his many considered judgments. It was not, alas, a life made for Husmann.

In 1881, he gave it all up—the appointments, the professorship—and headed west. California had called to him as a callow youth of twenty-two, seducing him to chuck his responsibilities on the farm in Hermann and venture west, like so many other Americans, in search of gold in the fever of '49. It called to him again as a middle-aged man of fifty-four, with its vast promise as a yet-untapped Vineland. A vineyard in Napa Valley, Talcoa Vineyards, needed a manager. And Husmann needed something, too. He needed to get his hands dirty again.

California was evolving. The completion of the transcontinental rail-

road in 1869 had made train travel cheap, fast, and efficient, almost single-
handedly altering the way business was done in America and transforming
California, previously inaccessible to consumers on the East Coast and in
the Midwest, into a commercial force, particularly an agricultural force.
The effect on the wine industry was profound. Because it was now possible
to ship goods to every corner of the country, winemakers in America were
no longer limited to the grapes they themselves had. They didn't even have
to buy the grapes. They could eliminate a step in the process and just buy
the juice—the nearly simultaneous arrival of industrial refrigeration made
it easy to preserve the pressed liquid.

Grapes grew year-round in California. Unlike in Missouri and the
Ohio Valley, there was no hand-wringing over frost and drought, no
despairing over mildew and rot. All these problems entailed higher labor costs for a grower, for the manpower needed to fight the elements.
California didn't have these elements. The climate was made for grape
growing.

By the turn of the century, growers in California could produce a pound
of grapes at half the cost of a pound in Missouri. As a result, three decades
after accounting for 42 percent of the nation's entire output of wine, Missouri accounted for just 3 percent.

Another, equally transformational change had already been underway
in the wine industry, one that was in progress by the time of the Weltausstellung of 1873. As late as 1869, the eminent wine critic Charles Loring
Brace in his book *The New West; or, California in 1867-1868* had given a
thumbs-down to California wines, identifying the climate as a probable
cause of their "bad name":

> In speculating over the apparent inferiority of California wines to
> European, I have wondered whether the defect could be in any
> degree due to climate. It is well known that the grape from which
> Sherry is made, if transplanted to the dry climate of the Cape of
> Good Hope, produces a very different and an inferior wine to the
> famous wine of Xeres.
>
> May not the dry and warm climate of California act on the

grape by intensifying the essential oils, which are at the base of
odors, and thus produce the peculiar and not agreeable bouquet
which distinguishes all these wines? It would seem as if the acetic
ether were the strong peculiarity of this bouquet. We know that
all odors and oils are strengthened by this wonderful climate.
Thus the mustard is said to be stronger than the European
mustard, the hops have a more astringent quality than our Eastern
hops, and I have myself observed the odor of musk in certain
grapes almost as strong as if it were an animal product. It may
thus be that some one essential oil which is formed in all wines, is
here intensified and becomes the prevailing property.

I throw this out merely as a suggestion. If it be a fact, the
inventive genius of the Californian cultivators will no doubt
eventually overcome even this obstacle.

Loring Brace was an enthusiastic proponent of the Norton, and he
mused in *The New West*, "The great wonder is that Norton's Virginia Seedling is so little known in California, where almost every European variety
of grape has been successfully introduced. No red wine has ever been produced in America equal to that made by the Germans of Missouri from this
grape."

His pronouncements capture an interesting moment in time, the apogee
of California winemaking ineptitude, just before the transcontinental rail-
road was finished, just before things turned. The fact was, the inventive
genius of the Californian cultivators was already at work, transforming the
industry. Not long after Loring Brace all but dismissed it, the state supplanted Missouri as the number-one grape grower in the country, and it
has never relinquished the title. Husmann did not venture west to found an
industry. The foundation was already there. He went to help it grow and
flourish, to nurture and cultivate it.

I put the question to Linda Walker Stevens, a Hermannite who used to
live in Napa Valley and who has curated a museum exhibit on Husmann's
life and written about his work: Did Hermann and Missouri go into decline

because Husmann left, or did Husmann leave because Hermann and Missouri had gone into decline?

"That's one of the big questions," she says. "Certainly, what you have happening at this time, is that the attention and the interest shifts to the West Coast, in great part because Husmann has gone there."

The small group of industry watchers who comprised the wine world of that time knew that it was more than one man lighting out for a new territory in pursuit of a new challenge. It was a symbolic journey, a symbolic passage. Husmann was passing the torch from Missouri to California. What he had given to his home state he could give to his adopted state. Missouri had done marvelously. But California, with its resources, would be more marvelous still.

In 1889, the same year the former Poeschel & Scherer, now called Stone Hill Winery, picked up yet another medal for its Norton at the World's Exposition in Paris, California wines—gathered by Husmann for exhibit—collected four golds and twelve silvers. And Husmann received a gold medal for his role as collaborator and promoter of the exhibit. "What was accomplished in that year was a glorious beginning . . ." Husmann said of the experience. ". . . I feel proud . . . of my sphere of work, which made the wines and brandies of California first extensively known to the world."

Whither the Norton?

He planted it, along with a number of other Missouri rootstocks, not long after he arrived in Napa. But it didn't take long to realize that California was not a home for it, just as Merlot isn't going to thrive in Missouri.

The Norton had been his pet project, but there would be other pet projects. If he had done it once, he could do it again. Of larger concern was the future of wine in America—*that* was the project that mattered; that was the project he was going to dedicate the final decades of his life to. It was not a new project, much as it might look like one. It was the continuation of the old project he had begun in Hermann with the Norton and other native grape varieties—the birth of a flourishing, self-sustaining wine culture in America.

It was an understandable outlook, thoughtfully reasoned. He had changed, the industry had changed, the country had changed. But it was hard not to think that he was exchanging the Norton for another, better lover.

I share my theory with Stevens, who chuckles at the analogy—and subtly reinforces it: "Well, he had to say, he couldn't help himself—California is the home of the grape."

POKING INTO the past in Hermann, I sometimes have the feeling I am on the end of a long and extended game of telephone, that enduring parlor game wherein the whispered secret is twisted and bent and entirely misconstrued by the time it reaches its destination. Hermannites have had nearly a century to stretch and distort the truth about their town's rise and particularly its fall. Even among those residents who are fascinated by the exploits of their forebears, it's not always possible to know just what happened when the town went dry.

"I'll see what sort of papers and whatnot I've got around here," Tim Puchta of Adam Puchta Winery tells me. "I can tell you, though, it's not gonna be a whole helluva lot. A lot of this stuff was lost when my dad died."

It's a familiar story. I talk to many people who bear a connection to the town's glorious and tragic past but who have no way of accessing that past, now that a parent or grandparent had passed and severed that link, and they are at pains to tell me where to turn, other than the handful of record centers. Many tell me they'll be interested in seeing what I find, and the eagerness in their voices and faces betrays a sadness over the loss of something vital—and over the idea that a stranger, an outsider, should be needed to help them make a connection to it.

Missouri's heyday had been reliably, if somewhat patchily, documented. It was the end that eluded wide description, as if the shutdown of its wine industry, a shutdown they were forced to undertake themselves, was too painful to record. From this sketchy documentation, it was tempting for succeeding generations to embellish the stories as the bootleggers had embellished the tales of their hooch. As the generations passed and the connection to Prohibition became more and more distant, the actual gave way to the possible, and thus the rampant myths, legends, and folklore of the era.

"Oh, yeah, the feds came in and the streets ran red," says Don Kruse, the editor of the *Hermann Advertiser-Courier.*

But then, before I can challenge the veracity of the story, it's as if his inner skeptic has reared up, his Missouri-born disinclination to embrace anything outright: "That's what they say, anyway, the old-timers."

"What do you say?" I ask.

"Well," he says, and chuckles. "Who knows, right? We have no way of really knowing."

"So what you're saying is, it doesn't sound like the truth to you—but that's not to say that it couldn't *be* the truth?"

"That's right."

Without proof, he isn't about to put his faith in that particular version of events. But he isn't about to dispute the given story, either.

GOETHE STREET would have run reddest. That was the public, unpaved road that cut through the property at Stone Hill, which was producing in excess of a million gallons of wine at the time of Prohibition. The draining of its oak casks would have constituted a violent bloodletting.

Stone Hill by this time had passed from George Stark to his sons, Ottmar and Louis. Ottmar Stark was the vice president; Louis, the treasurer. A generational shift was underway, bringing with it a change of priorities, a change of style. George Stark wore a long beard that stopped at his breastbone like a bushy bib, a style popular among German men of the mid-nineteenth century, connoting an air of studiousness and prosperity that suggested that its wearer was both a man of learning and a man of business. It was a style that aligned him with, among others, Michael Poeschel. His sons were modern men, indisputably rooted in the new century. Ottmar dispensed with the long beard, opting instead for a simple, well-kept

mustache that diverted attention from his dreamy dark eyes. Louis made
no concession to facial hair. His fastidious appearance was not simply a
matter of personal taste; it was a tacit argument on behalf of his willingness, his eagerness, to assimilate.

The sons reaped the benefits of their immigrant father's prosperity.
They were well educated and relieved from the burden of having to work
to earn their keep. They maintained homes in Hermann and St. Louis and
spent much of their time in the big city. They resided in Compton Heights,
a neighborhood that attracted many affluent German immigrants. Ottmar
was a director of a bank in Hermann, and operated a packet company in St.
Louis. The brothers ran a company called Stark-Inland Machine Works,
which manufactured spark plugs and piston rings; he had even applied for
and received a patent from the government for a special type of piston the
company had devised for use in automobiles. The predicted growth of the
auto industry excited the brothers and diverted a good deal of their entrepreneurial energy away from wine and booze. Cars captured their imaginations. Their father had been the first in Hermann to own a car, and the
brothers inherited his passion. They attracted attention for driving their
long, gleaming automobiles with obvious relish and speed.

Much less is known about the brothers' love for wine. Unlike Poeschel,
nothing of their attitudes toward viticulture or winemaking survives them
in documents or articles. The Starks saw themselves as businessmen, as
young, forward-thinking capitalists, and the company they presided over
would have been largely unrecognizable to Poeschel and those of his generation. It had become a sprawling, hydra-headed enterprise, with a bottling plant in St. Louis and even a distillery in Bardstown, Kentucky.

The diversity of their business interests, though interesting, does not
seem particularly significant to me until I stop one day to take in an exhibition wall of old wine labels at Stone Hill, many of them dating to the nineteenth century. The winery displays the labels in a glass case in a hallway just
off the light-filled tasting room. The hallway is adorned with framed portraits of the firm's owners, including Michael Poeschel, John Scherer,
George, Ottmar, and Louis Stark, and Jim and Betty Held. (In the main
room, an array of stuffed deer heads gazes vacant-eyed upon T-shirts, cheese

boards, and wine-drinking paraphernalia—the "experience enhancers" that seem to be a necessity for the wineries of post-Prohibition Missouri.) Jon Held, Jim and Betty's son and the man who today runs the winery, had just poured several of the company's excellent wines for me to try and was now leading me outside on a tour of his vineyards, after which we would descend to the winery's legendary arched cellars, walking among the shadows in the dank, echoing cave, where barrels upon barrels of Norton, pressed together like beads on a string, sat aging in American oak.

But first I pause at the board to linger over the old wine labels, dazzled by the nineteenth-century-style typography and design.

"Aren't these great?" Held asks, joining me in looking them over, his eyes big and avid and eager behind his glasses. The man I have just been listening to in the tasting room, a thoughtful and serious-minded man who, I was sure, could command an audience simply by sharing his vast knowledge about pH and fermentation, dissolves at the display case, and I see something of the boy in him, the seven-year-old who grew up at the winery and for whom every last little detail on the premises is a fascination.

I have always loved old stickers and mementos, loved the little window they give onto the past, and so I stand there for a long time with Held, converting the still pictures and florid typography into moving images, vital and alive. After a while, I realize that I have stopped noticing them individually and started to notice them as a whole. And what I notice—and why haven't I noticed it before?—is that many of them are not wine labels. In fact, the vast majority are for booze.

"Huh," Held says when I point this out to him.

Surely he's noticed this before. It's his board. Or maybe he's been conditioned not to notice, because to him Stone Hill was and always had been a wine company.

The original Virginia Seedling label is on display, but so are labels for peach brandy and grape brandy, for gin, for bourbon, for whiskey, even for slivovitz, the firewater-like plum brandy beloved by Eastern European Jews. (Slivovitz was being produced in rural Missouri? That was a mystery in itself.)

In 1883, Poeschel sold the business to George Stark and William

Herzog and retired. The company became Stone Hill, and Stark eventually turned it over to his sons, Ottmar and Louis. Whether the diversification of the company occurred under George's watch or his sons' is unclear, but the broadening of interests is a post-Poeschel development. Poeschel's focus was wine.

It may well have been that Ottmar and Louis were intent on building on the ubiquity and reputation of the brand in pushing the company to produce other kinds of liquor, leveraging the name in an attempt to expand and become even more dominant. It may also have been that they believed wine in Missouri to be a diminishing proposition, as Husmann's 1875 forecast of Hermann and of the Norton had eerily intimated—the industry was not to be self-sustaining for very long. The latter possibility did not negate the former. And the fact remains that, whatever their motivations, at the time of Prohibition, the Norton was an ever smaller piece of the picture at Michael Poeschel's winery. The times had moved on, and so had the Starks.

As it turned out, the diminishing proposition was alcohol itself. The warnings grew more numerous and more foreboding as the country entered World War I.

No one possessed a greater, more acute sense of anxiety over the direction that things were heading than Ottmar Stark. He had shipped a son, also named Ottmar Stark, off into the Armed Forces, but this fact alone, though significant, did not suddenly uncomplicate his feelings. Like a lot of German immigrants of the time, he remained conflicted. Many still had ties to, if not relatives in, Germany. This duality, and the success that many Germans had enjoyed for decades in Missouri in brewing beer and making wine, aroused the suspicions of a growing and increasingly rabid faction of anti-German citizens. The sense of threat in the air was becoming hard to ignore, and it was no longer possible to dismiss this sentiment as heated democratic discourse. There was no telling where or how far it might lead. It was wrenching to monitor the fighting in Europe from afar, to agonize over the fate of his son. But, increasingly, it was the war at home—a war that was every bit as senseless and terrifying as the war over there—that posed the greater threat to his and Hermann's safety and success.

Among the tactics used to whip up sentiment against German immigrants was to go after their native language, to equate the speaking and writing of German with a fundamental abhorrence of America. If the German immigrants wished to demonstrate their allegiance to America, if they wished not to be questioned as to their intentions, then it was incumbent upon them to embrace English as their language. Prior to World War I, there were three daily German-language newspapers, twenty-five weeklies, and twelve monthlies in Missouri. The era of German cultural preservation, a particularly important concern for the Hermann settlers, was brought to a sudden, swift end. Some papers converted to English; others refused and held on, but lost large numbers of their subscribers.

Among the treasures at the Deutschheim State Historic Site, a museum that documents Hermann's colorful past, is a reproduction of the following resolution from the Missouri Council of Defense, which powerfully illustrates the nakedly nationalistic appeals that aimed to isolate and alienate the Germans in the hope of driving them out of society:

> To the People of Missouri: The Missouri Council of Defense
> heartily approves the patriotic effort of Governor Frederick D.
> Gardner to abolish the use of the German language in this state.
> The Missouri Council of Defense is opposed to the use of the
> German language in the schools, churches, lodges and in public
> meetings of every character. The Council believes that the
> elimination of German and the universal use of English at all such
> gatherings, is essential to the development of a true, patriotic
> sentiment among all the people. The general adoption of English
> by all patriotic German organizations is a national duty and
> prompt action by all such, will be regarded by loyal Americans as
> the clearest evidence of loyalty and a sincere determination to help
> and not hinder the American Nation in this war.

The warning that ended the paragraph—"Loyal and zealous Americans should refrain from violence and disorder and under no circumstances, and no conditions, should our own people be guilty of injustice, oppression or atrocious conduct toward any class of our citizens"——was akin to the modern-day disclaimers on packs of cigarettes, a conscience-cleansing exculpation on the part of those who peddle a dangerous thing. In Linn and Cass counties, the desire to crack down upon the enemy language was taken to such a frenzied extreme that officials made it illegal to talk in German on the telephone.

Worse, as the temperance movement became a prohibition movement and as the war raged on, antidrinking sentiment became conflated with anti-German sentiment. The Citizens' Dry Alliance fought hard for an amendment outlawing the sale of alcoholic beverages. It advertised heavily in Missouri newspapers. "A dry vote is a vote against the Kaiser," went one ad. The Greene County Dry Alliance was infinitely more heated in its rhetoric in an election-day ad of 1918: "The Kaiser Must Go! The Saloon Must Go! Both Menace the Welfare of Humanity."

The gulf between the idealism of the Dudenites and their descendants and the reality of America had never been wider or more forbidding. One of those first Dudenites, Hermann Steines, had entreated his brother in 1834 to join him in a "country where freedom of speech obtains, where no spies are eavesdropping, where no wretched simpletons criticize your every word . . . in short if you wish to be really happy and independent, then come here and become farmers in the United States. . . . Here no despots are to be feared."

No, the despots were not kings and queens and princes; they were ordinary citizens. Tyranny in America was not a function of the ruling class, as it was in decadent Europe. It was democratized; it belonged to "we, the people."

And we, the people were restive. From the final, unruly decades of the nineteenth and well into the early years of the twentieth century, America was in the throes of unprecedented social and cultural change, profound systemic disruptions that presaged the possibility of a new national identity. Nominally a war against drink, the war of the Drys was also indisputably a stand against modernity, against openness, against tolerance, against immigration, against the growing influence of the cities.

Right up to the end, Ottmar and Louis Stark, like many other Wets, must have been mystified that the idea of the temperance movement, so sensible and rational, had transformed into the rabidity of the prohibition movement, and that so restrictive and backward an idea could flourish and become law. No drinking? No wine? Did they wish to outlaw pleasure, too? Put a ban on happiness?

Carrie Nation, in her infinite wisdom, seemed intent on attacking any facility that had anything even remotely to do with alcohol. In neighboring Kansas, Nation's state, where animosity over the Civil War still smoldered, the Prohibitionists had taken to burning wine books, diaries, and journals. Books! What next? Where would it stop? In truth, they all feared what would come next.

Hermann, the land of promise, had become a target as one of the most prosperous, most visible German communities in the entire country. The New Fatherland, they had dubbed it, in a spirit of unalloyed optimism. Now, four decades later, the nickname left the town exposed. Anti-German sentiment had become so fevered, it was a wonder that armies of soldiers with bayonets and cannons had not advanced on the city. Who could doubt the possibility, with Carrie Nation wielding her hatchet at every opportunity, and with the furor of the mass public demonstrations across the Midwest, which linked all German immigrants with the Kaiser and drummed up suspicion about their every activity, especially those that yielded a tidy profit.

On July 1, 1919, the day Prohibition went into effect in Missouri, Ottmar Stark, who was born the same year that the Norton debuted on the world stage, gave his men the orders they all had been dreading, the orders that, right up until the end, he and they and the townspeople, too, had not believed quite possible: destroy the vineyards.

The vines were pulled up, the wine dumped, and the winemaking equipment destroyed. Like criminals being carted off in silence from the courthouse to prison, the hulking, hand-carved barrels known as the Twelve Apostles were hauled off the property. Everything that Michael Poeschel had built and that his father had continued to nurture—gone. Gone in an instant. Creation took time; it proceeded by small steps, a process of becoming and flowering. Death came suddenly and all at once.

The next day, the *Advertiser-Courier* marked the dawn of Prohibition, appropriately, with an obituary.

"Gone But Not Forgotten," read the headline. "John Barleycorn, Prominent Citizen, Passes Away After Long and Eventful Career—Thousands Visited His Bedside and Bade Him Farewell—End Came Peacefully at Midnight Monday":

> John Barleycorn is dead but not forgotten. He passed away very peacefully last Monday at midnight. He gave up without a struggle, nor were there any impressive obsequies. One thing noticeable was the fact that unlike the larger cities, the day here was about the quietest ever experienced. It was like a Sunday and with the exception of a fair sized attendance from the north side of the river, King Alcohol passed away on Monday without occasioning the least excitement among his many friends.
>
> Tho a hush pervaded the city on Monday, it was quite different on Saturday, when there were more people in our city than even the Frisco Travelers' days brought out. Two thousand people paid their final respects to the dying monarch. Two hundred touring cars lined the river bank on the north side and each trip of the ferry boat brought the mourners to Hermann. They came from sixty miles away, from south in Montgomery and Warren counties and from Osage and Gasconade counties, bearing with them, on their return, sweet memories of the departed one.
>
> John Barleycorn is no more. He resided here over eighty years and was one of the best known residents. He was a great factor in every improvement and in the progress of the city. He built fine macadam roads throughout our County. He made Hermann the business mecca for people from many neighboring counties and permitted everybody to share in his prosperity. He never abused nor was he abused by his fellow residents. He was welcome in nearly every home and his bearing was always irreproachable when in the company of gentlemen and ladies. He has now left us

as quietly and unostentatiously as has been his residence with us. Always a friend to the sick, a helping hand to all worthy causes, a power for the wheels of industry, we forgive whatever may have been his transgressions and thank him for the good he wrought.

Every one of the town's five saloons, the paper reported, had shuttered, and two already had been converted into "soft drink parlors." "It's all over but the shouting," the paper's editor observed, "and even that's taboo when you're too dry to shout and there's nothing here to wet your whistle."

A full decade before the stock market crash of 1929, Hermann was plunged into the Great Depression. And the dream of Jefferson, of Dr. Norton, of Husmann and Poeschel, the great and animating dream of wine in America, of American wine from American grapes, had turned to grotesque nightmare.

PART THREE

16

THE NORTON'S RETURN from the dead began one day in December 1965, in back of a hundred-year-old German schoolhouse in Gasconade, a town ten miles west of Hermann that hugs a slight bend in the Missouri River, when Jim Held stomped through the half-acre vineyard of an old bootlegger named Paul Rauch in pursuit of the gone but not forgotten grape.

A corn and hog farmer, Held and his wife, Betty, had just agreed to become owners of Stone Hill, having taken advantage of a sweetheart deal given them by the owner of the property, a man named Bill Harrison. Harrison had decided that someone young and enterprising ought to purchase the property and restore the button-mushroom farm to the winery it had once been. Restore Hermann to what *it* had been. Wine was the town's legacy; it needed to flow again. Nearly three decades after Repeal, there was only a small restaurant winery in nearby St. Charles and a bulk winery, which peddled its fermented grape juice in large, commercial quantities.

Held had never owned or operated a winery. He was poor. He had only a tiny parcel of land to his name, and he and Betty were busy raising four small children. Every week, every day, was a struggle. But he had always been attracted to a challenge—he could trace his ancestry all the way back to the first settlers who had arrived on that first boat at the Hermann settlement in 1837—and what he didn't know, didn't deter him. There were always books and manuals to fill the gaps in his knowledge. Besides, tinkering in the field came naturally to him. Years earlier, he and Betty had planted a vineyard full of Catawba in their backyard in nearby Pershing, Missouri, and shipped the grapes to New York for a small profit. Building on that small success, he purchased the Kemperberg vineyard, a couple miles southwest of Hermann, with the idea that he would continue to sell grapes. He devoted four acres to Catawba; one acre he set aside to experiment with some French hybrids.

With this meager résumé, he now found himself thrust into the role of that young and enterprising someone, entrusted with the daunting task of bringing an American legend back from the grave.

First things first, he told himself, attempting to allay his anxiety. Before he could bring back Hermann, he reasoned, he had to bring back Stone Hill. And before he could bring back Stone Hill, he had to bring back the Norton. The grape was his link. The project of restoring the winery was, in a very real sense, the project of restoring the grape. The glory of one was inseparable from the glory of the other.

Held had heard whispers that the Norton was not dead. Could it be true? Certainly he wanted to believe it was true. But he had no proof and a whole host of doubts. If the Norton was not dead, it certainly was not thriving. Where were these rumored grapes that had survived the destruction? How to get his hands on them? What hadn't been ripped out by the feds had been ripped out by the growers themselves, who in the dark and desperate years after Repeal had decided to pursue a sure thing and grow grapes for jelly and juice. Throughout the Missouri River valley, Concord—the basis for Welch's Grape Juice, which operated a processing plant in the neighboring state of Arkansas—had supplanted Norton as king.

Examining the wild vines in back of bootlegger Rauch's property, inspecting the roots of a flopping, three-pronged leaf with blue-black orbs, Held was relieved to discover the Norton had not been expunged from the state after all. Federal agents had undertaken everything in their power to wipe it out. Growers had given up on it and moved on. But it was here; it had survived; it was strong.

That in itself was cause for elation. But Held quickly realized that he had not simply happened upon a few rogue plantings of the grape. Rauch's

Norton was old Norton, pre-Prohibition Norton, and most likely had been in the ground since the Civil War.

Held had come in pursuit of a rumored artifact; he'd unearthed a sacred text.

As it had been for Poeschel & Scherer and Stark and Herzog, so would it be for him. Build with the Norton. He made as many cuttings of the vines as he could from Rauch's patch and the following summer, 1966, he planted them in a nursery row in the fertile river-bottom soil near his house in Pershing. Seven-year-old Jon helped to hoe the weeds around the fledgling plants, which were dug up the following year and lowered into the ground at his new Kemperberg property.

Held had not just collected cuttings. He had also bought an allotment of grapes from the old bootlegger, and that year he decided to see what kind of wine he might make from them—nearly five decades after Ottmar Stark had ordered his fields to be destroyed, the first vintage of Norton at Stone Hill since Prohibition.

WINE HAD NOT been a primary target of the Drys or later of the feds. It accounted for less than one-tenth of the amount of home brew that agents seized in 1932 and less than one-twentieth of the haul's alcohol content—but that hardly mattered. It had been swept up all the same in the puritanical campaign to rid the country of demon drink. The movement made no distinction, as Jefferson had once done when he warned of the deleterious effects of liquor and advocated for American viticulture. Wine to Jefferson was a civilizing force, a force for good. It improved the mind and it encouraged reasoned discourse. Whiskey was the drink of excess; wine was the drink of moderation.

Not to the Drys. Wine was bad. Whiskey was bad. Beer was bad. All inevitably led to social ills.

Actually, the Prohibition laws made one distinction—that between wine grown for religious purposes and wine grown for commercial benefit. Commercial wine was bad. Sacramental wine was good.

The Dry movement may have billed itself as a political entity, and the banishment of drink may have been its chief political weapon, but it was primarily moralistic in its mission, its rhetoric rife with references to retribution and purification. Prohibition unleashed a cleansing frenzy across the land, a vast, unprecedented effort to leech the country of all the impurities that had conspired to undo a virtuous Christian enterprise.

It accomplished what decades of political advocacy had not. If it could not put a stop to the forces of industrialization, the creeping urbanization, and the civilizing efforts of cultural sophisticates weaned in Europe and sneering at the frontier, all of which came under the banner of progressivism, then it could instill fear and perhaps stunt their growth. What had the vaunted American openness produced, the most passionate Drys asked, but a society that was veering perilously close to that of Europe at its worst, an indolent populace fond of drink and riven by ethnic strife?

Today we regard Prohibition as a catastrophe and cite its repeal as conclusive proof of its impotence as a national policy—in the long sweep of history, a statistical hiccup. But to a country that was in the midst of a great social change, a transition from the agricultural economy of the nineteenth century to the industrial economy of the twentieth century, it was epochal. Its influence can hardly be calculated, for it extends far beyond the decade-plus when it was law.

As with slavery, Prohibition was initially repealed in name only; its devastations, psychological even more than literal (and now transferred to the drug war), have grown even harsher. A culture of taboo, repression, and fear had been created and could not be shaken off. The liquor once again flowed, but wine is a vastly different beverage, not so easily generated. Many in the Missouri wine industry were simply too spooked by Prohibition to start over, presuming that the battle cry of purification was certain to be taken up at some later date, who knew when. And high liquor taxes and high license fees militated against the industry's rebirth. Many of those who chanced to start over did so elsewhere, heeding the American imperative to head west. California, as Husmann had shown, was where the action was.

Repeal had undone the law, but it could not turn back the clock. Nor could it curtail the evolution—the devolution—of taste. In the years of alcohol suppression, America all but lost whatever palate it had acquired for dry table wines. In the post–World War II era, sophisticates turned to highballs, martinis, and other cocktails. For thirty-five years after Prohibition, more than half the wine consumed in the country was fortified wine, which typically contains up to 20 percent alcohol—one and a half to two times that of table wine—and loads of sugar. Sweet wines, tipples, the crude legacy of bootlegging, dominated the market.

In a sense, this was the Norton's salvation: its grapey sweetness.

A raft of notorious policing strategies marked the Prohibition Era, from the Bureau of Prohibition's recruitment of young boys into "sleuthing" societies (government-sanctioned organizations meant to encourage them to rat out their elders) to an Air Corps that patrolled the Mexico border to the advent of wiretapping (J. Edgar Hoover was director of the Justice Department's Bureau of Investigation, a forerunner of the FBI) to an array of fear tactics, including evidence planting, arrest for "criminal intent," entrapment, and no-knock shoot-first raids. The surveillance of small-town markets was among these extremist measures. Those caught purchasing big, oversize burlap sacks of sugar were invariably fingered for making bathtub or basement wine. Like the Concord, which it was superior to in every important respect, the Norton produced enough natural sugar that there was little need to stir any into the barrel during fermentation. It gave bootleggers a chance at remaining on the down low.

"EVERYBODY," Jim Held says, "made homemade wine. My father did, and my grandfather, and so did I, and so did everybody else we knew." He declines to use the loaded term *bootlegger*, with its connotations of something wrong as well as illegal. Right up through the 1960s and even the 1970s, he says, this was simply how everyone who lived in and around Hermann, all along the old *Weinstrasse*, came by their wine.

We're sitting around a long table in a high-ceilinged conference room with his sons, Jon and Thomas, in the great house on the property, a room that, in earlier days, was the family's living room. Jim Held is seventy-six now, many years removed from running day-to-day operations at the winery, a great bear of a man with a brush-cut head of going-white hair, a full and scruffy beard, a potbelly that tents his hunter green shirt and stretches his red suspenders, and, last but not least, a twinkle in his eye that communicates everything from wistful remembrance to mischievous delight. I can't help thinking I'm watching a man who could play Santa Claus without resorting to costume. When he gets to talking about the old days, as he does now, the twinkle functions as a directional signal does in a moving car, alerting the listener that some crackling good tale is on its way.

Hearing my surprise that people were still making bootleg wine well into the 1970s, long after Repeal, Jim stares at me as though I'm the new recruit in the army, the one who hasn't figured out that he is about to be broken. He turns to his boys with a curl of a smile working at the corner of his mouth, eyes glinting madly. He's savoring this like a glass of one of his aged Nortons. Nobody says anything, but the sons smile back at him and turn to smile at each other, and my own eyes dart back and forth at this silent toast of their eyes in recognition of an inside joke at my expense.

"Those stubborn old Germans," says Thomas finally, breaking the silence, shaking his head.

"Oh, you weren't going to stop them," says Jim. "You have to understand: This is how they had been doing it. And this was how they were going to keep doing it. Right? Why not? Tradition! We come along, and we're trying to sell wine that we were making for money? We charged a dollar a bottle. They charged five dollars a gallon. And our wines weren't sweet enough, either."

I ask Jim whether his experience with homemade wine made it easier to run a winery when the time came. That glint again: "Nope."

"Not even a little?"

"A little. But not much more than that."

IN PERSHING, where he had been born and raised and where, before arriving in Hermann, he had lived and raised his own family—a town so

fearful of anti-German reprisal it had changed its name from Potsdam—
he had devoted four and a half acres of his lot to growing grapes and had
cranked out fifty gallons of wine a year. But fifty gallons was nothing. His
grandfather, too, kept a fifty-gallon barrel and drank a glass of wine every
morning, without fail, at 10:30. He doled out jugfuls for his friends down
the block. Jim had been watching his grandfather in the process of portion-
ing the wine when the old man collapsed of a heart attack and died.

The joy of homemade wine was that it didn't matter if the wine was
good or not—he and his family and friends would drink it anyway. A commercial operation could ill afford such blithe indifference. And what about
money? Held was not flush. Heck, he didn't even *have* a flush—that's how
poor he was (and poorer now, after the purchase of Stone Hill). They still
used an outhouse back in Pershing.

What he had going for him was his work ethic (no one would give a
greater effort), his pride (he could tolerate bad wine, but he would not abide
poor, shoddy effort), and his willingness to try anything—an admittedly
modest set of traits that had turned out pretty well for the original novice
winemakers of Hermann. There was something else that Jim Held had
going for him: a desire to live up to the promise of his surname—"hero,"
in German. Or at the very least, not to live it down.

The Stone Hill property had been a mushroom farm since 1923. Only a
monstrous renovation could reverse what four decades had destroyed.
There was, to begin with, the awful job of scrubbing the place down. As
Held reminisces, eyes glinting: "You still had a lot of cow shit in the
cellars."

"Compost, Dad," Jon corrects him in a slow, firm voice, his eyes wid-
ening beneath his glasses, the broad planes of his cheeks shading red.
"Compost."

The give-and-take of their joshing suggests the kind of abiding affec-
tion that can only come of deep mutual respect, a welcome and noticeable
departure from the subtle condescension that runs through too many of the
conversations between a middle-aged child and an older parent, even as it
confirms the reversal of roles that has been thrust upon them, subtly and
irrevocably altering their bond.

The Helds involved their kids in the operation. They had no choice—
they couldn't afford to hire a large staff. The boys and girls would finish
their homework, then do their chores in the cellar, washing the pumps. On
Saturdays, they helped with the bottling. They mowed the grounds. They
served as tour guides. Some of his other employees in those early years
were not much more experienced—a staff composed, in Jim Held's nostal-
gically colorful description, of "semi-alcoholics who would sometimes
steal wine out of barrels and spoke with thick German accents."

The Helds' first Norton was produced with the aid of an old cider mill,
used for grinding apples, with ten-year-old Jon Held turning the crank to
extract the juice of the dark-skinned grapes. Whatever winemaking equipment there had been had been destroyed when Prohibition took effect. The
Helds made 1,500 gallons and immediately wished they had made 15.

Nor did the batches of wine that followed represent a significant improvement.

They sold, though. Someone had been willing to buy them. It was enormously gratifying to think that they had not lost all their money on their
initial attempts, but it was not much of a comfort to think that they were
peddling inferior product. They had to improve. But how?

Jim Held read whatever books he could get his hands on, and he talked
to any- and everybody who had any knowledge of grape growing and
winemaking. Few of those old heads were around anymore, however, and
that was one of his problems. The knowledge and experience of making
wine had up and left; and the memory of what a good wine was had vanished. Husmann and the cultural ferment he had created, of wine as a great
and noble communal enterprise, were long gone. In its stead was the practical, corner-cutting know-how of the bootleggers.

"Oh, those guys were funny," Jim Held says. " 'Jim,' they'd say, 'you
don't want to bottle in those little bottles.' We were using wine bottles, the
kind you see today. 'You want to be making *gallons*, Jim.' "

I ask him if they taught him anything valuable about making wine.

That glint again. "They taught me what not to do," he cracks, chuck-
ling at the memory. "The big thing was, they tried to get me to make seconds," he says—to put the grapes through a second extraction in order to

produce more juice, and thus, more wine. In effect, to brew a second cup of tea from the same bag.

The old timers, the onetime bootleggers, stuck to drinking their cheap, sweet homemade wine, and the business at Stone Hill struggled mightily to stay out of the red, even as the Helds purchased the winery outright in 1968 and increased production. Operating in the black seemed a wonderful fantasy—something to aspire to but not something they could attain. They clung to their tenuous maroon existence. So much for the nobility of bringing back a piece of history.

A WORKING KNOWLEDGE of winemaking and viticulture was not all that had been lost in the intervening decades in Missouri.

A year after Held had got Stone Hill up and running, Mount Pleasant Winery, in Augusta, began producing wine on property that once belonged to Friedrich Munch, the cofounder of the Giessen Emigration Society. St. James Winery and Montelle Winery each followed four years later, in 1970, and Hermannhof started up four years after that. Some winery owners began wondering whether the Norton they were reviving was really the Cynthiana, a grape that has done much to contribute to the air of mystery around the Norton. (Devotees of Cynthiana would likely argue that it is the Norton that has done much to obscure the history of the Cynthiana.)

As far back as the mid-nineteenth century, despite the pronounced similarities between the Cynthiana and the Norton—their distinctive vegetation, the character of their fruit—Husmann and others who had observed the grapes growing alongside each other reckoned that the varieties were different. As Cornell's U. P. Hedrick wrote in 1908, "The botanical differences of the two varieties are not greater than might be attributed to environment, soil, climate and culture; but side by side the two grapes ripen at different times, and the quality of the fruit, and more particularly of the wine, is such that the varieties must be considered distinct. The distinction should be maintained, for Cynthiana is the better grape of the two."

The question of whether the Norton and Cynthiana are different varieties, with distinct genealogical and oenological differences, or whether the latter is really just an offshoot of the former, has been debated for years with little consensus, and the disagreement continues to this day. In the decades after Repeal, as the Norton has made a comeback in many states and drawn new recognition, the question has returned with renewed urgency. But still the mystery persists.

In the early 1990s, two different universities took up the Norton/Cynthiana question, conducting separate trials in an attempt to arrive at a definitive answer. Researchers at the State Fruit Experiment Station of Southwest Missouri State University, after exhaustive study of twelve samples of Norton and Cynthiana grapes that had been collected in Missouri and Arkansas, concluded that the two varieties were genetically identical. Plant scientists at Cornell reached the same conclusion.

But just how conclusive are these conclusions?

It was not possible for researchers to perform isoenzyme analysis of vines that grew prior to Prohibition, for a great many of these vines had been pulled up to comply with the law. The parentage of most vines in Missouri and Arkansas can be traced to only one or two sources.

Might it be that the two grapes were indeed different varieties at one time but that after winemaking in America stopped, the few vines that had not been eradicated, that had been overlooked and left to grow untended, grew wild and grew entangled—grew, in other words, into the same plant?

Paul Roberts, who owns and operates Deep Creek Cellars, in Maryland, and who has written lovingly about both the Norton and Cynthiana in his engaging book about winemaking, *From This Hill, My Hand; Cynthiana's Wine*, believes Cynthiana is a clone of the Norton. He makes an analogy to Pinot Noir in France, which numbers "at least a half-dozen prominent clones in Burgundy."

In Virginia, the name Cynthiana is nonexistent, so there is no chance of engendering confusion in the consumer's mind with the Norton, but in Missouri, both names are used, with some wineries insisting that Cynthiana is deserving of the acclaim that the Norton has been receiving as the state's official grape. Arkansas wineries, on the other hand, use the term Cynthiana, never Norton. Their wines are, in general, lighter and softer than Nortons from Missouri and Virginia, and produced for immediate consumption, not aging and mellowing. Some are even sweet.

The debate is unlikely to be resolved, because many winemakers in Arkansas and Missouri simply refuse to accept the findings of the scientists, preferring to trust in their powers of observation and their well-trained palates, which tell them there are important differences between the two, however subtle.

On the website appellationamerica.com, the wines are presented together, as the varietal Norton/Cynthiana. A lively color illustration depicts a face that is half man and half woman. "Your history is crazy, even a little wild," the text reads. "You first surfaced in the state of Virginia as Mr. Norton, a man with a regal character. Proudly American, but respected in Europe where they flattered you as the 'best of all nations.' Then we met you in Missouri, posing as a demure and elegant lady, impressing with subtle charm. The locals knew you as Miss Cynthiana, their 'Cabernet of the Ozarks.' As it turns out you were a little mad, for Mr. Norton and Miss Cynthiana, you are one in [*sic*] the same!"

17

IN 1974, Jim Held went west and took a few courses at the University of California–Davis in its nationally renowned program in winemaking and viticulture. The irony was not lost on him that he had gone off to California to try to learn and master the very things that Husmann had regularly imparted to the winemakers of Hermann—things that California now had and Missouri didn't.

Two years later, he packed Jon off to California State University–Fresno to study oenology full time in a four-year degree program. Jon's sister Patty would follow him, while Thomas would enter the wine program at the University of Arkansas, where he would stay after graduation to become the school's first research oenologist. (Only Julie, the youngest, did not pursue a career in viticulture, becoming a lawyer. "The black sheep," Jon cracks.)

The technology had become infinitely more sophisticated, with new techniques being introduced into the industry every couple of years, it seemed, but it was more than that. What Jon Held needed to know in order to bring Stone Hill up to competitive standards could no longer simply be handed down, as before, from father to son, from generation to generation. He had practically been weaned at the winery, reared on the cycle of the seasons and the imperative of working hard, on the importance of mastering the innumerable odd details of the winemaking process. And still, for all that he had learned, for all that he had grown, he and his father knew that it was not enough, that he would have to learn more and grow more if he was going to assume control of the family business, as they both hoped, and take the operation to the logical next phase of its development. How strange, and how exhilarating, too, to think that, having turned the crank on the cider press as a kid, he would be turning the crank now on the entire operation.

By the time he left for California, Stone Hill was producing around thirty thousand gallons of wine a year, a good number, and a sign of just how far his father had brought the business. But the old Stone Hill in its prime was producing an estimated 1.2 million gallons a year and winning awards at home and abroad. Quantity *and* quality. Granted, they were still a young operation, a comparative infant in the winemaking business—his father and mother, after all, had owned the winery outright for only eight years. The question was, Was the kind of quality and quantity that Stone Hill had stood for even within their reach? He was determined to find out.

He bore down on his studies in a way that he had never done as a slightly above-average high school student, bore down upon them with the methodical determination of a scientist desperate to unlock a secret. All around him, his classmates were reveling in the carefree, privileged life of college kids, many of them drifting in search of some nameless purpose. It sometimes seemed as if they attended a different school. His parents, struggling at the vineyard, desperate to stay afloat, had scraped to send him to school, and he felt an obligation to repay their investment, with interest. He had been working at the winery since he was seven; his four years of college were simply an extension of what his father had started. Others could afford to live for the moment; what animated him, what inspired him, was to take the long view. On the field trips to California wineries that constituted a vital practical component of his course work, he performed reconnaissance, looking for ideas he could swipe for the operation back home. In the rare moments of spare time he had, he game-planned revisions to Stone Hill, mulling more efficient ways to use the space. He fantasized about the midsize wineries of Beaulieu and Mondavi, made them his models, envisioned replicating their scale and success. He never attended a single football or basketball game. He graduated with a 4.0 grade point average. "I'm never gonna mean much to you," a girlfriend at the time told him. "You've got one thing you're married to."

He was young and naive, and everything he dreamed of, every big, bold dream—confronting history, recapturing the past—seemed within reach, seemed possible, just because he could imagine it.

His father, he saw, was the transitional figure, the bridge between the mushroom farm and a small winemaking outfit, between nothing and something. He had poured the concrete foundation; it was up to Jon to construct the house. In those moments of deep, sober-minded reflection, of reckoning with his future, his exhilaration at what awaited him modulated into a sense of the hugeness of the task, and he nearly became overwhelmed. He had watched, with admiration and a kind of awe, the almost superhuman effort it required of his father to run the place, the endless hours, the work in the field, the testing and retesting in the cellar. There was no leisure time, no relaxation. His father had left his life in that cellar, in those fields. And now he realized that he would be leaving his life in them, too. He craved the challenge, craved the responsibility and the authority and the feeling of control that came with being the person in charge. But it was sobering, too, to think that his future had already been chosen. The past had determined the present. *Legacy* was such a grand, impressive-sounding word. *Inheritance.* He began now to see their many shades of meaning.

One day, on Christmas break between his freshman and sophomore year of college, he was exposed to many more shades of many more meanings. Bill Harrison, the man who had sold the mushroom farm to his father, had summoned Jon to his house to talk.

Harrison's house sat high in the hills of Hermann, a sturdy, two-story brick édifice that had once belonged to Michael Poeschel's brother, William, and that looked out over the Missouri River. His father, Jim, had not been invited, nor his brothers or sisters—just him, just Jon. Harrison, a man he had known since he was seven, was dying of cancer. He wanted to speak in private.

It was an unseasonably warm day. They sat outside, without coats, in the yard. Behind them, he could hear the slow rush of the Missouri. How many times Jon had gone down there to fish for bass and brought some of his catch back to share with the old man. Harrison was like family.

The teenager's throat got tight as the old man revealed to him a secret that only his father had been privy to. The sweetheart deal was even sweeter than anyone at the time had realized. Harrison had given his father two years to decide whether he liked what he was doing; if at any time during those two years he should come to the conclusion that running a winery was not something he was interested in, he could back out and get his money back. Harrison had not just handed off the property. He was a patron. He was not going to leave things to chance, in hopes that the venture might succeed. He was going to make certain that it did.

The imminence of death had shortened Harrison's days but lengthened his perspective. With a calm that belied the urgency of his words, Harrison spoke of the future—a future he knew he was never going to see, a future even Jim Held himself might not see. He had invested wisely and widely. He had survived the Depression. He was a wealthy man. He had had a lot to be thankful for, a lot to be proud of. But his shepherding of the restoration of Stone Hill, which in turn had triggered the restoration of wine in Missouri and of the Norton—this was the thing he was proudest of. His legacy. And to this point an unfinished legacy. Where would it be in twenty, thirty, forty years? Would it one day earn comparison with the golden age of Stone Hill? He had learned over the years how vitally important it was to be patient with investments. It was years, sometimes decades, before they showed a return. And so, no doubt, it would be with this little talk of theirs today.

Did Jon know why Harrison was telling him these things?

Maybe not. It was many years before Jon Held, no longer a teenager, managing the company his father had restarted, realized how the words *privilege* and *obligation*—such seeming opposites—could come to be so entwined.

AT CAL STATE–FRESNO, Jon Held had relished playing the wine lover's version of stump the band, pouring glasses for his classmates of his father's Norton—Held's Virginia Seedling, Jim had initially called it, until some perplexed Missourians asked why he was selling Virginia wine in Missouri—and seeing if any of them could identify it. They never could. They'd never even heard of it. Norton? Was this a joke? It was not a joke, he'd say. Taste. Tasting was always the proof. The Norton was a real wine. A *serious* wine, in spite of its obscurity.

It was about to become more serious still.

While he was away, his father had decided to bring aboard a full-time winemaker at Stone Hill. Though the decision was born of desperation, because Jim Held could no longer run the operation without help, it was occasion for optimism, too, in that it represented the next step in the evolution of the winery. The first winemaker didn't work out, but his successor, a man named Dave Johnson, did. Johnson pored over the pre-Prohibition literature about the Norton, and he became fascinated by what he read. He had recently graduated from a winemaking program at Michigan State, and reading what his viticultural forebears had written about a grape he knew practically nothing about was confirmation of how much more he still had to learn.

It was like stumbling upon a secret history, and as Johnson read about the methods and techniques of the nineteenth century, and the characters who had developed them, it dawned on him: Nobody now was making Norton wine the way the literature described.

The other wineries were using the Norton in blends or to make a pale, sweet wine. The diluted wines, especially, were testament to the devastating effects of the rupture induced by Prohibition and the concomitant ascendancy of the bootlegger's art.

IT WAS JOHNSON who pushed Jim Held to try to make the Norton in the old style. That meant, Johnson believed, treating the Norton the way vintners in Bordeaux treated Cabernet or Merlot. This required extending two of the most important processes in winemaking—letting the grapes ferment longer in their skins, then aging the extracted juice longer in small oak barrels. The Bordeaux style of winemaking, applied to the native grape, produced a supremely drinkable wine, infinitely superior to anything that Held had achieved previously. It proved a popular wine, too, with wine lovers in St. Louis and Kansas City soon taking notice.

The success of their old-style Norton, however, would be measured not by its initial drinkability or even by its popularity, but by its ageability. Their method had been adapted from Bordeaux, and if the promising young wine that resulted from their experiments had anything in common with those complex, elegant wines, its charms would not be fully evident for years, when it developed a little bottle age and its character began to ripen and express itself more fully.

A good wine when young; a great wine when mature. It's what the best winemakers all aspire to. It takes more to achieve, however, than the sum of those usual success-story standbys, talent, knowledge, and hard work. It takes luck and patience. Because, having mastered the first half of the equation, it is premature to sit back and celebrate. A team with a commanding lead at halftime of a playoff game doesn't start popping the corks. But the temptation! The agony of waiting five, sometimes ten years! Winemakers are obliged to wait. By the time a wine has gone into the bottle, the process is effectively out of their hands. Conception has given way to gestation. They can only hope and pray that the wine in the bottle cooperates, that time does its slow, important work.

Held and Johnson were fortunate. The bottle cooperated. Time cooperated. The wine was a success early, and a success late, too.

The wine critic Paul Lukacs, in his book *The Great Wines of America*, writes about the difference between the two ages of Norton in his praise of Stone Hill: "When young, Stone Hill Nortons taste intensely fruity—grapey to be sure, but also redolent with an aroma resembling ripe blueberries. With time, the fruit calms down, and the wines develop earthy, even meaty secondary flavors, in this regard something like wines from the southern Rhône Valley in France."

. . .

AFTER WORKING at vineyards in Switzerland and Ontario for two and a half years upon graduation, Jon Held returned home in the spring of 1983 and went back to work at Stone Hill. He needed a place to live. His father had purchased Paul Rauch's property in the late 1960s, and so Jon settled into Rauch's old farmhouse. The nine-hundred-square-foot dwelling became his home for the next thirteen years. He had only to look outside to be reminded of his mission: The property lay fifteen feet from the same Civil War–era bootleg Norton vines his father had cut from to restart the wine industry at Stone Hill.

As he began assuming more duties at the winery, Held began pushing to increase the Norton's presence in the vineyard. It had not escaped his notice that in 1982 a Cynthiana from Cowie Cellars, in Arkansas, had taken home a silver medal at the International Eastern Wine Competition, in New York, which included more than seven hundred wines. The eminent wine critic Leon D. Adams, a founder of the Wine Institute, in California, singled out Cowie's Cynthiana for familiar-sounding praise, writing that it "could be discovered as the great American wine of an American grape." Held's classmates at Cal State–Fresno might have been ignorant of the grape, but clearly others were beginning to notice. Things were changing.

Beginning in 1984, Held added five new blocks of Norton in the vineyard. He also devoted more of the winery's acreage to establishing estate vineyards, low-yield plots where he could control the growing conditions even more carefully and craft the best, most expressive wines possible. Today there are six estate vineyards in addition to one that borders the winery, and four of them—one of which is Paul Rauch's old farm—feature the Norton.

The old-style Norton had proved something to him, and not just that the grape was capable of producing a good wine with age. It had proved to him that the mission of recapturing the past at Stone Hill was bound up in the mission of restoring the Norton to prominence.

Throughout the 1980s and into the 1990s, the winery was beginning to assert itself, like a tranquilized lion rousing from its long slumber and reawakening to its purpose. The Helds were making good wines, and they were growing. But the better they got and the bigger they got, the goal, paradoxically, seemed to Jon to move farther and farther away, and he was forced to reckon with how far they remained, still—in stature, in size— from the company they had once been. The fact was, aside from folks in Missouri and the four nearby states that carried their wines, who knew about Stone Hill? Who knew about the Norton? Who even knew about Missouri? Whenever he traveled to the coasts, people looked at him funny whenever he told them what he did—doubting him the way his classmates at Cal State–Fresno had doubted him when he first pushed a bottle of Norton under their noses.

Was recapturing the past even possible? he wondered. Had the rupture of Prohibition made it delusional to aspire to make great wine on that scale ever again outside of California?

So MUCH ABOUT the culture, and not just winemaking culture, had changed in the century since Stone Hill and the Norton had attained the pinnacle of renown. Tastes had changed; fashions had changed; winemaking itself had changed. Prohibition had KO'd California, just as it had KO'd Virginia and Missouri. But California had been quicker off the mat than either of the others. A man named Cesare Mondavi, an ambitious Italian immigrant who had established himself in California in the 1920s with a wholesale business peddling grapes and other fruit, took a gamble and plunged into winemaking after Repeal. So did another ambitious Italian immigrant family, the Gallos, brothers Ernest and Julio. They were joined by more than eight hundred other companies in those heady, early years in the Napa Valley, an entrepreneurial boom that amounted to a kind of second Gold Rush. The biggest gambler of all turned out to be Cesare's son Robert Mondavi, the family scion, who broke away two decades later after his father's death—and an acrimonious dispute with his mother and brother—and went on to found a winery that reigned over Napa in the 1960s and 1970s.

By the time Jim Held brought Dave Johnson aboard as a winemaker in the late 1970s, establishing Stone Hill as a serious commercial enterprise, more than a decade before wineries in Virginia began to reappear in significant numbers, California's best wines were acclaimed as being on a par with the best in France and Italy.

Throughout the postwar years, if Americans drank, they drank cocktails. Wine meant sweet wine. It meant Mateus, more beloved for its flasklike bottle than for what was inside. A candle holder and a beverage, all in one!

By the late 1960s and early 1970s, all that was in flux. The emergence of California as a winemaking force coincided with the coming of age of Baby Boomers, who had gone off to backpack around Europe and had become enamored of the good cheap wines they downed at nearly every meal. Americans began drinking wine in larger numbers than they ever had before. It was not only socially acceptable to drink wine, but it had now become socially prestigious to do so. California was teaching them how to drink, and it was teaching them *what* to drink, too.

A distinctive style had emerged. The wines from Napa were high in alcohol, a result of the long, hot summers—higher by far than the wines of Europe, where 7 to 8 percent alcohol was the norm. Some Napa wines were clocking in at 14 and 15 percent. There was also the matter of fruitiness. Europe emphasized low alcohol content and muted fruitiness. Wine was chiefly an accompaniment to a meal. In California, wines were ends in themselves, and it sometimes seemed as if they were trophies—the bigger, the better.

Cabernet Sauvignon, the most prized grape in Napa, is a big wine to begin with, opulent and mouth-filling. When it is crafted in the high-alcohol, "fruit-forward" style, it can produce a wallop of a wine, a struttingly aggressive drink intent on proving its manhood. The best Cabernet Sauvignons made in California possess, in addition to bigness, a grace, an expressiveness, that all great wines in the world display. They are the equivalent of Shaquille O'Neal in his prime, combining monstrous size with unexpected finesse. But most California Cabernets, like mosts in everything else, don't fall into the category of best. Most are middling. They are big, plodding, sometimes oafish, and generally lacking in either grace or subtlety: old Shaq, injured and in decline.

The harshest critics of this style of winemaking refer to these wines, with a dismissive sneer, as "fruit bombs," a phrase that conjures up the image of one of those iridescently colored popsicles from the Good Humor truck and suggests the utter lack of sophistication that "American" has long stood for in the minds of many aesthetes: big and bold and crude. It remains, however, an enormously popular style, both among wine drinkers and wine critics—a style that has come to appear definitive. For many Americans, this has quite simply become the profile of American wine.

The character of Stone Hill's best wines did not fit this template. Low in alcohol and with subtle fruitiness, they had much more in common with the wines of Europe. The Norton was not a modest wine, it filled the mouth, but it was not overwhelming to drink—it did not flood the palate like a California Cabernet. And it was companionable. A drinker could pair it with more than just a big slab of steak.

But now the Norton seemed to be suspended between two worlds.

Only a handful of people drank native varietals. Only a handful even knew that native varietals existed. And of those who knew they existed, most did not care, except perhaps as a novelty. A century earlier, the Norton had suffered for being an American wine that lacked the cachet of its European counterparts. Now, drinking American wine was not only desirable but, to some, preferable. And drinking American wine meant, for the most part, drinking one thing: the big, bold wines of Napa.

It was tempting for Held to wonder, What if? What if there had been no rupture? What if Virginia and Missouri had not had to start all over? What if they had not lost nearly fifty years to a political action intended to turn the clock back on immigration, urbanization, and industrialization—an action that had little to do with wine or grape culture?

Even so, no one who knew anything about wine and economic forces in late twentieth-century America would suppose that California would not still be the leading winemaker in the country and an enormous influence on public taste. But it did not require too much imagination to think that Virginia and Missouri would be regarded far differently than they are today. Not as competitors, exactly—California is simply too big and too varied a wine producer to possess a rival—but as vital alternatives, as regions with established traditions and deep roots. In every country where wine is drunk, beloved, and regarded as an intrinsic part of the culture, there is a universal recognition of the idea that regionality in winemaking is important and should be encouraged and preserved. France has its justly celebrated Burgundy and Bordeaux, but it also has the Languedoc. Italy is renowned for its magnificent Barolos and Nebbiolos, but it also produces the charming, rough-hewn wines of its southern coast. In America, however, the land where distinctions were supposed to be blurred, where the peasant was encouraged to dream of becoming a prince, the tradition of simple, rustic wines belonged to the distant, pre-Prohibition past. In the minds of the vast majority of Americans who bought and drank wine, there was still only the one region, the West Coast, and for the most part, they seemed to be satisfied that one was enough.

TURNING BACK the clock on taste—was it even possible?

Held was no longer young. He no longer thought that you could simply dream a thing into being. But if recapturing the past was out of his control, that didn't mean it was futile of him to keep working to recapture the glory of the Norton's past. Great wine is great wine—wherever it is made and whoever is making it.

One day, he felt sure, someone would come along who understood. One day, someone did.

THERE WERE thirty wineries in Missouri in 1992, when Gerald Asher, the wine editor for *Gourmet*, paid Jon and his sister Patty an official visit at Stone Hill as part of a tour he was making of the state's wines.

Thirty was hardly cause for taking notice, let alone proclaiming that an explosion was underway. It was a pitiable number compared to California, an eyedropper of liquid in an enormous oak barrel and, crucially, less than half the number that had existed during the state's nineteenth-century viticultural heyday. But considerations of quality, not quantity, drove Asher. There were good wines being made all along the old *Weinstrasse*. Among the recent newcomers when Asher visited was the Adam Puchta Winery, which the Puchta family itself had reopened in 1990, making it the only vineyard in Hermann to be owned and operated by a single family throughout its long, though interrupted, history.

If Jim Held had revived the industry, it was Missouri's Wine and Grape Advisory Board's decision, in the 1970s, to conduct extensive research to determine which grapes were best suited to the *terroir* of the state, with its harsh winters and pesky (but controllable) summer diseases, as well as to work one-on-one with winemakers, that fed and nurtured its growth. As a result of the board's research, French-American hybrids began to displace Catawba and Concord in Missouri's vineyards. A new movement was underway—ironically, a movement Husmann and others had championed more than a century earlier.

In a world in which *vinifera* wines are regarded as normal and natural, invoking the names of these French hybrids—Seyval, Vidal, Vignoles, Chardonel—is bound to prompt the sort of double take that sometimes results upon hearing for the first time the names of certain lifestyle drugs, which summon familiar-sounding words only to stunt and alter them. The wines are virtually unheard of on the two coasts and seldom, if ever, receive attention from the mainstream wine press, a phenomenon almost entirely unrelated to their quality. Asher was thus a rarity. Like another freethinking critic a century earlier, immune to faddishness and endowed with a need to communicate his own particular truths, he was concerned only with the quality of what was in the glass. As he pointed out later, Missouri's best wineries are capable of producing excellent wines from these French hybrids—distinctive wines that convey a strong regional character and impart what all good wines ought to: a sense of time and place. Seyval, Asher noted, "produces an excellent wine when barrel-fermented.... Vidal makes a delicious Champagne-method sparkling wine. . . . Vignoles, an unusual white hybrid genetically based in part on Pinot Noir, gives wines the rich texture and fragrance of Pinot Gris." A 1991 Vignoles from Hermannhof had just been declared Best White Wine of the New World at the

International New World Wine Competition in California a year earlier. At the same competition, an "excellent" 1991 Vignoles from Montelle was deemed "stiff competition" and took a gold medal. And then there was the Norton, which, owing to a proud and protective piece of legislation, had been declared the state grape, cementing its status as a piece of history and assuring its continued spread as a durable and productive asset in the vineyard.

Arriving in Hermann two days after the annual Great Stone Hill Beast Feast, Asher had missed out on the chance to dig into such local delicacies as possum teriyaki, raccoon pie, and beaver jambalaya. He dined, instead, on fresh venison steaks in a Norton wine sauce at Stone Hill's Vintage restaurant. (The deer had been caught munching on pre-Prohibition Norton vines by the proprietor of Vintage, Gary Buckler.) At Jon Held's urging, Asher tasted four vintages of Stone Hill Nortons, from 1984 and 1985, and from 1988 and 1989.

Held was intent on demonstrating to Asher the clear difference between the two sets of Nortons, how they performed when they were young and how they performed when they had matured a little. Had he known what was riding on the outcome of this visit, he might have been more nervous. Only Vizetelly's judgments on the panel at the Weltausstellung, handed down more than a century earlier, had done more for the grape his father had resuscitated and passed on to him, to grow and love and pass on to his own sons.

"Even after reading Vizetelly, and others," Asher wrote, "I was astonished to find the wines so remarkably good. They were more meaty than fruity, with something of the Rhône about them. The 1985, in particular, rounded out by its time in wood and fully developed by several years in bottle, was quite delicious. I finally understood, as I never really had before, why Vizetelly had been so confident of Missouri's wine future."

Asher had not seen enough to declare *himself* confident of the state's future as a world wine power, as Vizetelly had, but he had seen enough to believe that its future was promising and that the Norton possessed enormous potential. The April 1993 issue of *Gourmet* focused on the resurgent Missouri wine industry and, as Asher had written, on an "indigenous

American grape that might yet do for Missouri what Cabernet Sauvignon has done for California."

In Hermann and in all the winemaking towns along the old *Weinstrasse*, Asher's lengthy, substantive article was greeted with a sense of disbelief, as a windfall of good fortune. The stamp of approval of a prominent East Coast periodical, the product of big-city people who tended to sneer at the Midwest as "fly-over country," was a major development for the nascent industry, proof that Missouri was again producing good wine and that the Norton, the varietal that many of them had put their faith in, as their nineteenth-century predecessors had done, was worthy of their devotion.

There was wariness, too, in their response, a characteristic Show-Me-state skepticism that was loath to give in to optimism over Asher's pronouncements. That caution proved to be well-founded, because the article in *Gourmet* did little to generate interest in the wines outside Missouri and the surrounding states.

Wine writers and wine lovers talked often of the distinctions between Old World and New World, particularly as they pertained to the process of aging wine in barrels (new oak versus old oak, and the degree of time a wine spends in the oak) and of the respective styles of there (low alcohol, muted fruit) versus here (high alcohol, fruity). What was seldom, if ever, discussed was the fact that wine was a closed world. There were France, Spain, and Italy in Europe, and there were California, Oregon, and Washington in America. And then there were the up-and-coming wine regions: South Africa, Chile, and Australia. Everything else—well, what else was there? A wine that came from an area that fell outside these known regions was not necessarily regarded as suspicious; it was often not regarded at all.

Americans have always prided themselves on a belief that they are not bound by the old orthodoxies or enslaved by the old hierarchies. The French, for instance, employed a number of classification systems for their wines, denoting certain wines in Bordeaux and certain vineyards in Burgundy as special (*premier cru* and *grand cru*, respectively). It was hard to imagine any such system, any such official classification, gaining traction in America. But that's not to say there wasn't an unofficial system, one that enforced its own unspoken hierarchy. Whenever I flipped through the glossy wine magazines, like *Wine Spectator* and *Wine Advocate*, or read the wine columns that appeared in the country's most important papers, I tried to imagine what Jon Held or Jenni must have felt. And I imagined that they must have felt the way a soccer (or lacrosse, or women's basketball) fan must feel whenever he or she reads the sports pages of a major daily newspaper or national magazine. *My world does not exist. No matter how great I am at this thing that I do, I am doomed to a life on the margins.*

Somehow, there was a finite amount of capital that could be expended on wine, and so the editors and writers decided that they would devote almost all their available resources to covering Europe and California. And why not? After all, these editors and writers often said, this was what the audience wanted. This, of course, was not an argument; it was specious chicken-and-egg reasoning. The audience wanted it, because that's what the audience had been conditioned to want, having been fed the same thing over and over and over again. No, the truth was that it was a matter of money. The PR machinery had its interests to advance and protect, and journalism, particularly food and wine journalism, is a comfortably status quo profession, which is to say, an exceedingly lazy profession, disinclined to probe for truths and content to convey news of prevailing trends. Journalists are prone to ascribing their decisions to the importance of serving the needs of their readers, which presupposes that readers—who are, after all, waiting to be told what to drink and buy and cultivate tastes in and talk knowledgeably about at cocktail parties—know what is best.

One article, then, was not going to change the wine culture in America.

Could the wine culture of Hermann, which *had* changed—changed for the worse—since Prohibition, be brought back and revived? Asher's article seemed to have answered the question in the affirmative.

AT DINNER one night at Vintage, the restaurant where Gerald Asher had been persuaded of the wisdom of Henry Vizetelly, Jon Held and I drink a couple bottles of aged Norton and feast on plates of schnitzel and schweinshaxe, the latter a massive hog hock, flanked by generous mounds of braised red cabbage and potato salad, that the kitchen presents, Tom Jones–style, with a steak knife jammed into its roasted flesh.

The food is good; the wine is even better. His Norton is everything I love in a red wine: It is complex and expressive, with a strong, identifiable character that only being bound so intimately and rigorously to a specific time and place can produce. It tastes like nothing else in the world, except perhaps another Norton. There is the wild earthiness I love, which seems to conceal within it a hundred unknowable mysteries, but it changes over time as we drink it, a living, breathing thing that opens up like a flower to become softer, more supple—a more subtle and interesting wine.

The copious quantities of rich, heavy food together with the big pours of robust red wine, after a long day spent in the cellar and out in the sun-baked vineyards, have a narcotic effect, dulling our earlier, animalistic attack at our plates and dimming the animated edge of our conversation. The rolling hills of Hermann, which presented a lovely picture postcard to gaze upon through the back window of the dining room during our meal, have gone dark. The staffers, hovering politely, profess that they haven't the slightest interest in hurrying us along so they can clean up and go home. The restaurant is otherwise empty.

Held and I, meanwhile, are borne along a current of wine into the kind of easygoing fellowship that good drink makes possible, which men can only ever seem to find otherwise if they played a team sport together and have reunited after many years. Hours earlier, when the meats dominated our plates, and the bottles had only just been opened, Held had been talking about the growth of the vineyard and Hermann's wine industry with all the pride of a civic booster, and I had not let a pause go by without asking another question about the winery, about winemaking, about life in Hermann. Now, in this new, more reflective mood, with our bottles empty, testaments to our gluttonous stupor, our conversation drifts into musing and contemplation, to ruminations on time and loss.

"Let's kill the Norton," Held says now, tipping the last of the two bottles into my glass, and something about the phrase jostles my drink-addled brain, and I remember to tell him about my lunch that afternoon at Trapper's Grill, on the corner of Main and Fourth, when I washed down my burger and fries with a glass of Norton from Adam Puchta Winery.

A Norton by the glass: this was a first. But my elation yielded to a stunned incomprehension when I read the list more carefully as I waited for the food to arrive. There were thirty-three wines on the menu, and only eleven of them were from Missouri. The majority of the others came from California.

The waitress shrugged when I asked why. "The owner likes California wines," she replied.

It was no different at Rivertown Restaurant, a diner on First Street where I dropped by one day for breakfast.

The owner, Jack Stoyanov, swung by my table, introduced himself, and invited me to come out to his tavern, the Silver Dollar, in nearby Swiss, Missouri. We got to talking about wine, and I asked Stoyanov if he liked the local wines. A few, he said, listing wineries (including Stone Hill) but declining to name varietals. He much prefers California wines, and his wine list at the Silver Dollar reflects his tastes. He serves a number of Missouri wines, but if "my customers want something better, I'll break out my stash"—a small collection of premium California wines.

Another day, it was lunch at a place called Wings A Blazin, a shiny, plasticky wings-and-beer franchise that seems incongruous with such intrinsically local places as Trapper's Grill and Rivertown, but which is popular with Hermannites all the same.

A hockey game was on the tube. I hopped a stool at the bar next to a florid-faced, glassy-eyed man in a Harley hat who quoted lines from the movie *Slap Shot* ("That's a fuckin' classic, right there"), advised me on the tendencies of the police ("If you're gonna be out partyin' tonight, watch out for the blue lights"), and engaged me in a conversation about wine after I asked to look at the list of choices.

He complained about the prices of local wines, which broadened into a rant against the marketing practices of the wineries, the appeals to affluent weekenders from St. Louis. "You're sellin the 'experience'? Well, your 'experience' just got up and walked away, bro. I can go down the street to the market and get me a fifth of Merlot or Cab from Australia or Napa for five or six bucks, and you're chargin' twelve? Come on, bro. You know, support the industry—that's cool. But I gotta support me, you know. That fifth, that tastes just as good to me."

I asked him what he did for a living. He said he worked as a pruner in the vineyards at Stone Hill.

At this litany of the various misdeeds of Hermannites against their own, Jon nods solemnly. It is the nod of a man acknowledging the inescapability of a complex truth he has tried to bury and forget. His eyes are level and wide behind his glasses. He doesn't blink as he tells me that there are about sixty B and B's and inns in and around Hermann. "Sixty B and B's versus how many wineries? A handful," he says. "Nothing like the early days."

Beyond the B and B's and inns, there are the museums and the cultural centers that keep alive the story of the town's glorious winemaking past. Promoting wine and wine country would seem to be more popular than actually producing wine, a striking and ironic reversal of the nineteenth century.

Another piece of irony: Norton was the foundation for the vineyards' revival and is today at the heart of Stone Hill's mission, but it is not its biggest seller. Concord, the basis for both Welch's grape juice and the treacly-sweet Manischewitz, is king in the Missouri marketplace; Norton lags in the bottom third of sales. If not for the financial windfall of sweet wines like the Concord, Held suggests, he probably could not afford to keep making the Norton. I am reminded, listening to him talk about the popularity of the two wines, of the now-vanished Biograph Theater in D.C., a house of worship for devotees of film as literature. At night, Hitchcock and Godard played to small but enthusiastic audiences; by day, the theater did a brisk business showing skin flicks.

Jon says, "We brought back the industry. We brought back the wine. What we haven't brought back is the wine culture. That'll take time."

Something tells me Jon doesn't actually believe this will happen. Or if he believes it, he doesn't believe he'll be around to see it.

· · ·

ONE AFTERNOON in Hermann, I drive out to Oak Glenn winery to tour the estate and drink the Norton.

George Husmann bought the land just before the Civil War and planted grapes in the fields, but sold it before the house was completed. The winery is perched on densely forested bluffs that loom like vaulted cliffs above the churning gray waters of the Missouri, which Kerouac in his letters described as "a great river of rivers. . . . wild & beautiful." On this day, the sky is overcast, and there is a light fog, which shrouds the tableau in a gauzy, myth-making mist. It's not Napa, but the rough, untainted grandeur would have appealed to the artists of the Hudson River School, and I can imagine a duel breaking out among them for the chance to preserve the scene on canvas. Few sights I have ever beheld are more breathtaking, and as I walk along the gravel parking lot toward the tasting room I find myself moderating my pace, the way I do with a book I don't want to finish too fast.

This attempt to savor and preserve a moment begins to feel like so much romantic foolishness, though, as I approach the winery. The idea of a winery as a respite for customers to fantasize about the possibilities of the good life, a place of quiet contemplation, is swept under the tidal wave of AC/DC's "Highway to Hell" crashing over the George Husmann Pavilion. If I didn't know any better, I would have sworn I'd wandered into a kegger.

"It's a bachelorette party and a birthday party, together," the woman administering the wine tasting tells me. She pours a bottle of the estate's Norton into a tiny plastic cup. It's a dead ringer for the kind my dentist, filling with a splash of mouthwash, bids me to use to rinse. "No glasses?" I ask. "No glasses." The Norton I taste here is everything its critics say it is: It's big, and sweet, and grapey, and unsubtle.

I find a man named Glenn Warnebold in a rumpled polo shirt and white baseball cap manning an umbrella-topped brat station just off the tasting room. A St. Louis accountant, he bought the land in 1997 with his wife, Carolyn. I ask him if he knew about Husmann when he bought the property—if the connection to history is what, in part, drew him to make the purchase.

"Nope," he says, and smiles, and doesn't immediately surrender anything else by way of elaboration. I'm confused for a moment by the meaning of this *nope*, thrown off balance, conversationally speaking. This is not the admission of a man who did not understand the significance of what he'd stumbled into but has since been privileged to discover a vast new world. This is the declaration of a man who lives in the now. "This was all poison ivy," he says, gesturing at the dramatic, sloping land where rows and rows of vines now flourish, and his meaning is clear: *You want to talk about Husmann and his accomplishments? Husmann was then; I am now. This place was a dump; I restored it.* Behind us, on the patio at Husmann Pavilion, two women are dancing to Billy Ray Cyrus, bumping hips as they shimmy to the rollicking beat. Bottles of one of the vineyard's sweet white wines— adorned with the stately, serious image of Husmann—collect in a bucket like empties at a beer bash.

Taking my leave of him, I thread my way through the party, past the dancing, around the bucket of empty bottles, and walk upstairs to the sec-ond floor of the tasting room. Linda Walker Stevens's museum exhibit on Husmann is here, the panels tacked up to the attic walls. If it's a tribute, it's an odd one, an acknowledgment of the man and of the past that comes across as almost obligatory. Below the images chronicling Husmann's life and times is a surfeit of tchotchkes for sale: key chains and souvenirs and wine-related tchotchkes. I spend twenty minutes reading about Husmann. No one else comes up.

Downstairs, it's Ike and Tina Turner, now. "Proud Mary." Snaking through a clump of partygoers, I hop in the car and head out, down the long, descending entrance of the estate.

I find myself thinking, as I drive back into town, about Jon's soulful Nortons, as if drinking a glass or two would wash away the memory.

18

D ENNIS HORTON'S HEAD of thick, tinseled brown hair is bi-
sected by a part as precise and clean as a farmer's row in a corn-
field. He wears a long-sleeved checked shirt with a pen jutting up from the
front pocket. His gold-rimmed aviator glasses are both out of fashion and
too big for his face. In Hollywood, these details are shorthand for nerd, but
that is not the impression that Horton conveys. His appearance, rather, is
an assertion of his sturdy Midwestern roots and seems to argue for the su-
periority of the 1950s.

When I first meet him at his office supply business, ASI Supplies, Inc.,
in an industrial park in Springfield, Virginia, a Washington, D.C., exurb-
turned-suburb, the first thing he does is puts down a Swisher Sweets ciga-
rillo, sidles up to me, extends his hand, and asks, in the slow, even tone of a
town sheriff: "What can I do for you?"

What can you do for me? I reply. You can connect the dots: Norton's
past and its future, Missouri and Virginia.

THE CATACOMBS, Horton remembers, were dark, mysterious, and unfathomable, a fascinating subterranean escape for a young, restless boy
looking to rid himself of the boredom and arbitrary confinements of the
adult world, exactly the sort of secret passage that another Missourian

would have dreamed up for his crafty alter egos, Tom Sawyer and Huck Finn, a place to lose and then find oneself in.

The place reeked, but not in an off-putting way—in a fascinating way. It was the smell of earth, of something profound and alive—the smell of mushrooms. And the tunnels! They seemed to go on and on and on. If you didn't have a good sense of direction, or if you wandered for too long, it could take you hours to get yourself out of there. Of course, that was the whole point.

"Oh, man, we had some fun in there," Horton says, recalling the Hermann of his youth. His enthusiasm is palpable, the enthusiasm of a boy who became a man but who never forgot that he was a boy. He is sixty-three years old, with a sun-baked face that he tends to hold cocked at a slight angle when he listens—as if he were duty bound, by training and by temperament, to suss out foolishness or imprecision, the correction of which seems to bring him endless joy.

Like most boys who grew up in Hermann in the 1950s, Horton came to the catacombs with his friends to play hide-and-seek. The catacombs were his alternate reality, a place of innocence, of fantasy.

It was not until he was an indifferent student at the University of Missouri in Columbia, that he came home one weekend and discovered that the great, secret place of his childhood itself contained a secret. It was 1966. Jim Held had assumed control of operations at the mushroom farm, and now he had begun the arduous task of restoration and recovery, of returning the catacombs to their long-ago purpose.

It was as if a veil had been lifted on the past. His hiding place had been a winery, a famous winery. The catacombs had held casks of legendary wines. And he'd grown up at 327 Stark Boulevard, a block away. A block away from history. Who knew?

Well, no one. That was the thing. It was three decades after Repeal, and it was not just that knowledge of making wine that had been lost. It was history itself that had been lost. There were people growing up in Hermann, in the 1960s, who had never known what the town had been, who were ignorant of the boom years, of the wine that had flowed like water.

The catacombs had sat empty for so long that many people forgot what they had been built for—a monument to forgetting.

Horton was still too young to understand the meaning of a legacy. Still too young to know that we aren't as free as we think we are, that the past is an invisible tether, never to be cut.

He went back to school, back to drinking beer and chasing girls and pretending to be a student, and the excitement of the discovery receded into the past, as everything generally does in the life of a college student, one experience among many. Who could have guessed that drinking a glass of Jim Held's Virginia Seedling at Stone Hill one day years later would lodge itself in the recesses of his mind and never leave? His biggest worry at the time was avoiding the army. Anything to avoid enlisting in the army. The problem was, he had gotten booted out of the University of Missouri for failing to maintain a 2.0 grade point average and had received his induction notice.

"Do you know why they have young men fight wars?" he asks me over a crab-cake lunch at a nearby restaurant.

"Why's that?"

"'Cause old men won't."

I ask him if he was a conscientious objector. He chuckles at my hastily reached conclusion. Not the military, but the army. "I could see myself doing something stupid with an airplane," he explains. "I couldn't see myself doing something stupid with a rifle."

He'd done two years of ROTC and taken the exams, and he was intrigued by the air force. He went to the recruitment office on Olive Street in downtown St. Louis one day and begged to be taken. "Get me the results of your exams," a recruiter told him, "and I can have you on a train to San Antonio tonight."

He arrived just in time to catch the midnight train to Texas. Not long after, an army officer came knocking on his parents' door.

"Sir, your son is AWOL."

"My son," came the reply, "is in the air force."

In air force parlance, he was a 462—it was his duty to make sure the "weapons release systems" of the planes that flew in missions were in proper working order. In Horton's parlance, "From the time the fighter pilot pushed the button till the time it went away, I had to make sure it all went off without a hitch."

I ask how long he was in. He rattles off his oft-repeated reply: "Three years, six months, and nine days."

It wasn't all bad. For a time, he was stationed at the Bentwater Air Force Base, outside Ipswich, England. English food was legendarily terrible, but the beer was good, and so were the wines. It surprised him. The English didn't make the stuff themselves, like the French, who had elevated wine to some saintly level, or the Germans, who came close, but they knew what was good. And there was always a lot of it at hand. He was not a rube when it came to wine, not like a lot of Americans he knew in the service, and that was surely a product of having grown up in Hermann. Wine was always around. His parents drank it every night at dinner. Everybody, it seemed, had a little wine in the back. They didn't call it bootleg wine. Bootleg was such a loaded word, so fraught with importance. It was homemade wine, like homemade vinegar or homemade pickles.

His exposure to wine gave him an edge on his friends, but he was, all the same, ill-prepared for what he tasted. There was a big difference between Missouri hooch and European table wine. The difference was as big as the distance between the two countries. It fascinated him. He became a wine drinker. He made trips to France and Germany, tasted the wines there, and began making all sorts of mental notes about what he liked, and why. And what he didn't like, and why. A wine lover—him, Dennis Horton. Things had a funny way of working out sometimes.

HE RETURNED to the States. He got serious.

The University of Maryland at College Park had agreed to accept the credits he had earned in Europe, as part of the university's extension program. He took twenty-one credits a semester, working a job in a furniture store in his spare hours, and finished with a degree in marketing in two and a half years. He'd wasted three years, six months, and nine days; he wasn't about to waste any more time. He went to work for an office supply business in Rockville, Maryland, rose quickly, and turned a marginally profitable company into a successful one. He did it again, several years later, with another, larger office supply business, this one in Washington, D.C.

It was time to work for himself, to enjoy his share of the money he was so obviously skilled at making. He and his wife, Sharon, moved to Aroda, Virginia, about thirty miles northeast of Charlottesville, in 1977 and with a business partner, Joan Bieda, opened Automated Systems, Inc., in Springfield that same year.

Business was good, and so, naturally, life was good, too. But his time in the military had trained him to be "tenacious," to never be idle, to take nothing for granted, and it was not in his nature to sit around and watch TV or play golf or putter around the house. He had a notion that he might grow grapes and make wine, just as his neighbors back in Hermann had done. Why not? You wanted wine, you made it yourself. He had the time, and he had the inclination, too. He had always liked figuring things out, solving problems, and at its most basic, winemaking was simply problem solving. He began carting books around in the backseat of his Cordoba, wine books. On climate, on soil, on grapes. The three dozen volumes scattered across the back seat comprised a library and a growing obsession. One in particular fascinated him, and he returned to it again and again. It was a volume on pre-Prohibition grapes, on the grapes that had been lost and forgotten. The vanished grapes of a vanished America.

He laid the vines in rows in front of his house in Aroda, the first thing he saw when he walked out the door and the first thing he saw when he returned home. He tended them with care and devotion. The air force had drilled into him the importance of detail, and his grapes would be the beneficiaries of his lessons learned. It was like making a bed with tight, military corners. You're gonna do a thing, you're gonna do it right.

With the book as his guide, he focused on native varieties, including the Concord and the Niagara. He couldn't resist planting Cabernet Sauvi-

gnon, too, but he noticed one day that after an inch of rain the previous
night, the chemical levels of the grape fluctuated wildly, while the Cabernet Franc he'd planted nearby—it, too, produced a big red wine, but according to the books, it was better suited to the growing conditions in
Virginia—held steady. The soil and climate, it wasn't too hard to see, were
made for certain grapes. *God help us, we can't change that shit, so why don't
we work with it instead of against it?* he wondered.

IN THE MID-1980S, his business took off. An unexpected assist from an
unexpected source sent his sales soaring. He couldn't have foreseen it, just
as he couldn't have foreseen becoming a lover of wine, but one day he met
a new client in a parking lot of Tysons Corner Center, near McLean, Virginia, to deliver three commercial-size shredders, a relatively recent inven-
tion. Ordinarily, Horton did not make personal deliveries. But he made an
exception in this case because the client, a government official, had emphasized to him that he could not wait, that he needed the shredders right away.
Not a week from today, not tomorrow: today. The recent revelations that
John Anthony Walker and Michael Walker had been working as Soviet
spies had rendered obsolete the notion of "burn bags," government vernacular for containers, typically paper bags, containing sensitive or classi-
fied documents that, upon transfer from one insider to another, are set
aflame and destroyed. The government official proved his seriousness by
showing up in the parking lot with $6,000 in cash. From that point on, a
government agency would cut Horton a check for his equipment, but that
day Oliver North was desperate and paid the money himself.

There's a long-standing joke in the wine world: Wanna make a small
fortune in wine? Start with a big fortune. He didn't have a big fortune. But
Ollie North and his boys had made him very, very comfortable.

He had, by this time, begun to think seriously of starting a vineyard, a
real vineyard, calmly enduring the good-natured gibes of his friends, who
were quick to paint him as a man entering the first stages of a midlife crisis.
How could he explain it? It was not a crisis. There was nothing agitated

about it. No attendant anxieties, no escalating fears. It was less than that, and more. It was another realization, or rather, a continuation of the first realization.

Like his famously straightforward forebears, Horton is an avowedly plain-spoken sort, beholden, as he says, to "what is"—the simple, unvarnished account of things—and so the notion of being haunted, of even allowing such a lofty, momentous word to attach itself to him, is personally troubling, an admission, perhaps, that he has gotten fancy. Yet how else to describe what he was feeling? It was the past, coming to get him. The past, telling him he had a responsibility.

He had read enough books and talked to enough people to know that it was not the height of foolishness to try to build a vineyard from scratch around the Norton. Not the height, no. A gamble? Yes, and an enormous one.

But he was fearless. How those higher-ups in the air force had liked to take credit for turning him into a tough cuss, when all they had done, really, was to hone his innate fearlessness into something useful, practical. It had been in him from the start, like his sly wit, like his discerning palate.

He knew that the Norton had already made its reappearance in Missouri, but the idea of returning home to Hermann to launch his vineyard didn't interest him. What, and leave his thriving business, his house, and every other part of his life too? No. Virginia was where he belonged. And not merely where *he* belonged—where *it* belonged. It boggled his mind that, aside from a handful of small, experimental plantings in the state— and what were these but toes dipped into the wading pool—nobody had thought to bring the Norton all the way back, to restore the pride and glory of antebellum Virginia's vineyards to the cradle.

A man named Bruce Zoecklein, the head of oenology and grape chemistry at Virginia Tech, had cautioned him against investing too heavily in the Norton. Zoecklein had been convening groups of winemakers and winery owners for a variety of roundtables, short courses, and seminars since he'd arrived at Tech in 1985, with an emphasis on making better, more consistent, more expressive wine. At the University of Missouri, in the early 1980s, he'd done similar hands-on work, helping winemakers in the field and in the cellar, exposing them to new techniques. Zoecklein was not opposed to the Norton. In fact, he thought it had great potential, that the grape was not only ideally suited to Virginia's climate, but also that the wine the grape could produce was distinctive and sometimes worthy. His first exposure to Norton had occurred a little more than a decade earlier, at Cal State–Fresno, where his four-year stint as a professor just happened to have coincided with that of an industrious student named Jon Held. The Stone Hill Norton that Held had turned him on to that day had made enough of an impression on Zoecklein that a year after arriving on campus, he hosted a "brown bag" tasting at his Blacksburg, Virginia, house: five wines, all Nortons, for the thirty-five winemakers who were then working in the state. He didn't tell his guests that they were drinking Nortons, and none guessed. Much of the discussion centered on whether the wines were "Left Bank," where Cabernet Sauvignon grapes predominate, or "Right Bank," where Merlot grapes are more prevalent. Lacking all identifying information, the Virginia winemakers presumed that the Nortons from Arkansas and Missouri, some dating back as far as 1972, were premium French wines. "The aged varieties of Norton," Zoecklein says, "can be quite alluring."

But aging meant waiting, and waiting on a wine to find itself, to fulfill its potential, was not something most new winery owners could afford. Nor was the Norton particularly easy to make, being difficult to start and offering generally lower yields than other grapes.

And why make a wine that nobody was likely to buy? It was hard enough to get people in the state interested in wine again. But to get them interested in a difficult, challenging wine like the Norton? No one in Virginia was growing it, so no one was buying it or drinking it. The fact was, no one had heard of it, not even the wine writers or critics. Seventy years after the start of Prohibition, the grape had vanished, a casualty of the erosion of collective memory.

Well, here's to nothing, Dennis Horton thought, and in 1989 he bought a small patch of land in Gordonsville, in Orange County, Virginia, an hour-and-a-quarter drive southeast from Springfield. Horton Vineyards became the state's fortieth vineyard.

Logistically, it was an ideal location, an easy drive from the office park, allowing him to shuttle between both businesses without, he hoped, running himself too ragged. Historically, it was even more ideal. His vineyard lay twenty minutes north of Charlottesville—smack dab in Jefferson country.

NEARLY SIX DECADES after Repeal, winemaking in Virginia was again starting over. The state seemed to be constitutionally fated to the false start, the abortive dream.

Recent advances in technology had made it possible to make wine from *vinifera*, which made it possible to produce wan, watery versions of Cabernet Sauvignon, Chardonnay, and Pinot Noir. The state was imitating California, and badly. It was astonishing, Horton thought. In the interest of producing wines that were familiar, and thus marketable, they were simply repeating the earlier failures of Jefferson and countless others. Virginia was doomed to fail when it came to wine, a tragicomic version of the myth of eternal return.

"Grapes," he says, "are kinda like men. The preamble says all men are created equal, and we know that's horseshit. Not all grapes are created equal." Trying to grow *vinifera* grapes in the *terroir* of Virginia, he knew, was disastrous. "God can't grow Pinot Noir in the state of Virginia. He'd give up and go back to Jerusalem."

Didn't they know their history? Hadn't they learned their lessons? How could they have overlooked the rich potential of the Norton? Prohibition hadn't lasted thirteen years; it was still going strong. Memory, knowledge—gone, vanished. The pioneering insights of Daniel Norton might as well have been the fossilized remains of an ancient civilization. Winemakers operated out of fear.

"The thing of it is," he says, "you've got a grape that originated here, a strong, disease-resistant grape, a good grape, that went all the way from here to Cincinnati, and then all the way from there to Missouri, producing good wine and winning all kinds of awards, and you're not gonna plant it here?"

Here was the problem, though: finding it.

It was one thing to talk with passion and purpose about your very high-minded intentions, and another to do something about them. You can't start a revolution without a rifle.

He didn't have the grape. Federal agents had swept the state and ripped out the Norton vines, along with every other winemaking variety that had flourished in Virginia in the 1920s. It was possible that the feds, despite their zeal to expunge every last wine-producing vine from the state, had not gotten everything, that there were some strays growing in the wild some-where, but he had gone looking and looking, and he hadn't found a thing.

"Not a stick," he told me. "Not a one."

It was time for plan B. Time to go home.

THE STRANGE ways of fate and time.

The Norton had migrated west from Virginia to Missouri. Now, in its improbable second act, it was migrating east from Missouri to Virginia. *He* was the migration, Dennis Horton thought, as he rang up Jon Held at Stone Hill in the fall of 1988 and requested a shipment of vines, laying the foundation for his new vineyard. And what about his own migration? He had left home, joined the air force, gotten married, graduated from college, and started a business, and here he was, coming back to find what had been there waiting for him all along, one block from the house he'd grown up in. Like coming home to collect the mail.

He buried the borrowed roots in the soil that spring, eight acres' worth of Norton—the first planting of the grape in Virginia since Repeal.

And then he waited. It takes a cutting of grape vines about three years from the time it is planted in the soil to flower. It was a long time to think—too long. Had he known then that the grape's capacity to endure is perhaps its greatest trait in the soil—"This thing'll grow through asphalt; at least a crack in the sidewalk"—he might not have been so anxious.

How to explain this uneasiness? Who but he knew what exactly was at stake? In truth, of course, nothing was at stake. If he failed, who would know? Who would care? What would it matter if a grape that no one remembered or cared enough about to keep alive all these years failed in the field? But he had come to believe that he was a node of linkage, a go-between who kept the past alive in the present, and if he failed, then something of the past was going to die out because of him.

The Norton, however, did not die. It lived. It grew. And grew. And grew. There was something to this *terroir* business, after all.

It was not simply that the grape was well-suited to the soil and climate. No, something more than that. Something deeper: The grape was meant to be here. Was bred to be here. He had effected a homecoming. He had returned it to its roots, to its habitat, and it had rewarded him with great, blooming growth.

In three years, he celebrated his first grape harvest and a year later, his first vintage. The Horton Norton. It hit the shelves in 1992.

With the regenerated grape as his centerpiece—his conversation piece—the vineyard became a kind of experimental laboratory for varieties that nobody had dared to try in Virginia. In 1993, he released his first Viognier, a sweet, fruity, and voluptuous white wine made from a European grape—one of the rare instances of a *Vitis vinifera* that is able to grow and thrive in Virginia. The following year, Robert Parker, the most respected and most feared wine critic in the world, awarded Horton's second vintage of Viognier a score of 91 out of 100. In Virginia, the wine was little understood—many of his customers referred to it as "VOG-ner," which Horton with shrewd slyness informed them was the "German pronunciation"—but the vintage was a huge success, wowing a number of winemakers in California at a blind tasting and winning several awards.

He was succeeding; he was not yet a success. Recounting the travails of the first-time winery owner, Horton speaks in tones of biting irony: "Year one: Write a lot of checks, zero revenue. Year two: Write a lot of checks, zero revenue. Year three: Write a lot of checks, zero revenue. Year four: You can make some wine and, if you're lucky, generate a little revenue, but nothing to cover the costs of year four. And probably not year five, either. Year six: Now, if all goes right, you're just starting to cover expenses."

But already, because of these two wines, he had developed something of a reputation as a maverick, a man bucking trends and the fates, a man in defiance of history. Which only made him the latest incarnation of the man who would put Virginia wine on the map.

In this new role, which he had not sought but which he had not rejected, either, he saw that it was not enough to just grow grapes and make wine. "With the Norton, and with these other grapes, you don't just have to sell the wine," he says. "You have to sell the grape, too."

Restoring the native grape was a cause, and a cause demanded a champion. He would have to get out there and stump on behalf of his beliefs.

19

M ICHAEL MARSH* arrived early at the American Society for Enology and Viticulture conference and snagged a seat in the front row of the conference room of the Omni Hotel, right by the downtown pedestrian mall in Charlottesville, Virginia—mere miles, the thought struck him, from where Jefferson had tried to make wine.

His suit and tie were an outward denial of his inner anxiety: killing time was killing him. The prospect that something, or someone, at this ASEV conference might open a door to a new and different future was thrilling and unsettling in equal measure, and impatience being one of his weaknesses—being, in fact, his biggest weakness, as if he had been cursed with a condition that made him unable to sit patiently and let things take their natural course—he couldn't wait for someone to step up to the podium and *begin* already.

It was July, 1995. Two weeks earlier, he and his partner had struck a huge, life-changing deal in a Wall Street boardroom and sold their company to a rival, and that had been both thrilling and unsettling, too. Thrilling, because they had made a more than $40 million fortune, which, in the spirit of the go-go 1990s, they immediately dipped into, celebrating that night at a midtown Manhattan restaurant with gargantuan slabs of

*Not his real name.

beef, multiple bottles of aged Bordeaux, and long Cuban cigars. Unsettling, because now that part of his life was done and gone. The long hours, the constant complaints, the hassles with staff, but also the daily camaraderie, the ceaseless drip, drip, drip of adrenaline, the primordial chase of success. It had been his twelfth and most successful business—the business all the others had been building inevitably toward. And now he found himself in an odd and unprecedented position: He no longer needed to work.

"You've gotta slow down and smell the coffee," his mother urged him.

Coffee? Not roses? Whatever it was, coffee, roses—they were not things he was particularly interested in taking time out for. Stress, with all its attendant complications, was a strain on mind and body, depleting it of resources and denying it the sense of perspective that kept a person in balance; but the way it adrenalized him, the way it thrust him into action and kept him going, was absolutely addicting. Was necessary. He was not built for slowing down. He was built to rush at life—to take things on, not slough them off.

His mother knew this, of course, which was why she was so vehement in her insistence. And why she could not have been surprised when he politely brushed her off. "Yes, Ma."

Exactly two weeks later and he was driving north to Jefferson country to meet his next challenge in a symposium on "alternative wine varieties."

The notion of alternative varieties appealed to him for a multitude of reasons, not the least of which was the fact that it chimed with his perception of himself as someone who could not be fit into the usual boxes. But more than that, it was the suspicion that there were more great wines in the world than the same half-dozen varietals always touted by sommeliers and wine critics. Just as people were infinitely more complex than the umbrellas of identification they often squeezed themselves under in their quest for belonging, so must there be other wines out there to cultivate and love and drink.

This was not his first fact-finding mission. Months earlier, seriously mulling the possibility of starting a winery, he had taken a couple of exploratory trips out west, touring Napa and Sonoma in California and the fertile Rogue River valley of Oregon, the last the source of some of the most interesting, exciting wines that were then beginning to come out of the West Coast.

The wines he drank were good, some of them great—no surprise there. The best wines in the country were coming from a stretch of land that extended from Northern California through Oregon and the midsection of Washington. As he had always done, wherever he had traveled, he tried hard to visualize himself living there, nestled among the moneyed elites— many of them, like himself, people who had made fortunes elsewhere— making ripe, fruit-forward wines and leading the sun-dappled good life. But he couldn't.

For one thing, he had reached the stage in his wine education where he had become a disciple of ABC—Anything But Chardonnay—and California was Chardonnay country. Lord knows, he hadn't made the safe, conventional choices in life; why should he make the safe, conventional choice now? Oregon, at least, held the prospect of being an alternative to Napa and Sonoma. There was only one problem: "It was all brown. They'd had years of drought. I'd grown up in Florida, where everything was lush and green. Where was the green, man? Everything was brown. Brown, brown, everywhere you looked. Yuck."

But more important than the surprising unlushness of Oregon or the boring sameness of the wines he drank up and down the West Coast was the realization that to plant roots in Napa or Sonoma or even Oregon was to do what had already been done by thousands of others, to be a copycat, a follower. The thought pierced him. It was a negation of self, a blotting out of his singular, hard-won identity. *I'm Type A, I'm a builder, I build things. I don't follow others, I never have, I make my own way in the world.*

He asked himself: Do I want to make the 375th best Merlot or Pinot Noir or Cabernet Sauvignon in the world? Or do I want to make the best fill-in-the-blank?

What that blank was, he did not yet know. But he knew enough, then, to know that he would not be satisfied until he had figured out what it was.

. . .

ONE DOES NOT suddenly decide to become a renegade, any more than one suddenly decides to become a genius.

Filling in the blanks without prompting, coloring outside the lines, challenging and defying convention—these things were as hardwired into him as his suspicion that Michael Marsh, his vessel, the outward manifestation of the person he was, was not like other men, that he did not have the same impulses, that something was wrong, oddly wrong.

The suspicion had been there all along. Standing one day in the door of his parents' bedroom, which was empty, he saw his mother's silk pink pajamas thrown over the back of a chair. He loved them. He coveted them. The thought came to him: *Those should be my clothes.* He was four or five.

He said nothing to his mother, or to anyone, and promptly buried the thought, as all good boys with complicated, complicating ideas are supposed to do.

But the thought did not go away. It stayed. It lodged itself and would not leave, a boarder who took up residence in a back room of a house and disturbed no one but could not be uprooted, either.

Nor would the image go away: the clothes he wanted and should not have. Could not have. The strange, exhilarating feelings he should not, could not, talk about.

As he moved through adolescence, another thought came to him, a related thought: *I'm in the wrong fuckin' body.*

But what could he do about it? He was a teenager. Sublimate it, and try to forget about it.

There was another memory, and he tried to sublimate that, too. It haunted him for years. The sound of his mother's cry, "Boys! Boys!" Racing into his parents' bedroom to find his father seized up, in the throes of a massive heart attack. What to do? There was nothing *to* do. The body was in control now, ringing its changes, and they were reduced to watching, helpless, as the vital man they knew and loved and thought indomitable vanished before their eyes, shed the vessel of his flesh and bones.

He was fifteen: a kid. He didn't act like a kid, and he didn't feel like a kid, and he sure as hell didn't want anyone thinking of him as a kid, with his cocksure sense of himself and his shrewd business acumen. But in that instant, he felt something break in him, and all he had been pushing toward and yearning for was as nothing, and he felt hopeless and alone.

His subconscious, that rogue director, had repackaged the images of that day into a continuous loop of pain and terror, but it was the eerie symmetry of the numbers that he kept returning to in his conscious mind. His father was fifty-two. His father's father had been dead and gone at fifty-two as well.

The idea of predestination ran counter to his brash teenage conviction that we are all given a chance to shape our futures. But what was this, if not a kind of predestination? Fifty-two. It was like clockwork. Like fate.

And it awaited him, too. That was terrifying to comprehend. Thirty-seven years more, at most. If he was lucky. If everything went right. That was the line of descent. That was the genetic parameter.

It changed him, changed him utterly. He knew everything would be different, knew it more than he knew anything else in the world, even before he knew exactly how. His father's death plunged the family of five into near-poverty and a reliance on government assistance. It wore on him. It was demoralizing.

He had thrown himself into his first business at fourteen. He'd thought it up with a friend of his who lived in the neighborhood, and the two of them would ride their bikes up and down and all around Dade County, Florida, snapping pictures of houses for a photographic directory that they would then sell to local businesses. Making money, being your own boss. What a gas, so much better than being cooped up all day in the classroom, listening to others tell you what they themselves had discovered. Show, don't tell, the English teachers all preached. But what was school itself? Telling, not showing. And waiting, not doing. He was a doer.

The idea of relying on handouts had become too much to bear, and so one day, with food scarce, he hopped into the family sedan and set out for the swamplands around Dade County.

Five bucks in his pocket, and a Harrington & Richardson single-shot shotgun, was all he needed. At the time, two bucks could buy you a full tank of gas. The other three bucks he spent on shells for the gun. He would shoot quail in the morning and afternoon and sleep in the car at night, going for days at a time until he had enough of a haul to bring back to the family.

In retrospect, he could look back and allow that these exploits were worthy of Daniel Boone, but at the time, it wasn't nearly so romantic-sounding. There were mouths to feed. And he was desperate.

Who knew what he might have become, had his father lived; now he had no choice but to accelerate the process of discovery, to hurl himself at experience. He smoked pot every day. Smoked pot and dreamed his big dreams. It was no longer enough to be equal to a challenge. He would cultivate a brash fearlessness. He had always taken risks. Well, so now he would go a step beyond: He would take gambles. Diamonds were created from the extreme pressure that a lump of coal was subjected to, and maybe a new, better, stronger self would emerge from his trials and travails.

And then he was sixteen. Coming into his body, beset by an urge for independence that felt just as strong and relentless as those other urges, he took off one day for Jamaica. All he told his mother was, "I'm going away for a while. I'll be back."

He boarded a boat from Miami, arriving in Jamaica a day later. He knew no one. For six weeks, he lived off his wits, making friends wherever he went, smoking spliffs with the natives, roasting goats over an open pit, riding horses, gnawing sugar cane, drinking 150-proof rum.

It was more of an education, and a better education, too, than he had been getting at Palmetto High.

College was more of the same, an empty-hearted flirtation. By sophomore year, it had become apparent that staying enrolled was a joke. As if the University of Miami, Party U., was not its own joke. Studying? Better to call it what it was: going through the motions. Whereas, in business— and it didn't matter the kind of business it was, just the fact of it, just the idea of business itself—there was always the feeling of constant, accelerating movement. The movement forward, the rush toward destiny. There was money out there to be made, lots of it—ripe for the plucking, like the ripe, sweet mamey sapotes hanging low from the tree in his parents' backyard.

THE FEATURED speaker at the conference was a plainly dressed man with a plainspoken demeanor, a sly sense of humor, and the kind of passionate idealism that cannot be faked—that inclined you to trust whatever he had to say, regardless of whether or not you were prepared to believe him.

Dennis Horton told his story by way of making his pitch to the fifty or sixty participants, many of them winery owners or winemakers in the state who were looking to broaden their educations. The catacombs . . . the legend of the Norton . . . bringing the vines back to Virginia, to the would-be cradle of American winemaking, to replant them in the same soil from which they came. . . .

His was a kind of experimental vineyard, founded upon the brave new idea that little-known varietals that were disease-resistant and could survive the vagaries of the climate held the best possible hope for the state's winemaking future. Virginia was not California and never would be. There the weather always cooperated. Here it was something to manage, a variable that proved enormously difficult to solve for, with as many as fifty days of thunderstorms a year, up to forty inches of rain, ten tornadoes, the occasional hurricane, and even a spring frost. It was largely the weather that accounted for the great difficulty that many Virginia winemakers had long experienced in growing Chardonnay with any consistency and quality. But this same fickle weather was of little concern to the red Norton and the white Viognier, making them ideal grapes with which to begin populating a vineyard, hardy and resilient and vigorous. In fact, it would be tough to imagine grapes that were more nearly ideal for the radical enterprise he'd outlined. Add the fact that they were also capable of producing excellent and expressive wines—wines as good, as complex, as rewarding, as those made anywhere in the world. Well, hell: This is a no-brainer, folks! These grapes are the future! This is nature, telling us what to do. Why fight it?

As Marsh sat there and listened, Horton's exhortation sounded in the depths of his being, and he began to think that after all his travels and all his explorations, he had finally found what he was looking for. What he was hearing, in Dennis Horton's story, was in some measure his own story, a parallel narrative of his own wild desire to break out from convention and try something else, something new. Dennis Horton was talking his language. Even before Marsh took a sip, he felt an odd affinity for this grape, the Norton, he had never heard of before, this grape that Horton, like some shaman, had brought back from the dead. Who knew but that its rebirth was, in some strange way, a kind of parallel to his own?

WHAT THE HELL? he thought, sticking his nose into a tasting glass that had been set out on a long side table.

He swirled the glass, sniffed again, then tipped it back and drank. All that he had learned about wine, all those books he had read and tastings he had attended had left him somehow ill-prepared for his encounter with the Norton. It was big. As big as the Cabernets he'd tasted on his tour of Napa. And funky. It had the intense earthiness of some of the Spanish wines he liked, the rustic character that was soulfulness itself. And yet it was fundamentally unlike these European wines too, so much so that it was like comparing singers from different eras and slighting both in the process.

He took another sniff, another taste.

He must have looked like a crazy person, with all that sniffing and tasting, someone who had wandered in off the street for the free booze. Sniffing and tasting, as if he had never tried a glass of wine.

Well, not this wine, he hadn't.

He would not leave the building until he had burned the precise memory of that nose and that resonant taste into his brain.

It was mysterious, haunting, alive.

It was different, and seemed to make a virtue of its difference.

It was not sophisticated; it did not strain for a refinement beyond its reach.

It was absolutely and utterly itself.

20

HEADING SOUTH on the drive back to Florida, Michael Marsh's mind was ablaze. His thoughts were racing faster than his car.

Dennis Horton had only touched on the basic story in his talk, a cursory outline of the Norton's rise and fall. He had come to tout the viticultural virtues of the grape, after all, not deliver a history lesson.

Marsh wanted more. He wanted a meal, not just an appetizer. Who was this Daniel Norton? Why had he succeeded where Jefferson had failed? How could a grape that had showed so beautifully in the glass be so obscure? Why had it vanished in the first place?

There was no buried history when it came to the European grapes, no secrets. He knew them all. Collected them. Stores were full of them. Wine lists, too. Pick up a wine magazine, and that's all you ever saw—poetic, impassioned testimonials to the great wine grapes of the world, Pinot Noir, Cabernet Sauvignon, Merlot, Riesling, Chardonnay, all of them European.

But Norton? Nothing. Not a word.

And not a word about any other American grapes, either. Californians could claim Zinfandel as an American grape all they wanted, but he knew better; he had done his reading: it originated in Hungary.

Reading the wine press, it was as if no American grape was good enough to produce good wine. Could that be? And if so, how? *You mean to tell me,* he thought, *a continent as vast and varied as this, as rich in crops as this, could not lay claim to a single grape that could make a good table wine?*

Nope; couldn't be. Not only was the contrarian in him compelled to reject that notion outright on principle, but he had just tasted delicious and irrefutable evidence of a native grape's worth.

Not since he had walked into Big Daddy's Liquor Store on Christmas Eve, 1977, on the Miracle Mile in Coral Gables, and sat down over dinner that night to drink a 1971 Château Léoville–Las Cases, a Bordeaux, had a bottle of wine provoked so much excitement. *Fuck*, he thought, savoring his first sip, *this is fabulous*. For a long, heady moment, he forgot where he was, forgot even that it was Christmas Eve.

Until then, weaned on Boone's Farm and Strawberry Hill, he had been innocent of the power and complexity, the mystery and wonder, of a good wine, qualities that can turn otherwise sane, sober-minded people into obsessives, given to devoting their lives to amassing collections of wine as large as that of some libraries.

Eventually, he found his way to even better Bordeaux, but nothing compared to the power, the sheer revelation, of that first sip.

Norton had restored his sense of innocence and wonder, made him feel like a wine virgin all over again. And now, like someone smitten by the flush of first love, he couldn't stop thinking about it.

MANY MONTHS after the Omni tasting, Horton invited Marsh to his vineyard in Orange for another tasting.

He pulled out two bottles of Norton and poured a glass of each. One was a young Norton, his current vintage; the other, an older Norton, from his first vintage.

Marsh picked up a glass, agitated the contents with a violent swirl that sent the dark, purplish liquid circling the globe like a tornado, dug his nose in, repeated the swirl, sniffed again, then drank. He paused a moment to provide a needed interval between tastes, but also to mentally register his sensual impressions of the wine, and to translate those impressions into words and images.

Now he did the same with the other glass: swirl, sniff, swirl, sniff, sip.

All the while, Horton eyed his eager protégé, wondering what exactly he was tasting, wondering what was going through his mind, wondering whether he was getting the point he was trying to convey.

Oh, my, Marsh thought.

The differences were dramatic. The aged Norton was markedly softer, much less racy, and—here was the impressive thing—it had not sacrificed too much of its fruit in the process of mellowing. It reminded him of the aged Bordeaux he loved. Fruit *and* ageability.

He hadn't needed convincing that it was the right thing to come north and grow the grape and start a vineyard, at great personal cost and despite long odds. What this second tasting confirmed for him was that the Norton was even more special than he'd first suspected.

IT CONFIRMED something else for him, too, and that was that he was awfully lucky to have met someone with the knowledge and passion of Dennis Horton to shepherd him into this new venture, this new life. When he was most in need of guidance, he had stumbled upon a teacher.

The tastings had exposed him to a way of looking at and thinking about wine, a kind of philosophical grounding in viticulture, but he needed practical help, too, and Horton had also supplied that.

If not me, who? Horton thought. It was hard enough to start a vineyard. But to start a vineyard in an unforgiving place like Virginia? And to do it with the Norton? Horton knew it was like playing three games of tennis with one ball.

Marsh was struck by Horton's selflessness. Who could have asked for such generosity? He was struck, too, by the fact that Horton did not believe in hoarding his knowledge. Dennis Horton wished desperately to see Horton Vineyards succeed, to be a strong and self-sustaining venture. But he was not a ruthless competitor; the enterprise he was ultimately engaged in was nothing less than the revival of the state's entire winemaking culture. He had not imported cuttings of Norton from Stone Hill only to have the grape be regarded as some kind of a novelty in its original home. If no one picked up the thread, if no one continued his project, then what was the point of the whole thing? What would he have achieved?

There was a kind of spiritual dimension to this assistance, a notion of partnership that could not have been more different from the intensely competitive tech world Marsh had just ditched. It staggered the mind to think that he was entering an industry that was not consumed with profit only, the almighty bottom line. Making wine was not cranking out a product. It was coming into intimate contact with history, tradition, and culture. It was these things that a winemaker trusted in and leaned on amid the uncertainty of the seasons and the vagaries of taste and the market. It was these things that mattered and needed to be preserved. In handing down what he had learned, then, Dennis Horton was transmitting more than a method; he was transmitting a system of values, and ensuring their survival.

And now he made Marsh the next chain in the link with a gift of vines from his vineyard in Orange County, a chain he had not started but merely continued. By this simple gesture, he connected the eager newcomer all the way back to the bootlegger-sustained Norton vines from Paul Rauch's farm, the vines that had revived winemaking at Stone Hill in Missouri.

THE GRAND VISION that Marsh had glimpsed for himself in southern Florida had begun to coalesce into a distinct and terrifying possibility, the double helix of a new and uncertain existence.

All his life, he felt, had been leading him to this precipice, and now that he had arrived at its edge, he was frightened and exhilarated. He knew he would only be doing himself further injury to delay the inevitable, the decision to change himself, to radically remake his body, no longer a vague, romantic notion, but an urgent, practical need.

Michelangelo had famously written of the sculptor's art, of bringing forth what was already within, the release, through the black magic of art, of the human presence the marble contained and concealed. The surgeon Marsh had found and come to trust was not Michelangelo, nor could the clinic where the reassignment would take place be confused with the soaring, majestic cathedrals of Florence. But this exceedingly difficult, delicate process he was about to subject himself to was nothing less than a release from the block of marble that had contained him for four decades. He had spent his life in solitary confinement. Something, someone, needed to be set free.

Thus let loose, that something, or someone, could not return to what was, to the old assumptions, the old cares.

In his *Metamorphoses*, Ovid wrote:

> *How many creatures walking on this earth*
> *Have their first being in another form?*

How many creatures? How many *things*, wine among them?

A new life as a freed woman. A new life in the vineyards. It was almost indescribable. It sounded like heaven.

IF MAKING the change was anything close to as liberating as making the decision to make the change, Marsh thought, he was going to be one high and happy woman. He felt emboldened. Anything, now, seemed possible.

Even when he was feeling most fanciful and optimistic, the idea of starting a vineyard had seemed to him an enormous and daunting undertaking, a project far beyond his know-how and experience, a great and lunging reach that might exceed his grasp. Now, as 1995 turned into 1996 and he gave himself over to the first small steps in the arduous and painstaking process of radically remaking his appearance, it was as if he saw and felt things with a new eye, a new confidence. He felt newly powerful.

The great and unspoken benefit of making the change, he was beginning to understand, was that any other upheaval in his life, any other challenge, became suddenly less impossible. Set alongside his resolution to start over as a woman, his determination to establish his winery in Virginia on the forgotten promise of the great American grape was emptied of its ability to intimidate.

It was more than just a matter of perspective, though. More than just a question of context.

The two resolutions had come to seem entwined, each enabling the other, to the point that it had become difficult, at times, to think of becoming a woman without also thinking of growing Norton. The separate but related dimensions of a new, altered existence.

He was a novice at making wine, and the Norton was a leap into the great unknown. But just as the surgery would come with no guarantees or promises, so he could not expect to reap the immense satisfactions of taking a risk without also experiencing the pains along the way. He would teach himself to be a woman. He would teach himself to grow Norton. *I'm a builder; I build things.*

He had also learned the hard way that building takes time.

21

～～～

S HE HURT. Every day, she hurt. It was normal to hurt.

    Ha, she thought: normal. Now there was a word. Was there even such a thing?

Sexual reassignment surgery had left her in a kind of daze, a survivor of war. Yet, paradoxically, she had never felt better.

ACCORDING TO the dictates of *terroir*, every vine has a home, a zone, a patch of earth that is indisputably its own, where its identity will take root and flourish. Conversely, if that same flourishing vine is uprooted and subjected to soil that does not suit it, forced to accommodate itself to a strange and inhospitable circumstance, it may wither and die.

Is it any different with people? Why do some of us fail at one job but succeed at another? Why do some of us exhale when we leave the congestion of the city and unwind in the country, while others, after several days of simplicity and placidity, feel small and confined and long for the stimulation and variety of a busy metropolis? Why do some of us decide that changing our lot in life, at great odds and enormous personal risk, is preferable to dying slowly in our present circumstance?

From the colonists at Jamestown to the pioneers at Hermann and beyond, what was the American story but the story of starting over, of willful reinvention, the restless search for the true and proper identity? She had only to look at her own family's history as proof. Her father's ancestors had arrived in Jamestown in 1635, less than three decades after the first boats dropped anchor in the James River, while her mother's ancestors had been German immigrants in Missouri, in Westphalia, in the 1840s.

Her pioneering was figurative, metaphorical, but did that make it any less eloquent an expression of self-determination? She had ceased to be able to find meaning as a man, and the body she had found herself enclosed within at birth had left her feeling alienated and lonely. The soil and climate of Virginia, Jenni hoped, would nurture and sustain her, allow her to flower and thrive as she started over and tended the land—tending the land as a way of tending a wound.

Little by little, as she healed, she became stronger; and as she became stronger, she grew more confident of her ability to take on life as a woman. Indeed, during the lonely, difficult weeks of recovery, it occurred to her that, if she could get through this, then there was nothing to prevent her from doing anything else she dreamed. Even the ridiculous idea of making wine.

The name of the venture, Chrysalis, was the christening of a new existence. What could be more fitting, what could be more perfect—"the miraculous transformation of an ordinary thing." Grapes into wine. Man into woman.

THE FIRST BOTTLE of wine she produced was not the Norton that had given her the courage to plow over her old life and start over; it was a Chardonnay, made from purchased New York state grapes and made by Alan Kinne, the man Dennis Horton had entrusted with making the first Nortons in Virginia since Prohibition. His name graced the label that year, 1996, and for the next two vintages of Chardonnay, too.

These were finger exercises, for the most part, rough drafts that existed as much to relieve the anxiety of waiting on the Nortons to take root, flower, and grow grapes as to allay her anxieties over a winery that existed more on paper and in her head than in reality. She had yet to move into her estate at Aldie, Virginia. Operating out of her home, a rented townhouse in

Old Town Alexandria, she outsourced all aspects of production and set to work devising a devilishly unorthodox roster of grapes, three Spanish varietals—Albariño, Tempranillo, and Graciano—and four French—Petit Verdot, Tannat, Fer Servadou, and Petit Manseng—to supplement her lead red and lead white.

The Chardonnays made for a good and promising start, and she was ecstatic to see them in the bottle and on the shelves. Her wines! Her bottles! But the creation of the product was ultimately less important to her than the exposure to the process, the unofficial short course Kinne had provided in the rudiments of winemaking, whose innumerable details she absorbed the way an anemic absorbs a transfusion of blood.

The Norton was her baby. It was personal. If she was going to commit to growing it, she was going to learn everything she could about it, and that meant every single aspect of the process—how to plant it, how to trellis the vines, what the grapes needed to thrive, how long to leave the grapes on the vines, how much time the juice needed in the cellar, how to make the adjustments needed to balance the competing elements in the wine.

She had absorbed enough, she thought, from working with and watching Kinne that she decided to give winemaking a go on her own. By 1998, she was ensconced at her estate, and by 1999, she was not only running her own winery but also making her own wines.

In retrospect, she could accuse herself of indulging in hasty, impetuous thinking, of forcing things. She was so eager to master all the stages of the winemaking process, so eager to make herself expert, that she was racing through the stages of her own development as a winemaker. There was much she still needed to know, particularly about the Norton, and so the next year she brought in "the only white Trinidadian lesbian winemaker in the world" to work with her.

The Norton was a handful. Stubborn, independent, with a mind of its own. Oh, it was a marvel in the vineyard once it got going, requiring far less pesticide and fungicide than other grapes, particularly *vinifera* grapes like Chardonnay. In any given season, the Chardonnay grapes needed as many as fifteen sprayings; the Norton, just three. The problem was getting it going. As the doctor himself and later Prince and Husmann had all pointed out, it's an exceedingly difficult grape to propagate and has an un-usually high mortality rate. On the other hand, if it survives its infancy and is then left too much on its own, it can become unruly and unmanageable, taking over the vineyard.

Still, the bigger challenge—the bigger mystery—was in the cellar.

The Norton was not like other grapes. It did not do what it was sup-posed to, not even what its own chemistry seemed to tell it to.

A high-acid wine with a high pH doesn't compute, chemically speak-ing. But the Norton's acidity is offset by an alkaline component. In order to bring the pH down, forced to add tartaric acid to the juice as it ferments in the barrel. The result of this tinkering is, paradoxically, a liquid that is far more acidic to the palate than what they'd started with. To eliminate some of that excess acid, they have to tinker again, subjecting the liquid to a pro-cess called cold stabilization—freezing it at 24–26 degrees Fahrenheit—to correct the pH.

It was a 180 from just about every other kind of grape she'd ever heard about: a dream, once it got going, in the vineyard, a bitch in the cellar.

Wasn't that rich? A total inversion of the known! A complete flipping of the script!

It was precisely this need for fixing and tinkering, this need for constant attention, that was such a turnoff for most winemakers and winery owners. All that work for a wine that nobody had ever heard of and that was never going to rival a Cabernet Sauvignon or a Pinot Noir in the consumer's af-fection?

The fact that it wasn't easy to love, that it was different and quirky, that it had a mind of its own—these things spoke to her. And the fact that it didn't speak to everybody—that spoke to her, too.

SHE BOTTLED her first Norton, the Norton Locksley Reserve, in 2000. The name paid homage to the name of her property, the former Locksley estate, but the reference to Robin of Locksley, more commonly known as Robin Hood, could not be ignored. If Chrysalis was an allusion to her transformation, then Locksley could be read as a statement of intent when it came to making the Norton. The benevolent outlaw. The crowd-pleasing rebel.

The Locksley Reserve was a premium wine, to be set aside for cellaring and aging, and its list price, $35, reflected this intention. It would take a decade or two before she knew whether she had succeeded and to what extent. The wines of her beloved Bordeaux needed at least that long to fully reveal their complexity and charm.

It was not possible to operate a successful winery by relying on inter-mittent sales of premium wines, and so she was also putting out a "junior Locksley," her Estate Bottled Norton, which listed for $16. Its returns were more immediate, as she discovered when she tasted her first vintage, the 2001. If it lacked the finesse she was seeking from the Locksley Reserve, the soft suppleness that aging would bring, it exploded in the mouth with a burst of ripe, concentrated fruit. It was fresh and alive. A good and inter-esting table wine, she thought, and one that would be helped only by pair-ing it with the right kinds of foods, with venison, with duck. This is the way Europeans have always looked at their table wines—as companions, not trophies, not ends in themselves.

Another vision took shape in her mind. Not only was she going to grow the Norton, but she was going to grow a lot of the Norton. In fact, she was going to grow the largest planting of the Norton anywhere in the world.

BY HER OWN high standards, this was a comparatively modest vision, paling beside her more recent, more radical reinventions. In the world of Virginia wine, however, it appeared so odd and so risky as to cause indus-try observers to speculate that she had overreached in putting nearly all her chips down on one grape. One day, she would learn what they had learned. The Norton, interesting though it might be, was not a workhorse; you couldn't make money off of it. No less a champion of the grape than Dennis Horton had recently begun to doubt its potential in the marketplace. He was selling thirty thousand cases of wine annually, and Norton accounted for only a tenth of that total. It was an interesting grape, a good grape, an important grape. But how much Norton, Horton wondered now, could you grow and produce and still be considered a viable commercial winery?

From the eight acres of Norton that Horton had started with at Orange, he had expanded to twelve. A fifty percent expansion.

Jenni was thinking forty-plus acres.

If Horton, determined to shake up the wine establishment in Virginia and widely considered a rebel, had not been so daring as to make the Norton the centerpiece of his estate, then what did that make this brash upstart, who had seen his twelve and was going to raise the stakes by more than three times? A rebel's rebel? A holy fool?

As curious as her plan appeared in context, it appeared even more curious out of context. There was simply no precedent for what she'd envisioned. The grape was being grown now in nearly two dozen states, including Missouri, Arkansas, Ohio, Illinois, Iowa, Oklahoma, Kansas, Louisiana, Tennessee, Florida, and Pennsylvania. In nearly every circumstance, however, it was limited to a handful of acres, one among several different red wine grapes, as though winemakers were unwilling to commit more time and attention and resources to it. The Norton was a hot little number, a dalliance, not something that was likely to be monetarily rewarding over the long haul.

To grow and yet not invest, to try and yet not risk failing—it bespoke, she thought, a stinting vision, a pinched ambition. It was not going at things with gusto. It was proceeding with fear.

She had not spent her life following anybody else, and having reinvented herself not once, but twice, she was not about to do so now. The more other people talked about something being the truth, the path, the way, the less she believed it. Maybe they knew something she didn't. It was possible. But it was just as possible, she thought, that she knew something they didn't.

If the Norton had ageability, as Horton had demonstrated to her, why not invest in it long term? Why not stake her entire reputation on it?

HER CONFIRMATION came in 2003, an unlikely year to have come to a confirmation about anything positive about wine in Virginia, unless it was to confirm that the business of making wine is a fool's errand, its practitioners captives to chance and caprice.

That was the year she had chosen to debut the wine that was to be her flagship: the Barrel Select, her in-between Norton—less premium than the Norton Locksley Reserve, more refined than the Estate Bottled Norton. The year 2003 stands as one of the worst years ever for wine in the state, with precipitation eclipsing the previous recorded high by six inches. Excessive rain is among the greatest nightmares for winemakers, because there is so little that can be done later to correct or subdue its damage. Heavy, continuous rain dilutes the fruit on the vine, resulting in thin, watery wines. The effect is not unlike that of pouring gallons upon gallons of water into a wine barrel.

What to do? Jenni gambled, deciding not to pick her Norton grapes until the last possible moment, in this way allowing the sun more time to dry them out and concentrate their juices. She waited until November 5, more than a month past the usual harvest day. This was not the eleventh hour. It was a few seconds short of midnight.

At a Wines of the World competition at the Los Angeles County Fair in 2005, the 2003 Norton Barrel Select from Chrysalis won a Gold Medal. It was not the Weltausstellung, but it was *something*, it was a start. A victory—a *validation*. Jenni had judged shrewdly in opting to pick the grapes late—a testament to her belief that winemaking required art as well as science, required intuition, love, patience, attention. But if not for the Norton's resilience, would she have looked so shrewd? How many grapes, after all, would have emerged from such a long and soggy season to not only produce decent fruit, but award-winning wine, too?

What a fucking grape! she thought, and added eleven more acres of the Norton that year.

There was something about this all-or-nothing zeal of hers that was oddly resonant with the grape's boom-or-bust fortunes, something Nortonian. It was Nortonian to flout the experts and make more Norton. Nortonian to confront long, impossible odds. Nortonian to stand alone.

22

~~~~~~~~~~

I'M ON THE HUNT one afternoon for a bottle of Tylenol for my teething seven-month-old son, roaming the back aisles of my neighborhood grocery store, when the voice on the other end of the phone wants to know if I'm up for taking on a project, a special project.

"I was thinking that maybe you can help me get my hands on the Norton portrait."

My cell phone is wedged between my shoulder and my ear, which makes me cranky, and my son's gums are killing him, which makes him cranky, and so my question comes out much louder than I'd intended: "Where is it?"

A pharmacist who is scrutinizing the top shelf through a pair of thick spectacles turns around wearily: yet another rude and testy customer demanding something of him. I wave him off and mouth an apology.

"It's at the Virginia Museum of Fine Arts, in Richmond," Jenni says, "but it's in a back room there, just gathering dust probably. Just gathering cobwebs. Out of sight, out of mind." Amid the chaos, my initial reaction is to wonder if I'm being enlisted in some covert operation to steal the picture of the doctor.

For the next ten minutes, as I pay for the Tylenol and push the stroller through the parking lot and strap my son into his car seat, I listen to Jenni, her voice strident through my crummy cell phone, as she gives full vent to her rage: about bureaucracy, about abiding by arbitrary rules, about the importance of history and knowing and honoring our past.

And that's when it occurs to me: I am no longer a student in Jenni's tutorial. I have graduated to become a confidant, a sounding board, a sympathetic ear, a defender, a conspirator, a dependent.

We talk at least once a week. We e-mail. We go to dinner. We share our Norton bond.

"So, wait," I ask, cutting her off as I put my cell on speakerphone, "what are you trying to do, exactly? You want to buy the painting of Daniel Norton?"

Her ongoing harangue is about the worst possible thing for my son to be hearing at this moment, the very opposite of soothing, but for some reason I can't locate my earbuds. He's crying again. The car has become a surround sound of complaint.

"Well, yeah, that'd be great, but no, just to make a copy of the thing. That's all I'm asking. Shoot, if I could buy it, that would solve everything."

"But why?"

"Why? Why not? Why does anyone buy anything?"

The cry from my son in the back turns into a wail, and Jenni says, "Oh, boy, I remember those days. Hey there, little guy. How's your daddy treatin' you?"

"Apparently, not so hot."

"Oh, I don't believe that. I don't believe that at all. You getting any sleep at all? The early part's rough."

"An hour or two."

"Not bad," she says, "not bad."

I'm just about to recount the story of how our baby, uncannily, woke us up every hour, on the hour, the night before, but I've misjudged in thinking we've moved on to another subject. The cessation of rhetorical fire is temporary.

"So, anyway: the portrait. You know, it's really pretty simple when it comes right down to it. I just want the image. That's all. Just a good photographic reproduction. A picture! A freakin' picture. Not even the painting itself. A picture! And all I keep hearing is: 'Well, I'm sorry, Ms. McCloud, we don't have ownership of the painting in question.'"

The harangue does not end when, pulling up to my house, I plead fatherhood duties and end the call. She promises to forward a copy of a letter she'd banged out a while ago to her state delegate.

The next day, I click on and read the "nastygram":

> . . . Bob, you've probably gathered by now that I'm not very "political," that I can be painfully direct, and generally just come right out and speak my mind, expletives and all. Well, this is no exception.
>
> Frankly, I don't have the time, or patience, to be playing patty-cake, dancing around with, or stroking a bunch of self-aggrandized bureaucrats at the Virginia Museum of Fine Art. Actually, it pisses me off that I'm out here bustin' my butt growing grapes in this state, spending millions of bucks, promoting Norton and Virginia like a tireless evangelist, and then getting stonewalled on something as simple as letting me take a picture of a portrait to help out in this very worthwhile endeavor. Shit, these folks ought to be saying, "Hey, thanks, Ms. McCloud, this is all very exciting. We'd be happy to help promote Norton and Virginia. When would your photographer like to come? We'll have it all set up." Instead, this response smacks of the same kind of elitist, "how dare you bother us," pompous, mumbo-jumbo crap I've gotten from these jerks for 3 years now.
>
> Jeeze, did you know that your own counterparts in Missouri just passed a resolution naming Norton the state grape of Missouri! And I can't get our own state museum to let me take a picture of the Virginian who created it. What's wrong with this picture!

Bureaucratic obstinacy had not stopped her from chasing her goal, and neither would getting absolutely nowhere with her state delegate. Jenni persisted in her efforts to either make a copy or acquire the portrait out-right, and eventually squeezed from the museum the information that the portrait was on permanent loan from a relation of the family in Williams-burg, many generations removed from the doctor. Last name: Ambler.

She wrote a letter. The response was even more galling than the muse-um's had been. The response? No response.

SHE OFTEN imagined the portrait propped up against a wall in the back room, and her heart plummeted: dusty, unloved, forgotten. Two hundred years, and what had changed? Still the outcast, still on the margins. But those eyes!—dark and flashing—and that stare, brooding and knowing.

She understood something when she first glimpsed the doctor's picture. Something that not even a hundred, a thousand, sips of his wine could tell her.

That something made her want to rescue him, restore him, redeem him. She had already written the doctor into a variety of roles at the estate, a versatile and important star. Watching over the tasting room at Chrysalis, a memorial to the passionate, freethinking man who created this fruit of the vine. . . . staring out from the label of her bottles, connecting the wine to the man, the present to the past. . . . looming over her office, a haunting reminder of the need to work harder, smarter, better on his behalf. . . .

The most important thing was simply to bring him home. Quite clearly, no one else cared enough to give the portrait a proper resting place.

She alone, she understood now, was responsible for his memory. She was the rightful inheritor of his legacy. And as the inheritor, she was de-termined to resuscitate his name, just as he himself had resuscitated Amer-ican wine.

EVENTUALLY Jenni tracked down the name and address of another Am-bler, living out west, and called me: Would I please make her case about the portrait? "You're a writer, Todd, you can put this into words in a way I can't."

I have never been a joiner, have never sought community or formed lasting attachments with other people based simply and solely on our mutual love of some shared interest, but I realize I now must count myself a member of a secret society, a world of extravagant outsiderness, of tilting at windmills, of being utterly and hopelessly occupied with something that most people have never heard of, a genre within a genre within a genre within a genre.

Or is drawing nearer to the obsession the whole point? Is total devotion to a thing the only way to truly understand it? Living within a world, as the only way to function in and make sense of the world itself?

I write the letter.

The response? No response.

"I GET CHILLS, just thinking of him," Jenni says of the doctor one afternoon.

She points to a small, cordoned-off patch near the front of her estate as we rumble past in the Outlook, heading out to a wine tasting. In contrast to the vines that are proliferating in leafy, dense rows nearby, the patch is almost barren.

"Is that a nursery?" I ask.

"Nope," she says proudly. "That's my version of Magnolia Farm."

With the garden map Cliff and Rebecca Ambers unearthed and with Cliff's assistance, she decided to re-create Dr. Norton's experimental garden. Same grapes. Same layout.

"Why?" I ask.

It's a little like asking Sir Edmund Hillary why he climbed Everest. She looks at me with incredulity, that I should be so constrained in my thinking.

"Why?" she says. "Why not?"

After all, she says, what's the risk? The grapes don't grow? She fails? Big deal. That's no risk. And consider the potential reward. New insights into grape cultivation. And who knows? Maybe one of those new insights leads to a breakthrough in understanding the role that chance played in the creation of the grape that now consumed her.

"I don't know, seems pretty obvious to me," she says, gunning the engine. The Outlook hurtles on.

Making Norton—and, after a half dozen years, good Norton, award-winning Norton—was deeply rewarding. Having the largest planting of Norton in the world was deeply rewarding, too. But season by season, year by year, the obsession had intensified to the point that she was not simply producing wine; she was exhuming the dead, bridging the past and the present. Was it so hard to project herself into the antebellum South, a suffering melancholic tending a tiny plot of land as a last resort, relying on the steady cultivation of grapes as a means of salvaging a broken heart? Conversely, was it so hard to project the doctor into the twenty-first century, a wild iconoclast making his own way in the world, bucking the system, bucking trends, perhaps even bucking biology? A couple of lonely outsiders, mavericks on the margins, finding purpose and passion in their grape, triumphing where Jefferson and the Jamestown colonists had failed.

She was him, and he was her.

While she waited impatiently for bureaucracy to come to its senses and grant her the portrait to watch over and be watched over by, she would content herself with his garden.

ONE NIGHT I decide to go in search of Jenni's past. Of who Jenni had been, that is, before she had become Jenni.

I have a last name, I have the name of a company in Florida, and I have Google.

It isn't much. Nor does it bring much in return. It is my experience with the Weltausstellung writ small, only in this case, it is not time and neglect that have paved over the details, but Jenni herself. She had not just changed her first name and her last name; she had changed all her documents, as was her right and prerogative as a man who had become a woman and had to start all over. Who she was, was no more. Gone. Wiped clean from the record. A new face, a new body, a new name, a new life. The ultimate in reinvention. Which is to say, the ultimate in American life. Gatsby. Twain. Jesse James. Irving Berlin. The dreamers, the schemers, the obsessives, the think-biggers. The present a holding pattern, a way station from which to escape the haunting past and rush into the great, glittering future.

There is *something*, though.

My eyes widen as the page comes up and I click on the picture to enlarge it, and there it is. There *he* is: Michael Marsh. In a dress shirt and dress slacks and a tie, sitting next to his partner at the company, posing for a portrait in front of the company logo. How can I be sure? The eyes. Searching and kind, full of intelligence and full of mischief—full of fire. I recognize them immediately. They haven't changed, though everything else has. I can't help thinking of Hermann, of the houses I saw, with their foundations of stone, holdovers from the glory years, atop which sat 1960s-era homes of pastel-colored siding. And of the doctor, whose farm had long since been buried somewhere beneath the campus of Virginia Commonwealth University, with only a street sign to keep alive his memory.

I stare at the photo for a long moment, as if I can somehow understand the man Jenni was and the woman Jenni has become, as if these things would be revealed to me simply by staring, but I am no more enlightened when I turn off the computer than when I began.

The mystery is hard and impenetrable. As a mystery should be. Some things are not meant to be solved or known, and we have to learn to dwell in the wilderness of not-knowing, rather than continually force ourselves into the sanctuary of certainty. Wine is like that, too. It is irreducible and mysterious, and part of its appeal, part of its enduring fascination, is its elusiveness, despite all the centuries of testing, despite all the attempts to code and classify and corral it. *Aromas of tar and black cherry and pepper.* What are these words, if not testaments to the very unknowability of wine? You can tell yourself that you smell tar and black cherry and pepper, but that doesn't bring you that much closer to the meaning of a good glass of wine than saying that it's good. We throw words at art, as if words will frame and explain, but art, good art, doesn't need words. Good art eludes words. Good art is wordless and all the more profound because of it.

. . .

NOT LONG AFTER, I am browsing the aisles of Kramerbooks, in Washington, D.C., one of the city's best bookstores, when I spot, propped up by the register in the back room as if it were the kind of book you gave as a gift, a slender paperback titled *Conundrum*.

Its cover is adorned not with an image but with words: "I was three or perhaps four years old when I realized that I had been born into the wrong body, and should really be a girl. I remember the moment well, and it is the earliest memory of my life."

I buy the memoir, by the British author Jan Morris, and rush home to read it. It is an exceedingly beautiful book, an honest and enthralling piece of writing about identity and change, and I finish it in a single sitting, in one night.

But first I flip through the pages, and there, on the very first page I stop at, as if my discovery of this book had not been an accident but somehow fated, I read: "The world would take me or leave me, and one day, I was sure now, I would emerge from this bizarre chrysalis if not a butterfly, at least a presentable moth."

Reading these words, it is as if something has become dislodged in my memory, and I go back to the web page I'd stumbled upon several days earlier to confirm my suspicions. There is Marsh, wearing a tie, a dark tie with butterflies. Set against that dark, depthless background, they appear to float, free and light and fluttering.

It feels like trespassing, to have stumbled upon this image, but it is exhilarating, too, and my heart beats wildly in my chest. To be privileged with this glimpse into the inner life of another being, of a soul suspended between worlds, in the midst of one life and on the cusp of creating another, in the process of becoming. . . . It is too intimate, too profound, to keep looking, even more than it would have been to discover someone's diary and keep reading. I turn off the computer, chastened. But the memory of the butterfly tie does not go away. It remains with me for many months after, a lingering afterimage.

23

THE E-MAIL ARRIVES in my in-box at the end of a long, tiring week, of a long, tiring month, and near the end of a long, tiring year. My father has been in and out of several hospitals, and his problems seem to be multiplying, and the roster of doctors I have committed to speed dial on my mobile phone is as long as a grocery list. Little things with my father become big things, and as they do, my life becomes more and more about his life, and when things are most desperate and I feel that I have become paralyzed by fear, I compound problems by brooding on them. And then I click on the e-mail from Jenni: "Wanna roadtrip it this Monday?"

The insouciance of this offer is so incongruent with my state of mind that I don't bother to read further, dismissing it as an activity for another time, another place, an escapist fantasy incommensurate with the gravity of things I am now forced to contemplate. But as the day wears on, I find myself brooding, now, on the possibility of breaking away, if only for a little while—of getting some distance on my cares and worries. By the end of the afternoon, the idea, like some squatter, has taken up residence in my imagination and refused to leave.

I go back and read the e-mail. Jenni has been invited to give a toast at the Virginia state capitol, in Richmond, on the occasion of the twentieth anniversary of Virginia Wine Month. In the hours preceding the big event, winemakers, winery owners, and wine writers will gather in a room at the

Virginia Wine Board Office for a "heritage tasting" of Virginia wines going back twenty years, including Chrysalis's 2000 Locksley Reserve Norton, the first Norton she'd ever made.

What the hell, I think, after hours and hours of weighing the pros and cons, and e-mail her that I'm in.

ON THE MORNING of the big day, I arrive late at the compound at Chrysalis, and my lateness, which Jenni won't verbally blast me for, but which her face nonverbally does, only adds to her mounting tension.

She moves sweaty-faced through the great house in her cream skirt and print blouse like a mother with three toddlers and neither enough arms nor time to spare who is also running late for work. I stand watching her, feeling guilty for not helping, feeling, in truth, a little like one of those oblivious TV sitcom husbands. Jenni, sizing up the inequity, quickly puts me to work retrieving bottles of Albariño and Norton to box and take out to the Outlook.

The gate's open. I heft the box of wine up onto the lip of the trunk, propping it there with my hand while looking over the rest of the cargo that's already been packed and pondering a quick rearrangement of the space. The dogs are hovering at my legs, yapping, demanding my attention. Jenni, coming up on my shoulder, gives the boxes a shove, tosses a bag in there too, and, in search of catharsis, slams the gate shut with such force that the dogs scamper away as if repelled by a violent thunderclap. The sound echoes over the valley.

"Let's roll."

She hops up into the driver's seat and blasts the A/C. The fact she has to deliver a toast at the capitol rotunda, in front of the governor and with all her winemaking colleagues in attendance—a speech she has written and practiced many times already, but which she remains uneasy about, like a paranoid student who lives in fear that every memorized fact will flee her brain at precisely the most inopportune moment—is not the only source of her anxiety.

The previous week, while I had been agonizing over my father, she had been monitoring the future of Wall Street. Citibank had filed for Chapter

11 bankruptcy protection, and, Jenga-like, the financial system, with all its intricate, interlocking blocks, tottered toward collapse, as if everything, every last corporation or concern, had been dependent on the integrity and stability of that one block. On Friday, waiting for my reply to her invitation, she'd e-mailed me: "I've got my eyes glued to my trading screen, trying to recover some lost dough."

There is, too, the recent arrival of fall, heralded by a new clarity in the light, a new sharpness, and a turning of the leaves on some of the trees, which give off flashes of orange and red as we barrel down the highway, leaving northern Virginia behind. I marvel aloud at the gorgeousness of the landscape.

"Fall is melancholic for me," Jenni says. "It's the end. I like beginning. I like spring. It's creation and nature coming alive."

In the Outlook, she rehearses her toast for me, her audience of one, as she drives. She glances down at a copy of the speech on her lap every few words—exactly the sort of multitasking the authorities have begun to crack down upon, and I find myself instinctively reaching for something to hold on to. The only time she stops doing double duty is to implore her fellow drivers to pick up the pace. "Come on, guys. Put the fuckin' pedal down. Jesus." Sweat rains down the sides of her flushed face.

When we'd hopped into the Outlook, Jenni had handed me a printout listing the wineries and the vintages they would be pouring at the "heritage tasting," and as she gives her speech for the second time, I scan the printout.

"What do you think?" she asks, having concluded her speech with a flourish.

"Good job," I say.

She beams as if she's just been awarded a gold star.

Then I recite the names of the wines on the list, and the beam is gone. It's as if it had never been there to begin with. Jenni frowns, the frown of deep and abiding frustration: the frown of a parent who, no matter what she does, no matter how hard she tries, cannot persuade her obstinate children to adopt her values.

"Yours," I say to Jenni, "is the only Norton on here."

The face she makes now is similar to the one she made at her computer the previous Friday, I imagine, as she watched her stocks plummet. The features collapse all at once. Everything goes slack. "Yeah, well."

"How can that be?" I wonder.

"How can that be?" she asks, her voice rising. "That can be, because too many of the people who are making wine in this state are afraid. That's how that can be."

In some people, you do not have to poke all that hard or all that long at the concealing membrane to find a welter of pain and hurt and insecurity. Those with the deepest vulnerabilities are those for whom the concealing membrane is a necessary mask, who understand that the real person exists many fathoms beneath the level of what can be seen and that society itself is a necessary mask too, an arrangement that often obscures what is most vital and most alive.

INSIDE THE marketing office of the Virginia Wine Board, a suite of offices inside Old City Hall on East Broad Street, we find a couple dozen wine industry people milling about the conference room, nibbling chastely on cheese and crackers and waiting for the tasting to start.

The main event won't take place until later that night, the big, industry-wide gala to be held inside the rotunda. The afternoon tasting is a private affair, an intimate gathering for winemakers and a few invited journalists, and it comes at a time of unprecedented optimism in the Virginia wine industry, with increasing attention being paid to the wines by national and international media. If the gala tonight is meant to encourage industry insiders to look ahead, this smaller tasting has been convened as an opportunity for winery owners and winemakers to look back, to survey past efforts and gauge progress.

As Jenni goes to greet her colleagues in the business, I stroll about the room. Munching Brie and eavesdropping on conversations, I think back to my first dreary tastes of Virginia wine more than a decade ago, how I had found the Chardonnays and Cabernet Sauvignons to be overpriced swill and how I had all but written off the state's emerging wine country, deciding it to be a beautiful weekend getaway, so long as you didn't expect to sip anything decent. I was not alone.

In 1999, a frustrated Dennis Horton sent a beseeching letter to a man named Ben Giliberti, at that time one of the wine critics at the *Washington Post*. Horton had tried for years to persuade the critic to devote a column to Virginia wines. To Horton's thinking, Giliberti traveled far and wide to sample wines, to France, to Italy, to Spain, and here, right in his own backyard, he was missing out on an important story. As an enticement, Horton offered to send a limo to come and collect Giliberti and take him back home when he was done. That way, he could drink as much of Horton's wines as he pleased.

The letter, its note of desperate grandiosity, caught Giliberti's attention. The critic responded, claiming that his choice of subject matter was a function of his audience. His audience didn't ask about Virginia wines, much less clamor for him to write about them. And there were too many other good wines from all over the world that he simply didn't have the space to tout the local vintages.

Giliberti was being charitable, though he angered Horton all the same. What Giliberti did not say was that, with few exceptions, Virginia wine simply didn't merit the attention of a major publication ten years ago.

Since then, however, winemaking in the state has improved dramatically, so much so that I now find myself prowling the aisles of wine and liquor stores in and around D.C. in search of the best Virginia wines, often preferring them to their West Coast counterparts, particularly since, being low in alcohol and high in acidity (like many European wines, but unlike many West Coast wines), they go so well with food. Not coincidentally, coverage in the media has increased dramatically, too. In that time, the number of wineries in the state has also more than doubled. Insiders project a figure of 460 wineries by 2028.

But if the industry is no longer lacking in either quality or quantity, the future is not a smooth open road stretching toward infinity. The fact remains that only 5 percent of the wines sold in Virginia are produced in Virginia. Its wines remain obscure even to its own residents.

And that troubling fact is actually less significant than another, more troubling fact, a fact that no one in the room, smiling brightly and focused on the positive, on the desire for commonality and unity, is likely to bring up, a fact that is, in fact, bound up in the other fact: the industry is at war with itself. It is a war over mission, a war of ideals and principles, a war of *terroir*.

Recent technological advances have made it possible for vintners in Virginia to realize, finally, the great dream of the Jamestown colonists and all those who came along after and took up the cause, the dream that sustained and ultimately eluded Jefferson and all of his spiritual descendants, too: the dream of making *vinifera* wine. It is possible now for winemakers to grow acres of *vinifera* grapes in Virginia without having to worry that they will succumb as a matter of course to disease and mildew and rot. It is possible now to make decent, sometimes good and occasionally very good, Chardonnays, Merlots, and Cabernet Sauvignons in the state.

Possible; but desirable?

Some wineries seem to think so. Rebecca Ambers put it succinctly to me when Jenni and I spent the day with her and her husband, Cliff, at their small, experimental vineyard, Chateau Z: "If you want to make money from wine, you make *vinifera*."

Kluge Vineyards in Charlottesville, Virginia, a firm bankrolled by the wealthy socialite Patricia Kluge that features a number of *vinifera* wines, created a stir a couple of years ago when it engaged the services of Michel Rolland, an international wine consultant as renowned as he is reviled. Rolland was the antihero of sommelier-turned-director Jonathan Nossiter's controversial wine documentary, *Mondovino*, tooling around in his chauffeur-driven Mercedes, a cell phone pasted to his ear, imploring his French clients to "micro-oxygenate" their wines—a process of introducing small bubbles to mute the effect of tannins, which can be harsh, and accelerate the aging process. If the goal was to be able to compete in the chaotic global marketplace, then distinctiveness and *terroir* did not much matter; what mattered was smoothness and drinkability.

The arrival of Rolland in the Old Dominion was, without a doubt, a validation of progress, proof that the state was coming up in the world of wine, but to Dennis Horton and Jenni and other *terroir*-ists, who are committed to emphasizing those varietals that thrive in the soil and climate of Virginia, and who fervently believe that Virginia wines ought to taste like Virginia—not France, Spain, California, Oregon, or Washington—it was also evidence that some winemakers were willing to sacrifice regional character in order to produce good, drinkable, marketable wines.

The *terroir*-ists are not categorically opposed to *vinifera*. Some *vinifera* grapes, like Viognier, Cabernet Franc, and Petit Verdot, are an excellent match for the microclimate of the state. All three seem to flourish in the field and are capable of producing good and sometimes elegant wines.

But how, they ask, is Virginia supposed to distinguish itself from California, Oregon, Washington, and Europe, how is it to find its niche in a confusing and highly competitive market, if it produces so many of the same wines, only not nearly as well and not nearly as cheaply?

The problem is that so many of these alternative varietals are not widely known properties. Most wine drinkers have never heard of them, making it difficult to sell a Viognier outside a controlled setting like a tasting room, where a winery can explain and contextualize it.

In a sense, then, the *terroir*-ists are not in a fight with those in the *vinifera*-or-bust camp, though they tend to regard the latter with the kind of contempt that only true believers can muster. They are in a fight with a distant enemy; they are in a fight with California. California's influence cannot be calculated simply by how much product it generates and how many awards its estates garner, or how many tourists traipse through lush, sun-dappled Napa Valley every year. California is a style, an identity, a brand. To make wine in America that consumers will want to buy is to make what is familiar and popular: Chardonnay, Cabernet Sauvignon, Merlot. In other words, to make the brand that is synonymous in most Americans' minds with wine.

All wineries are, at bottom, businesses, but not all winery owners are, at bottom, businessmen and businesswomen; the best are men and women who just happen to be in business. If I am sympathetic to the *terroir*-ists, it is not simply because I value the expression of passion over the pursuit of money. It is also because the *terroir*-ists are thinking less of their own individual needs than those of the industry.

What I cannot understand, however, and what I have come to the tasting and gala, in part, to learn, is why even among the *terroir*-ists, even among those who speak with such conviction about character in the glass and the importance of Virginia carving out an identity for itself that is distinct from the West Coast, so few of them are growing the Norton.

I SPOT A MAN in a terrific cream-colored suit that looks to be of Italian vintage or else a scary-good imitation, with its clean, sharply tapered lines, and I figure it's safe to venture a guess: "Luca?"

Luca Paschina, the winemaker at Barboursville Vineyards, nods and extends his hand. I have heard and read much about Luca. A native of Alba, which produces the best Nebbiolo in the world, he is widely reputed to be the greatest winemaker in Virginia, and Barboursville is considered to be among its greatest wineries. Luca is a sincere and self-effacing man, particularly for someone who is so admired, with a distracted, writerly air that can seem like aloofness but which betrays his passionate engagement with his craft. Though he is by far the best-dressed man in the room, he looks uncomfortable, like someone who is not accustomed to mingling in a suit, who lives to be in the field in rolled-up shirtsleeves and jeans, getting dirty, doing real work.

Barboursville was among the first of the post-Prohibition wineries in the state, opening in 1976 on a property graced with the ruins of a house Thomas Jefferson had designed, in Orange County, north of Charlottesville. It established itself quickly and soon won attention for the quality of its Cabernet Franc, Petit Verdot, and Merlot, all produced under the direction of Paschina, who approaches his work with an artisan's care and attention and carries with him an Old World notion that wine is a way of transmitting tradition and values—that it is not an emblem of the good life so much as an embodiment of life itself.

Barboursville doesn't make a Norton, and I ask Paschina why. He smiles, like a man who is cornered and has to resort to charm to connive a way out.

"Is a good wine," he says.

"It is." I smile back. "So why don't you grow the grape?"

"You should talk to Jenni," he says, and cranes his neck to find her among the crowd. "Jenni is the big Norton fan."

"Why should she be the only one?"

"She isn't."

"She's the only one here."

"But there are others, in the state. You have people growing Norton, now."

"But not you."

"For us, no. It doesn't fit into what we like to do at Barboursville. But as I said—is a good wine." It's as if I've been dismissed from his office and told I can expect a good recommendation from him in the future.

A WINE WRITER and consultant named Richard Leahy presides over the tasting and invites us to take notes as we work our way from lighter-bodied wines to rounder, more robust wines, in hopes of sharing our impressions with one another of their ageability.

Leahy is a slight, sandy-haired man with a nervous manner and a ruddy face whose intensity, when he is lost in thought or caught unawares, suggests an active inner life. He identifies himself as an unabashed *terroir*-ist and writes a blog, *Wine Report*, that chronicles Virginia's efforts to build a sustainable commercial wine industry. Leahy is also an unabashed partisan, as only someone can be who was born and raised in Virginia, who went to high school and college and graduate school in the state, and who watched up close as a culture was created before his eyes—although his sense of professionalism won't permit him to indulge in any boosterism on the national stage.

A little more than a year earlier, in 2007, Leahy had led a contingent of Virginia wine representatives who had traveled to London to mark the four hundredth anniversary of the landing at Jamestown. What they were also marking, though less obviously, was the fortieth anniversary of the re-emergence of the wine industry in Virginia.

France is generally reckoned to be the center of winemaking, but London today is the center of the wine trade, and many of the most respected voices in wine writing make their homes there. The contingent did not travel empty-handed. Sixty-four Virginia wines, chosen during a blind judging hosted by Dr. Zoecklein, also made the overseas journey. Andrew Jefford, one of the world's foremost authorities on wine, described the contingent's agenda in his column for the *Financial Times* of London: "It wasn't a sales trip; growers just wanted to see what British palates would make of them."

Jefford, along with two other experts—Hugh Johnson, author of the annual encyclopedia of wine, and Steven Spurrier, who orchestrated the now-legendary Judgment of Paris tasting of 1976—were invited to pass judgments on the wines.

On his blog, Leahy emphasizes the few positives of Jefford's tough-minded column. "Wines to Make a Founding Father Proud," ran the headline in the *Financial Times* several months later, but the prose was considerably less enthusiastic. Struck by the "petite dimensions" of the Virginia wines, particularly when compared with those from California, the "biggest-boned wines in the world," Jefford found their quality to be spotty at best.

And what were the first three wines Jefford mentioned in his review? Chardonnay, which "leads plantings," Cabernet Sauvignon, and Merlot. "The patchy quality of all three in the tasting suggested that consumer familiarity takes precedence over site aptitude," Jefford wrote, an opinion that echoes the most vociferous arguments put forth by the *terroir*-ists.

He also made mention of Viognier, Cabernet Franc, Petit Manseng, and Petit Verdot without remarking upon their worth, except to note that Hugh Johnson found the Petit Verdots to be "more than promising" and took a bottle of one of them home to drink with dinner.

The Norton? No mention at all.

Virginians had not expected their wines to cause a stir in London, much less for them to be embraced as the next new thing. It was enough, officials reasoned, to make the introduction, to provide the wines with some meaningful face time with the biggest names in the world of wine. Jefford was prickly and difficult to please, but he had not spoken for everyone. There were others in the press who were more intrigued. One, in particular, was quite moved by the Norton.

In 2004, the philosopher Roger Scruton, who writes an engaging column on wine for the *New Statesman,* Britain's premier current affairs magazine, gushed over a bottle of Horton Norton:

> Its inky contents stormed from the bottle like a cloud of hornets,
> clinging to nose, lips and palate and stinging us with intense
> flavours of cobnut, cranberry and molasses. . . . We recognised
> the authentic taste of Old Virginny—the rich red soil, the humid
> air, the insect-laden breezes, all squeezed into this deep black
> bottled-up grape, and then released in ecstatic clouds across the
> table.

Anyone who could feel and write like *that* was likely to gravitate to a wine like the Norton and find in its earthy wildness an objective correlative for his passionate inner landscape. Scruton, in other words, was the exception to the rule.

Two months after the London tasting, back on the home front, *Travel + Leisure* chose Virginia as one of five up-and-coming wine regions in the world—the only region in North America to be accorded the honor—and Virginia's moment seemed to have arrived. Again. The magazine's wine editor, Bruce Schoenfeld, singled out a Nebbiolo and Cabernet Franc from Barboursville Vineyards, a Chardonnay from Linden Vineyards, and a Meritage from Breaux Vineyards. The list of recommendations, extremely brief for a piece that was written in recognition of the work of an entire region, was as noteworthy for what it omitted as for what it included. There was no mention of Viognier or Norton.

As the state's reputation as a wine producer seemed to be on the rise, the grape that had established the wine industry there in the nineteenth century and helped to relaunch it in the late twentieth century was in danger of sliding into irrelevance in the twenty-first century, a curious footnote of history.

THE AFTERNOON tasting is a casual affair, with attendees chitchatting between sips, and so, after I've tried several of the wines, I approach Leahy and ask him if he believes the Norton to be a part of the future of Virginia wines he believes in so fervently.

"Absolutely."

"Then why," I ask, "aren't more winemakers making the wine?"

"That's a great question. I'd like to see more wineries working with it. I think it's a great grape, and I think it makes a great wine, with great potential for maturing and aging. I think what happens is, it's not an easy grape to deal with in the cellar. In the field, yes. But in the cellar, you've got the pH problems, and that's a lot for a winemaker to deal with. I think you really have to know what you're doing in there. And then there's the fact that not a whole lot of people have heard of it, compared with something like a Merlot or a Cabernet Sauvignon, so it's a tough sell."

"But isn't that getting into a kind of chicken-and-egg thing? It won't sell, so we won't make it. How do you know if you don't even try?"

"Agreed."

"And if you won't try it here, where it originates, where are you going to try?"

"Right."

At which point Leahy breaks into a nervous grin and speaks what he clearly believes to be the unspeakable—but softly, since Jenni is in earshot behind us, enmeshed in a conversation with Paschina, and he well knows just how passionate she is about the grape. It is as if to speak disparagingly about the Norton is to disparage Jenni herself.

The Norton is divisive, he says. There are some who like it, a few who love it, and many more who loathe it. "It's really a kind of love-hate thing."

Love-hate suggests that the violently opposing feelings are held to be in roughly equal proportion. However, I talked to many people in Richmond about the Norton, over many, many months, and it was hard to find more than a handful who were willing to declare themselves in the love-it camp. At the mere mention of the name, most would allow their mouths to curl in a little smirk of a smile, the way you would for the lovable class clown or the benign bad boy. It seemed to be regarded as an interesting cause, a great story. Something to wonder about and hope the best for, but not to plant in the vineyard. And not to drink.

ORGANIZERS had hoped that the "heritage tasting" would demonstrate the potential for aging of Virginia's oldest labels and best wines, ageability being the definition for serious wine lovers of greatness in a wine. On that score, the tasting is a failure, and not by a little. Some of the wines are too old and taste sour or raisiny—*cooked* is the term winemakers use. I sample most of the thirteen on hand, but there are only a few I enjoy and would gladly return to. Even so, the tasting does show how much progress has occurred in the past decade—how far Virginia has evolved in such a short time. New technology and new insights that have resulted from that technology have dramatically raised the quality, and I am struck by the enormous improvement over what I have been tasting in the past couple of years. Nevertheless, some of the wines I simply can't get down.

One of the few wines that shows well is Jenni's Norton Locksley Reserve, but oddly, it hardly tastes as though it's been aged. I share my observation with her and with Leahy.

"Yep, yep," Jenni says, "that's the fruit. That big, ripe Norton fruit."

Leahy nods, impressed.

Paschina turns from a separate conversation, hearing her voice, and gives an indulgent smile: *Ah, Jenni. Jenni, being Jenni.*

A couple of other winemakers and winery owners, listening to her gush at great length and with no obvious interest in moderating her remarks or the tone of her voice, just stare. It's like watching a roomful of concerned citizens at a town hall meeting being made uncomfortable by the loudest, most personally invested activist, the one whose passion dwarfs their own and exposes their engagement as less-than.

"This is what I'm talking about," Jenni says. "You take that wine, and you give it six, seven more years, and what are you gonna have? You're gonna have something very long, very Bordeaux-y."

"I agree," says Leahy.

"And that's why I believe in the Norton. Because of that potential right there—that potential to age in the bottle and soften and mature."

"Yep."

"I mean, you can drink it after a couple of years, and I think it's great, I like the fruit-forwardness, but all those people who go on and on about how they don't like Norton, and it's too this or it's too that, and blah blah blah—I mean, it's supposed to have some bottle age. You don't drink a Château Latour after a couple of years; it's too young—it'll rip your head off."

"I'm with you," Leahy says, as if to mollify her, as if to reassure her that she is not shrieking alone in the wilderness.

"I'm with you too," I say.

But Jenni is not fighting with us; she is fighting other battles. "No matter what I do," she says, "I can't make a Cabernet Sauvignon as good as the ones they make in France, in California, in Chile, in South Africa. I *can* make a Norton, and the best damn Norton in the world, too."

She cannot be impersonal about something so utterly, unmistakably personal. It is not just a grape, not just a wine, not just what she markets and sells and speaks out on behalf of. It is an extension of who and what she is.

THE ·TASTING, the emotions it has stirred up, and the anxiety over having to get up in front of a couple hundred people and toast the industry have gotten to Jenni, shaken her loose from her usual projection of cool, fierce competence, and by late afternoon she looks and sounds like someone who not only has spent the past couple of hours drinking wine but like someone who could use a drink—the stiffer, the better.

But rather than pop into a nearby bar, because there is no nearby bar, we walk from the tasting to the rotunda, where the gala will be held and where Jenni will deliver her speech, and from there we go downstairs to a sandwich shop and order a quick lunch. We're expected to be at the event in a little over an hour.

A TV looms on the wall above us, and as we take our food back to our table, CNN has just returned from commercials, and Jenni extends a halting hand, tilting her head up to the TV as if it were a papal figure and she were about to receive a blessing. If only. The crawl announces that the expected bailout of financial institutions has been delayed until the following week. "Oh, shit."

"What's wrong?"

"Fuck," is all she says for the longest time, eyes riveted to the screen.

She sighs, looks away, picks up her sandwich, puts it down again. "Remember what I told you I was doing on Friday? I put my money into Fannie Mae, 'cause the stock was so low—thinking they'd have this thing bailed out by now. And now I'm fucked."

We eat our sandwiches in a mood of thwarted hope as members of the Republican minority address the media and explain their decision to vote no.

Between bites of a steak sandwich, Jenni pops chips into her mouth without seeming to taste them, as if the goal were simply to keep her hand occupied and give her a nice change of pace from chewing on steak. But something else is going on. Something fascinating. The obsessive quality of eating chips without appearing to taste them has modulated into a kind of deliberative aggression—the whole thing so subtle, I don't notice the transition, only the transformation. She glances at the TV from time to time, but she doesn't talk about the market. She doesn't talk about anything. Each chew is a form of burrowing, a narrowing of her concentration, a rechanneling of her anger and anxiety about the tasting and the market into a kind of meditative state, a gathering in of her available resources, from which she can summon the necessary strength to give the toast without choking up or cracking.

Hitchcock once said that the duty of the filmmaker is to push his characters to the breaking point, because being forced up against a wall reveals who they really and truly are. I do not doubt that Jenni is made of stern stuff. But it is one thing to say that someone has a mental toughness and another to witness it up close, to see the transformation in process, the ability to turn the tap and change the direction and intensity of the emotion, redirect it from something negative to something positive.

We toss our trash and exit the sandwich shop, up the staircase and out, and I think about all the other turnings of the tap: after her father died, taking the sedan and a single-shot shotgun out into the wilds and bagging quail; starting and folding all the businesses; the change; leaving her family; coming north to make wine. A life of turning the tap.

Which is, Jenni's life seemed to be saying, life itself. The ability to pivot and not fall, to rush after and embrace a new thing, to change, to change.

The trees near the state capitol are being tickled by a light breeze, and the long branches sway gently against the perfect blue sky. It is the kind of picture-perfect day I have always associated with being on a college campus, and as we walk toward the capitol, taking our time, taking in the beauty of the day, my mind, which ought to have been put at ease by the sense of peace and quiet, is paradoxically astir, madly making connections. I am thinking about teaching Rilke, who knew well the importance of change. "You must change your life," he wrote, in one of his most famous letters. "Live the questions now," he also wrote, "and one day you may grow into the answers." I always urged my students to embrace this idea, to make doubt a companion, but now I myself am wrestling with my desire for answers, and this thought leads me from Rilke to my father, a vigorous and intense man who nearly eleven months earlier had a quintuple bypass and is now also in the midst of a battle with cancer. It had seemed to me to happen suddenly; one day he was healthy and strong, and one day he was not. He is struggling to walk, and I am struggling with the fact that he cannot walk, with the fact that without our ever agreeing to it or talking about it, our roles have switched, and probably not temporarily (though I can hope, and do). I am not possessed of the ability to turn the tap, and I know that this leaves me unarmed for the battle that looms, and unlikely to endure such a protracted existential crisis.

By the time we reach the capitol, Jenni is a new woman, fully composed and with the steely nerve returned to her voice as she mixes and mingles near a glowing marble sculpture of George Washington, and if I am honest with myself, I will admit that part of my interest in coming along with her on this trip is to hope for some kind of transference, as if courage, strength, the gathering of reserves necessary to make a big transition, to start all over, can be gained by mere proximity.

THE ROOM has the buzz of opening night in the lobby of a hotly antici-pated play. Free wine and food have a way of bringing out the best in people—or at least, bringing them out.

Wineries have been assigned tables in rooms just off the rotunda where the owners pour small tastes of their wines, and no one among the crowd of sommeliers, winemakers, winery owners, wine writers, politicos, and bankers isn't toting a glass. It feels like a grand cocktail party in the Old South, right down to the almost ritualistic separation of the sexes that oc-curs, so subtly nobody seems to notice, as the sound of polite chatter turns to a white-noise din. The women, in light dresses, congregate in clusters of two or three, engaging in chitchat about the wines and drinking white, while the dull-suited men, almost without fail in their allegiance to red, roam the room on their own or find a fellow to talk to (anything but wine: the economy, the election). What unites the sexes is their common desire to upgrade, which manifests itself in roving eyes that search the room for someone more interesting to talk to.

Ex-governor Gerald Baliles, a trim, watchful-faced man with glasses, a swatch of silvery hair, and a confidence born of having done just this sort of thing a thousand times, strides to the front of the assembly, cracking a joke about drinking that everyone, primed by drink to have a laugh, laughs at, and notes the dramatic changes that have occurred since he declared the first Virginia Wine Month twenty years earlier. Knowing the virtue of brevity, he keeps his remarks short, and cedes the floor to the current gov-ernor, Tim Kaine.

Kaine, in a white shirt and no tie or jacket, presents a stark and frankly shocking contrast to the older, coated Baliles, and I wonder who among the crowd is discomfited by the sight of the governor, at an official event, refusing to wear a coat and a tie. Richmond is a conservative city, and the

South is a conservative region. Traditions don't die hard here; they don't die. I'm wearing a jacket and open-collared shirt with no tie myself, and though I feel like an outsider as I traverse the glossy marble floors among the other, responsibly dressed men, I'm not the governor.

For months, rumors had him being considered as a vice-presidential candidate for Senator Barack Obama, but that matter has been settled with the selection of Senator Joe Biden—and presumably with it the stress of summer. As he addresses the crowd, he looks so tanned and relaxed, he might have just returned home from a couple of weeks at a tropical resort. Kaine reminds everyone that agriculture remains the leading industry in the state and that wine is intrinsically an agricultural product. But not just: It is, he opines, a "particularly human art form," an intimate thing that nourishes and sustains us in body and mind.

There is something Jeffersonian in this, the achingly idealistic notion of wine as a civilizing influence, a social unifier, and it is hard not to feel that Jefferson's spirit animates the room, a place he designed after all, whose soaring sense of space reflects a certain capacious, high-minded vision. And thinking, now, of Jefferson, I am thinking of Daniel Norton, because the two names have become entwined in my imagination, the founding father and the forgotten father, and also because we are only a few miles from Norton Street, the site of Magnolia Farm. And now Jenni, the one who made these introductions for me, who argued for the enduring connection between the two, who came to Virginia to pick up where they had left off, gets up to make her toast, succeeding first a man named J. Rock Stephens, the vice-chairman of the Virginia Wine Board, and then Paschina.

I am not surprised by the content, having heard her remarks twice in the ride down, but I am struck by her forcefulness and her naturalness, which changes things. She makes her predecessors in the industry look like schoolkids plowing dutifully through their book reports. Nor can the governors, though trained to be polished, match her intensity, her charisma. Her face is flushed, her brow is sopping, but there is no tentativeness in her voice as she brings her remarks to a close. It is clear, firm, commanding. She has turned the tap.

The meat of her remarks is to declare the wine industry in Virginia at "the tipping point." The title of Malcolm Gladwell's book has become as ubiquitous as some catchphrase from an old *Saturday Night Live* skit, spouted in the precincts of corporate America with a glee and assurance generally reserved for such enduring workthink clichés as "pushing the envelope," "outside the box," and "paradigm shift." I cringed when I heard her use the expression in the Outlook, yet somehow it doesn't come across as either forced or hackneyed, and the expected fingernails-on-blackboard moment never materializes.

But for me, the toast is less about the things said and more about the things unsaid.

Standing among the eager-faced crowd, all of us huddled around the glowing, imposing figure of Washington, wine glasses at our sides, I think of all those performers who are able to forget about their neuroses, fears, and doubts when they take the stage—or rather, who subsume these fears and doubts in their art, and exploit them to great advantage. Jenni is just this kind of a natural, emphatic when she needs to be, lightly teasing when it's appropriate, and nowhere more so than when she takes a moment to draw the listeners' attention to her cause, to the Norton—"the *real* American grape," she says, pausing, and it's as if the best man has just gotten off an inside joke at the wedding reception.

The crowd erupts in knowing laughter that rolls through the open, vaulted room. She knows that they know just how doggedly evangelical she is in her devotion to a grape and a wine that some of them neither like nor understand. But she also wants them to know that she can poke some fun at her own obsession, right down to the phrase she uses in all her promotional materials.

"You didn't think," she says confidentially, "I would pass up the opportunity to talk about the Norton, didja?" And they laugh again.

To speak of the Norton in an address that celebrates the growth of Virginia wine and projects its future is to align the Norton with that future, to assert that the one is synonymous with the other. How wonderfully shrewd and skillful, I think, to be able to suggest bonhomie while making a plea that affirms her own idiosyncratic path. And to have the crowd laugh and clap for her as if she had not done exactly the thing she just did.

But that's not all she has done. I hadn't picked up on it in the Outlook, riding down, but I do now, the third hearing making plain and clear what had escaped me or reinforcing what had not quite registered.

She has not just equated the Norton with Virginia. She has equated the Norton with America. She has asserted its importance, its centrality, to the American winemaking project. And this, too, sounds a distinctly Jeffersonian note.

On first hearing, "the *real* American grape" might come across as a sort of wine-based version of "Buy American," but it seems to me to have less to do with reflexively waving the banner of patriotism than with asserting and celebrating a hard-won American identity, a spirit of independence, of rugged difference. And no doubt because her words have been pinging around in my brain all day like some newly heard lyric, and no doubt because I have been spending so much time in her company of late, I think I can make out something distinctly Whitmanesque, too, in her meaning if I listen close enough. In art, poetry, filmmaking, theater, music, or comedy, there is room and recognition for a distinctly homegrown character, for the unbridled and unruly, the barbaric yawp, the pleadings of the holy outcast—a tone that is unmistakably American. More than a hundred years ago, American winemaking was in alignment with the thrust and tempo of a culture that was determined to make it *new*. Today? Today California and its West Coast followers, Oregon and Washington, stand atop a flourishing, multibillion-dollar industry that trades on the worth of European grapes. Its wines echo and mimic Europe; the best of them sometimes surpass it. But what are these top-flight wines improving upon? A model established by the Europeans. A new age of regionalism is upon us, a new agrarian age, with new ideas about buying local, supporting the independent, seeking out the heirloom. It is a chance to make it new again. Culture, real culture, is not something that can be imported, and it sure as hell isn't a top-down endeavor. It grows from the ground up, from the soil, rooted, authentic, chthonic.

Jenni lifts her glass now, bids the assembled to join her, and makes the toast official with a rousing, "Cheers!"

·   ·   ·

THE AFTERMATH of a public event is like the preceding two hours condensed into five to ten frantic minutes: the noise that skips past polite chatter and goes straight to room-filling din, the heads that crane for a final glimpse of the rich and famous, the quick good-byes and promises to meet again soon.

Amid the commotion, a couple of photographers want to take a picture, and so it happens that Jenni, the last one to address the group, is flanked by governor Baliles and Kaine. Their arms link in an exuberant show of unity and solidarity.

It is a great moment for Jenni, affirming her place in the firmament of Virginia, and in Virginia wine, and when she breaks free, I knife through the crowd and go up to her.

"How'd I do?" she asks innocently, sweaty-faced and keyed up, like an actress coming down off the high of opening night, and we embrace. I am thinking of the long and difficult journey—coming north from Florida, her radical reconstruction, taking on the Norton and making it her cause—and how much sweeter this night must feel because of all that she has sacrificed and paid to be here tonight.

"You were terrific."

"Really?"

"Really."

"So you think it went over all right?"

"You *killed*," I say, invoking the language of stand-up comedy.

I don't know why I've emphasized the point with such ferocity—she knows she did well; she wouldn't be buzzing like this if she didn't—except that Jenni needs to hear it emphasized.

The crowd has dispersed and gone. We push through the double doors and out.

Richmond at night is deserted, a ghost town, a set piece. Thin-branched trees swish in the cool night air. Government buildings, lit from below, glow like holograms.

"Pretty cool, huh?" Jenni asks as we make our way from the capitol toward the parking lot to hop into the Outlook and begin the long drive back north.

"I mean, to see you up there with the two governors, in the rotunda—this is a very conservative, traditional town."

"Very."

"And a very conservative, very traditional state."

"Very."

"And here you are. . . . You haven't been making wine all that long—what, ten years? You don't come from a winemaking family. You're espousing a grape that still hasn't been widely embraced. You're not a Virginian. You're not a Southerner. . . ."

And now Jenni leans in close in the parking lot and fills in the rest, shouting her joy into the darkness.

24

ON A GRAY, overcast day in Richmond, I rise from my perch in front of an old microfiche projector at the Library of Virginia, where I have spent most of the morning and a good deal of the afternoon poking into the life and letters of Daniel Norton, and walk.

After a certain point, working at anything becomes a matter of diminishing returns, and that's what poring over the correspondence of Norton and his ancestors has become for me. I am seldom alert to this need to stop and get up and walk around, however, or to stop and move on to something else, and when I finally think to peel myself away, many hours later, it's often too late, and I am dead to the present, a zombie among the living.

Exiting the library and emerging onto East Broad Street, my head—to spend six hours in a library is to lose all sense of your body, to become simply a head—feels all at once heavy and thick and weightless and light. A guy on the corner stops me to ask for change, and I am so slow to take in the moment that he gives up on me, frustrated, and keeps walking, muttering something unintelligible about me as he approaches another potential lender. I call after him and dig in my pocket. Catching up to him, I hand him fifty cents, and now he is the one who is slow to take in the moment, the idea that I have pursued a begging man to give him money, and he just stands there staring at me, searching my vacant eyes.

I drift to my car, taking in the hurried coming and going, the ubiquity of cell phones, the screaming ads on the bus that hurtles past, the flashing lights, the constant rush of cars, feeling out of joint with the here and now, its surreal assault of sound and light and motion. What feels real to me, what throbs in my head with the urgency of the actual, is the vanished world of the nineteenth century I have been conjuring up for the past six hours, a world of plantations and tobacco crops, of decorous correspondence and impeccable manners.

I get in and drive. From the library I head northwest through the stately, sleepy city center. I turn right onto North Harrison Street, amid the campus of Virginia Commonwealth University, passing the arena where the basketball team plays its home games, then make a quick left onto West Clay Street, driving slowly now, looking for Norton Street, an unremarkable two-and-a-half block stretch connecting West Marshall and West Leigh streets. The sign is not parallel with the street, but sits cocked at an angle, upward and out of joint. A fitting, if unfortunate, tribute, and I wonder what the actual tribute I am driving out to see will be: fitting and fortunate? fitting and unfortunate? unfitting and fortunate? unfitting and unfortunate?

I continue via Bowe to North Lombardy Street, make a gentle right onto Admiral Street, then follow Brook Road south until it becomes West Charity Street. From there the road signs guide me toward Shockoe Hill Cemetery.

What has compelled me to get in the car and drive, alone, to a cemetery I do not know, except that I am feeling a certain tug, an emotional need I can't fully express that operates at several fathoms below the level of reason. When I was younger, I sometimes would bring a date to one of the old cemeteries in Georgetown after a movie or after dinner. It was not something I was stupid enough to try doing very often, and that was because the result was always the same: no second date. Was I morbid? Death-obsessed? My dates all must have thought so, but I didn't and still don't. Cemeteries, to me, are places to slow down, to wander and think. Sometimes, when life crowds in on me and I find it difficult to breathe, I will hop in the car and drive out to a cemetery—any cemetery, it doesn't matter what kind, or for whom—and stroll the quiet, landscaped grounds, communing with the dead. When I venture back out into the world beyond the gates, I am a different person, a changed person, mind and body recalibrated by this reminder of the nearness, the inevitability, of death.

Driving along the redbrick walls of Shockoe Hill Cemetery, it occurs to me that it's been a while since I have ventured to a cemetery for the purpose of restoring my sense of perspective, for regaining my balance. There is no need to conjure death-in-life when the real thing is so inescapably close at hand.

I buried my father some months earlier. Every day since then, I do not move on with my life, but wake up and feel him die all over again, and die a little with him. I go about my days in a fugue state, functional but dazed, a kind of apparition, as if I now occupied a different dimension of time. Not the present, surely, and not the past, either, although it is the past I feel most keenly now. In some ways, it is not altogether different from what I felt on leaving the library, a sense of lostness, of not fitting with my surroundings, of being out of step with the passing parade, the getting, the going, the doing, the making, the striving. My balance has been tipped the other way, and it is a different kind of recalibration I have longed for, something to remind me of the vitality of living.

I park and get out. A dismal cluster of low-slung apartments borders the entrance. Little kids run in the dry, lusterless grass, their legs liquid as they chase one another around the development, their shirts off. Hip-hop booms from an unseen source, the treble turned down, the bass turned up, so the sound that carries in the humid spring air is a kind of heavy breathing. There's trash along the curbs, cigarette butts mixed with torn, desiccated leaves, twisted candy wrappers, bits of fast-food containers. Laundry on a long wire flaps in the wind.

It doesn't surprise me that the final resting place of the elite of nineteenth-century Richmond should be flanked by a housing project that contains the dispossessed of twenty-first-century Richmond. Actually, it shocks me. Shocks and delights me. The odd, ironic twists of history. The raging incongruities.

One of the kids, noticing that I've stopped to flip through the pages of my notebook and jot down a few notes, wanders over and asks if I'm going to the cemetery.

I mumble some sort of reply.

His eyes are big, alert, probing. "You look sad," he says.

It's as if someone has shoved a mirror in front of me, and I am forced to confront what the past few months have wrought.

The friends just stare, silent and unblinking, a mute chorus, as if they were too transfixed by my apparent sadness, by this intrusion of death-in-life in their midst, to speak. Looking at them reminds me of my own little boy, who is much, much younger than they are—who has yet to talk, in fact—but who is, all the same, astute in reading emotion and reflecting it in his wide, innocent eyes.

"Shouldn't you all be in school or something?" It startles me that I've asked, and also that the question has come out sounding more concerned than accusatory. But mostly it startles me that I should feel so suddenly—strangely—protective of them.

"No," the boy says, defiant. His ribcage is skeletal through his taut, unshirted skin.

"No?"

"We *been* to school."

My question has put a scare in them—either that, or a person is entitled to only so much sympathy, and they run off, now, into one of the buildings.

I enter the grounds. There's no directory indicating where anyone is interred, and for a long time, I wander uncertain as to how I might find the doctor. Uncertain, too, of whether finding him at all is not some hopeless excursion, and I have somehow gotten my information wrong and should turn back and return to my microfiche projector at the library.

In the middle of the cemetery, an obelisk, enclosed by a black steel bar fence, rises up from the earth like a monument over a city center. A magnolia tree provides protective cover. It is one of the most distinctive, most impressive headstones in the cemetery, and I am not surprised to discover whose plot it designates: John Ambler, Esq. Catherine Ambler, Norton's mother, is in the same plot. Not far away is John Marshall, the chief justice. So, too, is Polly, his wife. Something tells me I'm close.

I circle the grounds that encircle the encircled obelisk. But no: nothing; not a sign of Dr. Norton. I try again, this time with greater determination and intensity, like a detective scouring a crime scene for forensic evidence, crouching several times to inspect headstones and squint at their lettering. And still no doctor. It's frustrating, but I'm more puzzled than frustrated— my research into the Norton in microcosm.

Finally, it occurs to me to wonder, *What would make the most sense? Or rather, what is the opposite of my assumption?* In other words, not what place would be the most fitting, but rather, what would be the least fitting. Like the sign: the least fitting and most unfortunate.

At last I find it, in the far corner, at North Second and Hospital. It is a simple marker, so simple that I would not have thought to stop and investigate had I not been looking for it. Nothing rises into the air to proclaim the importance of the deceased; nothing encloses the tombstone. It lies flat against the ground, a thin, faded gray sheet. From a distance, it looks like a blanket spread out upon a grassy expanse. Why am I not surprised to discover that in death, as in life, the doctor remains the outcast, the misfit, the bad boy, shoved into the corner of the cemetery like the classroom dunce, far from the Amblers and the Marshalls and their world at the vital center?

I bend down onto one knee to try to make out the inscription. "SACRED to the memory of Daniel Norborne Norton M.D. Son of John Hatley Norton of England and his wife Catherine Bush of Winchester, Virginia born November 1794. Intermarried with Elizabeth Jaquelin Call and afterwards with Lucy Marshall Fisher. Departed this life the 23rd day of January 1842."

Parts of the words have been erased by rain and snow and time. Some have been spattered by bird shit.

It is no doubt a reflection of my state of mind of late, the moroseness that has seized me and darkened my outlook and caused my moods to gravitate toward the extreme, but crouched on one knee alongside his tombstone as if in supplication, I find myself unaccountably moved by the poverty of his circumstance; I feel protective of him and defiant on his behalf. My mind drifts to thinking about that period of the doctor's own suffering, his deep and persistent melancholia, his alienation from a Richmond society that neither recognized nor understood him, and I reflect on the crazy circle I have completed in coming here this afternoon, the discovery that was born almost two hundred years ago in pain and despair, that became an obsession and a mission, and how that same wild vine, which connects Jenni and the doctor and Husmann and Horton and Held, connects me, too. And I realize now that I have come to pay more than my respects. I have come to pay a debt. I am a part of you, Daniel Norborne Norton, and you are a part of me. And I promise to bring you to life in my book, to remember and to keep you, to resurrect and restore your name. And your wine, which I tasted once and could not forget, which launched me on a search for you until eventually I found you in it; your wine, which is the wine of the underdog, of the forgotten, of the dispossessed, of the despised; your wine which is the wine of love, and hate, and nothing in between; your wine, which is ours, unmistakably ours, whose every inimitable sip I take reminds me that the America I pledge my allegiance to, the America I willingly defend, is not the land of God-family-country and all the other pieties that are slung in the name of unity and conformity, but the America of outcasts and misfits, of restless seekers, of outsiders longing to reach the center, the America of blind hope, the America of impossible causes.

I pull out my cell phone and call Jenni. Who else, I think, would appreciate this moment, would alternately savor and rue the ironies? I detect a note of wry bemusement in her voice, a recognition of our mutual obsession: Her quest has become my quest.

A car careens past, oblivious of the thousands of dead. Its boom box thumps out a hard, stuttering beat, and I talk louder to be heard.

Here lies the father of American wine, the real father, not the commonly lauded father, with no marker to indicate his discovery or achievement. And then I look down. There, in the lower right-hand corner of the headstone, a small grape vine grows. Native. Wild.

BIBLIOGRAPHY

I AM INDEBTED to Drs. Rebecca Ambers and Cliff Ambers for their deeply researched paper, "Dr. Daniel Norborne Norton and the Origin of the Norton Grape," which provided me with an early understanding of Dr. Norton's discovery and colored much of my subsequent reading on the subject. Cliff Ambers later directed me to William Kenrick's *The New American Orchardist,* which shed additional light on Dr. Norton's unusual impregnation method at Magnolia Farm and helped to dispel a good deal of the mystery that has long been attached to the doctor's story of the grape's origins.

It was at the National Agricultural Library, in Beltsville, Maryland, that I turned the delicate, yellowed pages of a catalogue from the Prince Nurseries and learned that Dr. Norton's grape had been in cultivation since 1822, not 1830 as had been previously believed; sharing my excitement with the kind and cheerful staff was among the highlights of my research.

In Richmond, Beth Petty at the Valentine Richmond History Center directed me to several documents that illuminated the doctor's life and times. She also unearthed the letter from Dr. Norton that anchors chapter 2—a letter that helped me to understand the depth of his melancholy. At the Library of Virginia, also in Richmond, the letters in the collection of John Norton and Sons were helpful, as was the doctor's quickly sketched garden map, an immensely valuable and fascinating document.

I dug into Norton's correspondence at the Alderman Library, at the University of Virginia in Charlottesville. Included among a collection entitled "Records of Antebellum Southern Plantations" were more than two dozen of the doctor's heartfelt letters to his half-brother, John Jaquelin Ambler. The Alderman library is also where I read *Thomas Jefferson's Garden Book* for the first time.

I learned a lot about the vanished world of nineteenth-century Richmond through the kind and generous assistance of two men: Gregg Kimball, the director of publications at the Library of Virginia, whose knowledge and insights were invaluable; and Harry Kollatz, a senior writer at *Richmond Magazine* whose conversations with me about the city's history amounted to lively and fascinating walking tours.

Long before visiting Missouri, I immersed myself in the writings of Linda Walker Stevens, a Hermann resident and expert on George Husmann. It was through Stevens that I eventually found my way to Husmann's own books, which offered a rare personal glimpse into Hermann's early days as well as the heyday of nineteenth-century winemaking. In Hermann, the Deutschheim State Historic Site was a trove of information and insight, while Lois Puchta and the women at the Gasconade County Historical Society Archives and Records were gracious enough to let me sit and page for hours through the town's many decades of papers and letters. I came to believe that, in one way or another, every Hermannite is a curator, of sorts; I am indebted to three, in particular, for their time and conversation and knowledge: Tim Puchta of the Adam Puchta Winery; Don Kruse, the editor of the *Hermann Advertiser-Courier*; and the Helds—Jim, Betty, Jon, Thomas, and Patty.

I was lucky to find Mary Beth Brown, the manuscript specialist at the Western Historical Manuscript Collection at the University of Missouri–Columbia; she helped me to organize and streamline my research throughout the state. And I am glad I went against my instincts and killed a couple of hours one afternoon at the St. Louis Mercantile Library at the University of Missouri–St. Louis. I learned a great deal there about civil rights and the history of Prohibition.

SELECTED WORKS

ADAMS, LEON D. *The Wines of America*. Boston: Houghton Mifflin, 1973.

ADAMS, WILLIAM E. *Memoirs of a Social Atom*. Whitefish, MT: Kessinger Publishing, LLC, 2007.

ADAMS, WILLIAM HOWARD. *The Paris Years of Thomas Jefferson*. New Haven: Yale University Press, 1997.

ALBEMARLE COUNTY HISTORICAL SOCIETY. "Deep Roots & High Stakes." Exhibit on wine, 1994.

AMBERS, REBECCA K. R., AND CLIFFORD P. AMBERS. "Dr. Daniel Norborne Norton and the Origin of the Norton Grape." *American Wine Society Journal*, 36, no. 3 (Fall 2004).

AMBLER FAMILY GENEALOGICAL NOTES, 1826–1854. The Library of Virginia.

AMBLER FAMILY LETTERS. The Valentine Museum, Richmond, Virginia.

APPLE, R.W. "Jefferson Gets His Wish: At Last, a Decent Bottle of Virginia Wine," *New York Times*, September 13, 2000.

ASHER, GERALD. *Vineyard Tales: Reflections on Wine*. San Francisco: Chronicle Books, LLC, 1996.

BAILEY, LIBERTY H. *Sketch of the Evolution of Our Native Fruits*. London: The MacMillan Company, 1898.

BARNES, HARRY ELMER. *History and Social Intelligence*. Whitefish, MT: Kessinger Publishing, LLC, 2004.

BEHR, EDWARD. *Prohibition: Thirteen Years That Changed America*. New York: Arcade Publishing, 1996.

BEK, WILLIAM G. *The German Settlement Society of Philadelphia and Its Colony, Hermann, Missouri*. New York: American Press, Inc., 1984.

BETTS, EDWIN MORRIS, EDITOR. *Thomas Jefferson's Garden Book, 1766–1824, with Relevant Extracts from His Other Writings*. Philadelphia: The American Philosophical Society, 1974.

BOSWELL, PEYTON. *Wine Makers Manual: A Guide for the Home Wine Maker and the Small Winery*. New York: Orange Judd Publishing Company, 1952.

BRACE, CHARLES L. *The New West: Or California in 1867–1868*. Whitefish, MT: Kessinger Publishing, LLC, 2008.

BUCHANAN, ROBERT W. *On Descending into Hell: A Letter Addressed to Henry Matthews Concerning the Proposed Suppression of Literature*. London: George Redway, 1889.

BULLARD, FREDERIC L. *Famous War Correspondents*. New York: Beekman Publishers Inc., 1974.

BURNETT, ROBYN, AND KEN LUEBBERING. *German Settlement in Missouri: New Land, Old Ways*. Columbia: University of Missouri Press, 1996.

BUSH & SON & MEISSNER. *Illustrated Descriptive Catalogue of American Grape Vines: A Grape Growers' Manual (1883)*. Whitefish, MT: Kessinger Publishing, LLC, 2008.

CAMPBELL, CHRISTY. *The Botanist and the Vintner: How Wine Was Saved for the World*. Chapel Hill: Algonquin Books, 2005.

CATE, WIRT ARMSTEAD. "History of Richmond," 3 volumes (unpublished manuscript held at Valentine Museum, Richmond, VA), c. 1944.

CATTERALL, LOUISE F., curator. *Richmond Portraits in an Exhibition of Makers of Richmond, 1737–1860*. Valentine Richmond History Center, 1949.

CHRISTENSEN, LAWRENCE O., AND WILLIAM E. FOLEY, GARY R. KREMER, AND KENNETH H. WINN. *Dictionary of Missouri Biography*. Columbia: University of Missouri Press, 1999.

Commercial Relations of the United States with Foreign Countries During the Year 1876. By the United States Department of State, United States Bureau of Foreign and Domestic Commerce, United States Bureau of Foreign Commerce (1855–1903). Government Printing Office, 1876.

CONNOR, LEARTUS, ED. *The Detroit Lancet: A Monthly Exponent of Rational Medicine, Vol. VIII*. George S. Davis, Medical Publisher, 1885.

DEWAN, GEORGE. "The Blooming of Flushing." Newsday.com, 2009.

DOUGLAS, HENRY KYD. *I Rode with Stonewall*. Chapel Hill: University of North Carolina Press, 1968.

DRAGO, HOLLY. *Hermann's Haunts: The Wines and Spirits of Hermann, Missouri*. Grand Rapids: Virginia Co., 2007.

DRISCOLL, JAMES. *Flushing, 1880–1935*. San Francisco: Arcadia Publishing, 2005.

DUDEN, GOTTFRIED. *Report on a Journey to the Western States of North America and a Stay of Several Years Along the Missouri*. The State Historical Society of Missouri and University of Missouri Press. Translation of the 1829 publication.

DUFOUR, JEFF. "Fertile Ground: Virginia's Original Grape Puts Local Vineyards on the Map." *Piedmont Virginian*, Autumn 2007.

DUFUR, BRETT. *Exploring Missouri Wine Country*. Rocheport, MO: Pebble Publishing, 2006.

EATON, LORRAINE. "Virginia's Prohibition History." *Virginian-Pilot*, November 30, 2008.

ESCOTT, T. H. S. *Masters of English Journalism*. Westport, CT: Greenwood Press, 1970.

FAUST, ALBERT BERNHARDT. *The German Element in the United States*. Boston: Houghton Mifflin Company, 1909.

FULLER, ROBERT C. *Religion and Wine: A Cultural History of Wine Drinking in the United States*. Knoxville: University of Tennessee Press, 1996.

GABLER, JAMES M. *Passions: The Wines and Travels of Thomas Jefferson.* Baltimore: Bacchus Press, 1995.

GOODSPEED PUBLISHING CO. *History of Franklin, Jefferson, Washington, Crawford and Gasconade Counties.* Westminster, MD: Heritage Books, Inc., 1994.

GREAT BRITAIN, PARLIAMENT, HOUSE OF COMMONS. *British Parliamentary Papers,* Vol. 73, Part 4, 1874.

GREGORY, RALPH, AND ANITA MALLINCKRODT. "Wine-Making in Missouri's 'Duden Country'—1800s History and Customs." *Missouri Folklore Society Journal,* Vol. 6, 1984.

HAILMAN, JOHN. *Thomas Jefferson on Wine.* Jackson: University Press of Mississippi/Jackson, 2006.

HARRINGTON, GEORGE LEAVITT. *Brooklyn Medical Journal.* Medical Society of the County of Kings, 1888.

HARRISON, SAMUEL F. "History of Hermann, Missouri." Second printing, 1973.

HASE, EDWARD W., II, AND ROBERT M. HUBBARD. "Adolph Russow and the Monticello Wine Company." *The Magazine of Albemarle County History,* Vol. 46. Albemarle County Historical Society, 1988.

HEDRICK, U. P. *Manual of American Grape-Growing.* New York: Macmillan Company, 1919.

HOLLOWAY, CHARLES M. "Romancing the Vine in Virginia: No Wine Before Its Time." *Colonial Williamsburg Journal,* Summer 2002.

HUSMANN, GEORGE. *American Grape Growing and Wine Making.* New York: Orange Judd Company, 1883.

———. *An Essay on the Culture of the Grape in the Great West.* C. W. Kielmann, 1863.

———. *The Cultivation of the Native Grape, and Manufacture of American Wines (1866).* Bibliolife, 2009.

JEFFERSON, THOMAS, AND JOHN P. FOLEY. *The Jeffersonian Cyclopedia: A Comprehensive Collection of the Views of Thomas Jefferson.* New York, London: Funk & Wagnalls Company, 1900.

JEFFORD, ANDREW. "Vineyards to Make a Founding Father Proud." *Financial Times,* September 1, 2007.

JOHN NORTON AND SONS, PAPERS, 1757–1836. The Robert Alonzo Brock Collection at the Huntingdon Library, San Marino, California, available on microfilm at the Library of Virginia.

KENRICK, WILLIAM. *The New American Orchardist.* Boston: Otis, Broaders, and Company, 1844.

KNIGHT, EDWARD HENRY, SAMUEL DYSART, J. J. WILLIAMS, G. W. CAMPBELL AND T. R. FERGUSON. *Reports of the United States*

Commissioners to the Paris Universal Exposition, 1878. Government Printing Office, 1880.

LAWTON, CHILES A. *Barboursville Vineyards: Crafting Great Wines Inspired by Spirits of the Past.* Barboursville, VA: Barboursville Vineyards, 2008.

LEE, HILDE GABRIEL, AND ALLAN E. LEE. *Virginia Wine Country III: Stories and Wines of the 80 Old Dominion Wineries.* Charlottesville: Hildesigns Press, 2004.

LEWIS, HENRY, AND A. HERMINA POATGIETER, TRANSLATOR; BERTHA HEILBRON, EDITOR. *The Valley of the Mississippi Illustrated.* Minnesota Historical Society, 1967.

LUKACS, PAUL. *American Vintage: The Rise of American Wine.* New York: W. W. Norton & Co., 2005.

————. *The Great Wines of America: The Top Forty Vintners, Vineyards and Vintages.* New York: W. W. Norton & Co., 2005.

MALONEY, ELIZABETH, AMY SCHEIDEGGER, AND KELLY JAMES. "Prohibition: The End and Beginning of Stone Hill." *The Grapevine,* Hermann, MO, Spring 1996.

MANARIN, LOUIS H. *Richmond on the James.* San Francisco: Arcadia Publishing, 2001.

MARQUIS, ALBERT NELSON. *The Book of St. Louisans.* Chicago: A. N. Marquis & Company, 1912.

MARSHALL, GAIL. *The Cambridge Companion to the Fin de Siècle.* Cambridge University Press, 2007.

MASON, FRANCES NORTON. *John Norton and Sons: Merchants of London and Virginia.* New York: A. M. Kelly, 1968.

MCLEROY, SHERRIE S., AND ROY E. RENFRO JR. *Grape Man of Texas: The Life of T. V. Munson.* Austin: Eakin Press, 2004.

MOORE, JOHN HAMMOND. *Albemarle: Jefferson's County, 1727–1976.* Charlottesville: University Press of Virginia, 1976.

MORDECAI, SAMUEL. *Virginia, Especially Richmond, in By-Gone Days: With a Glance at the Present: Being Reminiscences and Last Words of an Old Citizen.* Michigan Historical Reprint Series, 2005.

MORRIS, JAN. *Conundrum.* New York: New York Review of Books Classics, 1974, 2002.

MUEHL, SIEGMAR, TRANSLATOR. "Hermann, Missouri: History Sources in German-American Newspapers, 1840–1854." Privately published. Iowa City, IA, 1992.

NORTON, DANIEL NORBORNE. Southern Agriculturalist and Register of Rural Affairs (1828–1839), Vol. 8, Iss. 2. Letter. February, 1835.

————. The Farmer & Gardener, and Live-Stock Breeder and Manager (1834–1839), Vol. 2, Iss. 40. February 2, 1836.

OLDBERG, OSCAR. *A Companion to the United States Pharmacopaeia*. New York: W. Wood & Co., 1884.

OVERTON, JACQUELINE. *Long Island's Story*. Garden City: Doubleday, Doran & Company, 1929.

PELLECHIA, THOMAS. *Wine: The 8,000-Year-Old Story of the Wine Trade*. Philadelphia: Running Press, 2006.

PERROTTE, KEN. "How Grape Thou Art: Norton Virginia Seedling Enjoying Old Dominion Rebirth." *The Fredericksburg Free-Lance Star,* October 8, 2005.

PINNEY, THOMAS. *A History of Wine in America, Vol. 1: From the Beginnings to Prohibition*. Berkeley: University of California Press, 2007.

POMOLOGICAL SOCIETY OF GEORGIA. Report upon grapes. *The Horticulturist, and Journal of Rural Art and Rural Taste,* Vol. 12. 1857.

POWERS, RON. *Mark Twain: A Life*. New York: Free Press, 2005.

PRINCE, WILLIAM ROBERT, AND WILLIAM PRINCE JR. *A Treatise on the Vine; Embracing its History from the Earliest Ages to the Present Day, with Descriptions of Above Two Hundred Foreign, and Eighty American Varieties; Together with a Complete Dissertation on the Establishment, Culture, and Management*. T. & J. Swords, 1830.

PUCHTA, LOIS, EDITOR. "An Unusual Obituary." *Gasconade County Historical Society Newsletter.* Vol. 20, No. 2. Summer 2007.

RAFA, CHERYL. "The Ambler Family in Virginia." nps.gov (US National Park Service). November, 1987.

RECORDS OF ANTE-BELLUM SOUTHERN PLANTATION FROM THE REVOLUTION THROUGH THE CIVIL WAR, SERIES E, PART 5: AMBLER FAMILY PAPERS, KENNETH M. STAMPP, GENERAL EDITOR. A microfilm project. University Publication of America, 2001.

RILEY, C.V. "On the Cause of Deterioration in Some of Our Native Grape-Vines, and One of the Probable Reasons Why European Vines Have So Generally Failed with Us." *The American Naturalist* 6, no. 9 (September, 1872).

RIPLEY, GEORGE, AND CHARLES A. DANA, EDITORS. *The American Cyclopaedia, a Popular Dictionary of General Knowledge*. New York: Appleton, 1870.

ROBERTS, PAUL. *From This Hill, My Hand, Cynthiana's Wine*. Baltimore: Resonant Publishing, 2009.

ROBINSON, JANCIS, EDITOR. *The Oxford Companion to Wine, Third Edition*. New York: Oxford University Press, 2006.

"The Rolla New Era." Extract from *The Hermann Advertiser-Courier,* November 2, 1889.

RUFFIN, EDMUND, EDITOR. *The Farmer's Register: A Monthly Publication Devoted to the Improvement of the Practice*. Edmund Ruffin, 1838.

SALA, GEORGE AUGUSTUS. *The Life and Adventures of George Augustus Sala, Written by Himself: Vol. 1.* Rye Brook, NY: Adamant Media Corporation, 2002.

SATTERFIELD, ARCHIE. "Missouri's Rhineland: West of St. Louis, Wineries Carry on a Tradition That Changed the Industry." *Chicago Tribune,* May 8, 2000.

SCHEEF, ROBERT F. *Vintage Missouri: A Guide to Missouri Wineries.* Toole: The Patrice Press, 1991.

SCHUCHARD, OLIVER A., ERIN MCCAWLEY RENN, ADOLF E. SCHROEDER, ANNA KEMPER HESSE, AND EDWARD J. KEMPER. *Little Germany on the Missouri: The Photographs of Edward J. Kemper, 1895–1920.* Columbia: University of Missouri Press, 1998.

SCOTT, MARY W. *Houses of Old Richmond.* New York: Bonanza Books, 1941.

SCRUTON, ROGER. "Wine—Roger Scruton Rhapsodizes Over Horton Norton." *New Statesman,* May 17, 2004.

SHERWOOD, M. E. W. *The Art of Entertaining.* New York: Dodd, Mead and Company, 1892.

SIEMON-NETTO, UWE. "In Missouri, a Phoenix Named Hermann." *Atlantic Times,* January 2007.

SINCLAIR, ROBERT JR., AND E. P. ROBERTS, EDITORS. *The Farmer & The Gardener, Vols. 1–52.* Sinclair & Moore, 1835.

SMITH, DANIEL BLAKE. *Inside the Great House: Planter Family Life in Eighteenth Century Chesapeake Society.* Ithaca: Cornell University Press, 1980.

STEVENS, LINDA WALKER. "Old Nick: Cincinnati Winemaker." *Timeline,* 13.2. Ohio Historical Society. March-April, 1996.

———. "The Making of a Superior Immigrant: George Husmann, 1837-1854." *Missouri Historical Review.* The State Historical Society of Missouri, Columbia, Missouri. January 1995.

———. "The Story of Wine at Hermann." *Missouri Folklore Society Journal* 21, 1999.

STONE HILL WINERY. "Photographs, Written Historical and Descriptive Data, Reduced Copies of Measured Drawings." Historic American Buildings Survey. National Park Service, Department of the Interior. Washington, D.C.

SUMNER, JUDITH. *American Household Botany: A History of Useful Plants, 1620–1900.* Portland, OR: Timber Press, 2004.

———. "The Spirit of George Husmann." *What Wondrous Life: The World of George Husmann: An Interpretive Exhibit.* Catalogue. Missouri State Museum's Traveling Exhibits Program, 2002.

TABER, GEORGE M. *Judgment of Paris: California vs. France and the Historic 1976 Paris Tasting That Revolutionized Wine.* New York: Scribner, 2006.

THUDICHUM, JOHN L., AND AUGUST DUPRÉ. *A Treatise on the Origin, Nature, and Varieties of Wine: Being a Complete Manual of Viticulture and Oenology.* London: Macmillan, 1872.

THURSTON, ROBERT H., EDITOR. *Reports of the Commissioners of the United States to the International Exhibition Held at Vienna, 1873.* Government Printing Office, 1876.

TUCKER, LUTHER. *The Horticulturist, and Journal of Rural Art and Rural Taste.* Luther Tucker, 1851.

———. *The Cultivator, A Monthly Journal Devoted to Agriculture, Horticulture, Floriculture, and to Domestic and Rural Economy.* Luther Tucker, 1845.

VAN RAVENSWAAY, CHARLES. *The Arts and Architecture of German Settlements in Missouri: A Survey of a Vanishing Culture.* Columbia: University of Missouri Press, 1977.

VINE, RICHARD P., ELLEN M. HARKNESS, AND SALLY J. LINTON, EDITORS. *Winemaking: From Grape Growing to Marketplace.* New York: Springer, 2002.

VIOLETTE, EUGENE MORROW. *A History of Missouri.* Cape Girardeau, MD: Ramfre Press, 1960.

VIZETELLY, ERNEST A. *Émile Zola, Novelist and Reformer: An Account of His Life & Work.* New York: Ayer Co. Publishers, 1979.

VIZETELLY, HENRY. *Glances Back Through Seventy Years: Autobiographical and Other Reminiscences, Vol. II.* Kegan Paul, Trench, Trubner & Co., Ltd., 1893.

———. *Paris in Peril, Vol. 1.* New York: General Books, LLC, 2009.

———. *The Wines of the World Characterized and Classed.* London: Ward, Lock & Tyler, Warwick House, 1875.

WALKER, MACK. *Germany and the Emigration, 1816–1885.* Cambridge: Harvard University Press, 1964.

WHITEHEAD, THOMAS. *Virginia, a Hand-book: Giving Its History, Climate, and Mineral Wealth.* Virginia Department of Agriculture. Richmond: Everett Waddey Co., 1898.

WRIGHT, RICHARDSON. *The Story of Gardening: From the Hanging Gardens of Babylon to the Hanging Gardens of New York.* New York: Dodd, Mead & Company, 1934.

ZRALY, KEVIN. *Kevin Zraly's American Wine Guide: 2008.* New York: Sterling, 2007.

ACKNOWLEDGMENTS

I USED TO BELIEVE that a writer worked alone, and that stories were born entirely of solitude. I know better now.

I am indebted to many, many people for many, many things, and I wish to take a moment to express my appreciation and gratitude for all that they have given to me in the making of this book.

Luca Paschina and Jason Tesauro at Barboursville Vineyards; Dennis Horton at Horton Vineyards; Michael Shaps at Virginia Wineworks; Cliff and Rebecca Ambers at Chateau Z; and Dr. Bruce Zoecklein at Virginia Tech for sharing their passionate knowledge of their craft.

Tim Puchta at Adam Puchta Winery; Don Kruse at the *Hermann Advertiser-Courier;* Steve Mueller at the German School Museum; Lois Puchta at the Gasconade County Historical Society Archives and Records; and Cheryl Hoffman at the Deutschheim State Historic Site for their time and assistance.

Jim, Betty, and Jon Held for letting me into their lives, and for the hours of good food, good wine, and good conversation.

Jack Limpert, Garrett Graff, Ken Decell, Bill O'Sullivan, Jill Hudson Neal, Harry Jaffe, Leslie Milk, and all the rest of my colleagues at *The Washingtonian* for their generous support of this project. And the magazine's food and wine staff, Ann Limpert, Kate Nerenberg, Rina Rapuano, and Cynthia Hacinli, for their friendship and encouragement.

Kelem and Adamu Lemu for providing the wonderfully strong coffee and an extra office when I needed it; Mike Franklin and Marc Heckrotte for all the good meals and good times at the restaurant; Leeann Irwin for the re-energizing

Wednesday sessions; Meg MacArthur and Leigh Altman for checking in on me periodically and pulling me out of my head.

Bill Thomas, Tom Bartlett, and Dave McIntyre for their excellent editorial advice and judgment; Nora Myers, Stephanie Haven, and Melissa Crawford for their dogged research assistance; Caroline Schweiter for her eagle eye and tenaciousness in improving the manuscript.

Bill Manion, Joe Taylor, Jack Russell, Donald Kleine, Michael Olmert, Rick Trethewey, Tova Reich, and Danar Eastnoor for their guidance and inspiration.

Phyllis Richman, Jody Jaffe, Don Rockwell, Deidree Bennett, Jim Link, Marianna Burt, Bill Culverhouse, Elva Myers, Andre Parraway, Marsha Weiner, Ben Clark, Indiah Wilson, Kerry and Lya Britt, Sean Mullin, Fred Uku, Pam Thomas, Gadi Ben-Yehuda, Genevelyn Steele, Michael Stearns, Dennis Blackwell, Vicki Gau, Dan Falvey, Marianna Ofosu, Sara Murphy, Debbie Lynn Kearse, Jennifer and Joe Goltz, and Andrea and John Goltz for all their many hours of conversation, laughter, and encouragement.

Colleen Fay for her wisdom, kindness, generosity, and devotion.

Sue Luker Johnson for believing in me, and for all the many hours of talk about writing and books and life; my protector, my compass, my teacher.

Jenni McCloud for the road trips, the seminars, the wine tastings, the meals, the many long conversations into the night. Her earthy good humor and her joyous and outsize passion for life inspired this book. I am much the richer for her friendship.

My editor, Rica Allannic, for her unwavering enthusiasm for this story, and her confident stewardship of the manuscript from start to finish; in ways big and small, she has made this a better, stronger book. I am lucky to have found her. At Clarkson Potter and Crown, I would also like to thank the following for their assistance and support: Marysarah Quinn, Ashley Phillips, Ada Yonenaka, Alexis Mentor, Gary Stimeling, Min Lee, Courtney Greenhalgh, Kate Tyler, Katie Wainwright, Donna Passannante, Philip Patrick, Andrew Stanley, Jill Flaxman, Doris Cooper, Lauren Shakely, and Jenny Frost.

My agent, Will Lippincott, who has been an advisor, a confidant, a sounding board, an editor, a cheerleader, a guru, and who has performed all these roles with wit, grace, and gentlemanly charm. I am in awe of his tirelessness, his conviction, his deep devotion, and his unfailing kindness.

Matthew Katz for his unflagging encouragement throughout this project—a source of great strength. Whether it was joining me on research trips, reading drafts of the manuscript, or checking in with me almost daily to ask about my progress, he has been tireless in his support. For three years, he has cared about this book as if it were his own. I am a better reader because of him, a better writer, and probably a better person, too. I am privileged to call him my friend.

My brother, Andrew Kliman, who eighteen years ago wrote me a wonderful check that made it easy to go off to grad school and write, and who has been unwavering in his support of my work ever since. I am grateful to him and to my sister-in-law, Anne Jaffe, for their love and friendship, and for their steadfastness throughout this project.

My parents, Ted Kliman and Itsy Kliman, the most passionate, most voracious and most unpretentious readers I have ever met. I owe my being a writer to them and to their creative and questing example. I lost my father during the course of writing this book, but every day I could hear his words of encouragement and exhortation in my head, and every day I could look at his brilliant and luminous paintings and draw inspiration to endeavor to see and say in my own way; his early excitement for the manuscript meant everything to me. Throughout this project, my mother was my first reader, as well as my first editor; also, my cornerman, my defender, my champion, my father confessor, my restaurant buddy. I could not have finished without her by my side.

My wife, Ellen, who has nurtured and sustained me throughout the researching and writing of this book, and who selflessly set aside many of her own performing opportunities in order to give her time and attention to this project. Her strength and wisdom and love have managed to keep me, just barely, on this side of sane, and every single day I find myself in awe at her uncanny ability to balance the practical and the spiritual. Without her, there would be no book. She is my first reader, my best friend, my rock.

Finally, my son, Jesse, my joy boy, whose exuberance and sweetness lifted me up on some very dark days and reminded me to laugh and wonder and be astonished.

INDEX